# CAMBRIDGE NATIONAL

## LEVEL 1/2

# Sport Studies

Mike Murray & Ross Howitt

An OCR endorsed textbook

HODDER
EDUCATION
AN HACHETTE UK COMPANY

The teaching content of this resource is endorsed by OCR for use with specification Cambridge Nationals Level 1/2 in Sport Studies (J813). In order to gain OCR endorsement, this resource has been reviewed against OCR's endorsement criteria.

This resource was designed using the most up to date information from the specification. Specifications are updated over time which means there may be contradictions between the resource and the specification, therefore please use the information on the latest specification and Sample Assessment Materials at all times when ensuring students are fully prepared for their assessments.

Any references to assessment and/or assessment preparation are the publisher's interpretation of the specification requirements and are not endorsed by OCR. OCR recommends that teachers consider using a range of teaching and learning resources in preparing learners for assessment, based on their own professional judgement for their students' needs. OCR has not paid for the production of this resource, nor does OCR receive any royalties from its sale. For more information about the endorsement process, please visit the OCR website, www.ocr.org.uk.

Although every effort has been made to ensure that website addresses are correct at time of going to press, Hodder Education cannot be held responsible for the content of any website mentioned in this book. It is sometimes possible to find a relocated web page by typing in the address of the home page for a website in the URL window of your browser.

Hachette UK's policy is to use papers that are natural, renewable and recyclable products and made from wood grown in well-managed forests and other controlled sources. The logging and manufacturing processes are expected to conform to the environmental regulations of the country of origin.

Orders: please contact Bookpoint Ltd, 130 Park Drive, Milton Park, Abingdon, Oxon OX14 4SE. Telephone: +44 (0)1235 827827. Fax: +44 (0)1235 400401. Email education@bookpoint.co.uk Lines are open from 9 a.m. to 5 p.m., Monday to Saturday, with a 24-hour message answering service. You can also order through our website: www.hoddereducation.co.uk

ISBN: 978 1 5104 5646 4

© Mike Murray, Ross Howitt 2019
First published in 2019 by
Hodder Education,
An Hachette UK Company
Carmelite House
50 Victoria Embankment
London EC4Y 0DZ

www.hoddereducation.co.uk

Impression number    10 9 8 7 6 5 4 3

Year      2023 2022 2021 2020

Cover photo © nd3000 – stock.adobe.com

Illustrations by Aptara Inc

Typeset in India by Aptara Inc

Printed in Slovenia

A catalogue record for this title is available from the British Library.

# Contents

# How to use this book

## Key features of the book

### Learning outcomes

**LO1** Understand the issues which affect participation in sport

**LO2** Know about the role of sport in promoting values

Prepare for what you are going to cover in the unit.

### How will I be assessed?

This is a compulsory unit. You will be assessed within a written paper, set and marked by OCR. The paper will last 1 hour and is worth 60 marks (60 UMS).

Understand all the requirements of the new qualification fully with clearly stated learning outcomes and what you will be assessed on for each learning outcome, fully matched to the specification.

### Links to other units

You can find further information on the synoptic links to this unit in **Units R052, 53, 54, 55** and **56.**

Relevant links to other units and learning outcomes.

### Key terms

**Tactics** Plans used against opponents' weaknesses and for own strengths

Understand important terms.

### Getting started

How much exercise do you get a week? Have discussions in class about how much exercise each member of the class does and what it involves – e.g. is a particular sport particularly popular or is there a range of activities?

Short activity to introduce you to the topic.

### Classroom discussion

As teenagers, what barriers do you face that you feel are particularly obstructive in allowing you to take part in sport?

Discuss topics with others and test your understanding.

## Stretch activity

Watch YouTube clips of two different performers from an individual activity who are performing the same skill. Make a list of the ways that their techniques differ.

Take your understanding and knowledge of a topic a step further with these stretch activities designed to test you, and provide you with a more in depth understanding of the topic.

##  Group activity

Conduct a survey of the activities in which people take part. Aim to produce a bar chart that shows how popular each activity is within the class.

Work in groups to discuss and reflect on topics, and share ideas.

## Know it!

1 Name five 'user groups' who face barriers to their participation.
2 For each user group, state a particular barrier to participation that is faced.

Test your understanding with this end of unit task.

## Assessment preparation

Think about the paper that OCR will set you to assess your knowledge of contemporary issues in sport. Make sure:

● You have visited: www.ocr.org.uk/qualifications/cambridge-nationals/sport-studies-level-1-2-j803-j813 to look at sample and past papers
● You are clear about examples of:
  ○ the features of major sporting events
  ○ the potential benefits and drawbacks of cities/countries hosting major sporting events

Guidance and suggestions on what you will need to cover for the OCR model assignment and a breakdown of what the command words mean.

## Read about it

Find out more about reaction time and decision-making in sport:
https://www.sports-training-adviser.com/reactiontime.html

Includes references to books, websites and other various sources for further reading and research.

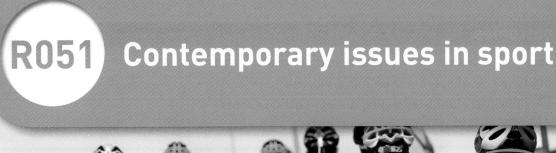

# R051 Contemporary issues in sport

## About this unit

Within this unit, learners will begin to understand the different issues which affect participation of different user groups. These user groups include ethnic minorities, retired people/people over 50, families with young children, single parents, children, teenagers, disabled people, unemployed/economically disadvantaged and working singles or couples. Learners will appreciate strategies that can be used to engage these groups. Learners will then develop an appreciation about how sport can be used to promote good values, locally, nationally and internationally. This includes looking at the Olympic and Paralympic movements and the values that the Olympic movement aims to promote. Through the appreciation of contemporary issues, learners will begin to understand the promotion of ethical behaviour within sport and the role of various national governing bodies and organisations. This involves looking at the aims of these organisations and how their funding is achieved.

## Learning outcomes

**LO1** Understand the issues which affect participation in sport

**LO2** Know about the role of sport in promoting values

**LO3** Understand the importance of hosting major sporting events

**LO4** Know about the role of national governing bodies in sport

## How will I be assessed?

This is a compulsory unit. You will be assessed within a written paper, set and marked by OCR. The paper will last 1 hour and is worth 60 marks (60 UMS).

During the external assessment, learners will be expected to demonstrate their understanding through questions that require analysis and evaluation in particular contexts.

### For LO1

Learners need to have knowledge and understanding of:

- the different user groups who may participate in sport
- the barriers these groups face to participation
- solutions to these barriers
- the factors which can impact upon the popularity of sport within the UK
- how the factors which can impact upon the popularity of sport in the UK relate to specific sporting examples
- current trends in the popularity of different sports in the UK
- growth of new/emerging sports and activities in the UK.

### For LO2

Learners need to have knowledge and understanding of:

- values which can be promoted through sport

- the Olympic and Paralympic movements
- other initiatives and events which promote values through sport
- the importance of etiquette and sporting behaviour of both performers and spectators
- the use of performance-enhancing drugs in sport.

### For LO3

Learners need to have knowledge and understanding of:

- the features of major sporting events
- the potential benefits and drawbacks of cities/countries hosting major sporting events
- the links between potential benefits and drawbacks and legacy.

### For LO4

Learners need to have knowledge and understanding of:

- what governing bodies in sport do
- governing body promotion, development, infrastructure, policies and initiatives, funding and support.

# LO1 Understand the issues which affect participation in sport

## The different user groups who may participate in sport

A wide range of people perform sporting activities. However, many groups face **barriers** or factors that may make participation particularly difficult. Those facing particular barriers to their participation can be categorised into different **user groups**, which include:

- ethnic minorities
- retired people/people over 50
- families with young children
- single parents
- children
- teenagers
- disabled
- unemployed/economically disadvantaged
- working singles and couples.

### Ethnic minorities

**Ethnic minorities** are deemed to be a group within a community that is of a different culture, religion or nationality from the main group in that area. Although Britain is a multi-cultural society, some ethnicities may be very much in the minority within certain areas – this is what makes them an ethnic minority.

### Retired people or people over the age of 50

These people may face certain barriers to participation. Although you can retire at any age, most retired people receive the state pension. The state pension age will increase for both men and women in future years. It will be age 66 by October 2020. The government is planning further increases that will raise the state pension age from 66 to 67 between 2026 and 2028.

### Families with young children

These families face certain barriers to participation, largely due to the time pressures involved in looking after and raising a young family.

### Single parents

**Single parents** are classed as any adult who is bringing up a child or children on their own. In 2018, nearly a quarter of all families in the UK were single parent families.

### Key terms

**Barriers** Factors that may make participation particularly difficult

**User groups** The different groups of people who face barriers to participation

**Ethnic minorities** A group within a community that is of a different culture, religion or nationality from the main group in that area

**Single parents** Any adult who is bringing up a child or children on their own

**Figure 1.1** Some retired people face barriers to taking part in physical activity.

## Children

Technically speaking, a **child** is deemed to be any human being under the age of 18 years of age, unless the law in a country permits otherwise (the United Nations Convention on the Rights of the Child).

## Teenagers

**Teenagers** are classified as human beings between the ages of 13 and 19.

## Disabled people

People with **disabilities** have a physical or mental condition that can affect their ability to carry out movement, use different senses or undertake everyday activities. There are many classifications of disability, which include:

- visual impairment
- deafness or hard of hearing
- mental health conditions
- intellectual disability
- acquired brain injury
- autism spectrum disorder
- physical disability.

## Unemployed people

These are people with no employment, whereas **economically disadvantaged** people simply do not have enough income to meet basic needs and therefore qualify for state-organised benefits.

## Working singles and couples

These people face the pressures and demands of the world of work and often struggle to find time to take part in physical activity.

## The possible barriers which affect participation in sport

Many of the possible barriers to participation are common to all user groups. These include the following:

- Lack of **time**: Not having enough time to take part in the amount of physical activity they may wish they could do.
- **Commitments**: Linked to lack of time, as prior or compulsory commitments may mean that time for physical activity may be limited.
- Lack of **disposable income**: Someone might not be able to afford to join in a sports activity. For instance, you normally need to be a member of a golf club in order to play golf. Membership can cost

**Key terms**

**Children** Human beings under the age of 18, unless the law in a country permits otherwise

**Teenagers** Human beings from 13 to 19 years of age

**Disabled** People who have a physical or mental condition that affects their ability to carry out movement, use senses or undertake everyday activities

**Economically disadvantaged** Someone who does not have enough income to meet basic needs and qualifies for state-organised benefits

hundreds or thousands of pounds per year, which means some groups of people cannot play the sport.

- Lack of **access**: Access refers to being able to get to or into a facility. Therefore, if a particular group finds it difficult to access a facility, it may prove difficult to take part in physical activity.
- Lack of **role models**: Role models are well known people who others aspire to be like. If a particular group has few or no sporting role models, they will not be inspired to try to emulate these people.
- Lack of **provision**: Provision refers to what is provided. If sporting activity is not provided for a particular group, clearly they cannot take part.
- Lack of **awareness**: Awareness refers to how aware or knowledgeable a particular group is about something. If a particular group has little or no awareness of what is available, then they will not know where or when they can take part.
- **Stereotyping**: A simplistic and sometimes unjust viewpoint of or idea about a particular type of person. Sometimes stereotyping of particular groups may demotivate them or lower their self-esteem. The portrayal of gender issues in the sports media may perpetuate stereotypes, for instance, that some sports are 'male', masculine, etc.

## Ethnic minorities

Ethnic minorities can face many barriers to participation. These are listed below:

- **Lack of awareness or information:** Ethnic groups might not know what is available for them – e.g. at their local leisure centre.
- **Cultural norms and lack of provision:** May mean there is more interest in sports not offered in the local area.
- **Lack of role models:** There may be fewer role models from the same ethnic group taking part in activities they may be interested in.
- **Lack of coaches of that ethnic group:** With fewer coaches to inspire and coach younger children of that ethnic minority, they may decide not to attend.
- **Fear of discrimination/racism:** Potential racist abuse from people at local clubs or at local facilities.
- **Language barriers:** If English is a second language it might prove more difficult to read adverts or understand the coaches and rules.
- **Religious beliefs:** Different beliefs may prohibit competition or activity on certain days; there may be certain dress codes which are not compatible with typical sportswear etc.

**Figure 1.2** Sports performers can act as positive role models to younger children.

> ## Key terms
>
> **Access** Being able to get to or into a facility
>
> **Role models** Well known people who others aspire to be like
>
> **Provision** What is provided or available
>
> **Awareness** How aware or knowledgeable a particular group is about something
>
> **Stereotyping** A widely held but simple and sometimes unjust viewpoint of or idea about a particular type of person

## Retired people/people over 50

People of retirement age or those over the age of 50 may face potential barriers to participation. These are listed below:

- **Not exercised or participated in a long time:** Therefore, unconfident, unwilling or too unfit. This may affect confidence to take part.
- **Lack of fitness:** May lack the fitness required to get started or to perform basic physical activities or skills.
- **Increased likelihood of illness:** Due to previous or likely illness or injury. Older people may be more prone to injury.
- **No or limited access to transport:** No easy bus route to a facility or lack of own transport. Some retired people rely on bus routes to travel around.
- **Cannot afford the cost of participation:** Perhaps only have a basic pension and very little disposable income.
- **Discrimination from others:** Perceived by others as being too old to join in or participate. May feel they are being judged so decide not to attend.
- **If still working, work commitments:** Resulting in very little leisure time to participate in physical activities as work commitments must be prioritised.
- **Family commitments:** Can mean that there is a lack of time to undertake leisure pursuits as it is common for grandparents to help look after grandchildren or pick them up from school.
- **Lack of self-esteem/low confidence:** Don't have self-belief to take part, may feel self-conscious about wearing a sports kit.

**Figure 1.3** Retired people often have to take public transport to travel to suitable facilities for physical activity.

## Families with young children

Families with young children face many barriers that can prevent them from taking part in physical activity. These are listed below:

- **Childcare costs:** Often mean that money should be prioritised for childcare ahead of any leisure activity costs.
- **Family commitments:** Can mean lack of time as looking after children can be very time consuming and there is little time left over for leisure pursuits.
- **Limited childcare:** Can be difficult to find suitable childcare which would have allowed parents to take part in activities and exercise.
- **No crèche or childcare at the sports centre:** Therefore, nowhere for the child to go whilst the parents are exercising.
- **Transport issues:** Partner may need the car (if a one-car family) and public transport may be awkward or difficult with children.
- **Lack of time:** Time is prioritised to work and/or family commitments.
- **Appeal of alternative leisure activities:** For example, attending parent and child groups or meeting with other young families.

**Figure 1.4** Families with young children often face barriers to participation such as a lack of time.

- **Partner may wish to exercise:** Difficult to find the time for both parents to exercise. One partner may be able to exercise more than the other due to time constraints.

## Single parents

Single parents face similar barriers to parents with young families but do not have a partner to help them out. Some of these barriers are listed below:

- **Childcare costs:** Often mean that money has to be prioritised for childcare ahead of any leisure activity costs.
- **Parenting commitments:** Mean lack of time as looking after children can be very time consuming.
- **Limited childcare:** It may be hard to have the child looked after whilst the parent is exercising. If there is no crèche or childcare at the sports centre, then there is nowhere for the child to go whilst the parent is exercising.
- **Transport issues:** Parent may not have access to a car or the ability or income to use public transport.
- **Lack of time:** Time has to be prioritised for work and/or family commitments.
- **Appeal of alternative leisure activities:** For example, attending parent and child groups or meeting with other young families.
- **Lack of role models:** Few single parent role models who make an elite level in sport.

## Children

Children face many barriers to participation, some of which are similar to teenagers. These are listed below:

- **Lack of role models:** Important sporting role models for children are often family members, and if there aren't any role models in the family, then the child might not be encouraged to, for instance, join a local club or league etc.
- **Lack of awareness:** Don't know that clubs or activities are available.
- **Lack of money/disposable income:** No job or obvious source of income and likely to be reliant on parental contribution.
- **Lack of access to facilities/transport:** Can't drive yet and may not be allowed to travel on their own.
- **Lack of appropriate activity options:** Low numbers of children participating as there may be a lack of appropriate activity options.
- **Negative attitude towards participation:** Would rather do something else that is deemed 'cooler', more adventurous or they simply 'can't be bothered'.

- **Poor body image/lack of confidence:** Fear of failure or unconfident in ability to join a club where others have already learned how to play.
- **Peer pressure to undertake alternative, more sedentary activities:** For example, playing together at home or gaming.
- **Distractions:** Children may get distracted watching television, using laptops or mobile phones.
- **School/work commitments:** It is possible that the child prioritises school work/homework ahead of other leisure pursuits.

**Figure 1.5** School work can be prioritised over exercise by some children or teenagers.

## Teenagers

Teenagers face many specific barriers which can prevent them from participating. These are listed below:

- **Lack of role models to inspire the user group:** Very few sporting teenagers are seen as positive role models.
- **Lack of awareness that suitable activities for teenagers exist:** Few teenagers in sport receive media coverage.
- **Lack of money/disposable income:** To afford entry, equipment or membership. Disposable income may be spent on other interests.
- **Lack of access to facilities/transport:** May not be able to drive yet.
- **Lack of appropriate activity options:** Activities available do not interest them or may not be inspiring.
- **Negative attitude towards participation:** Would rather do something else that is deemed 'cooler', more adventurous or they simply 'can't be bothered'.
- **Poor body image:** Do not want to wear or be seen in sports clothing.
- **Peer pressure to undertake alternative, more sedentary activities:** For example, socialising, gaming or attending the cinema. Teenagers may prioritise other social events rather than sporting events.
- **School/work commitments:** Prioritises school work towards exams or assessments rather than committing the time required to take part in activities.

## Disabled people

Disabled people face many barriers to participation. These are listed below:

- **Lack of access to (specialist) facilities:** Specialist facilities not available locally.
- **Lack of access to (specialist) equipment:** Specialist equipment not available at local leisure centre or sports complex.

**Classroom discussion**

As teenagers, what barriers do you face that you feel are particularly obstructive in allowing you to take part in sport?

**Figure 1.6** Accessibility into sports complexes can cause a problem for disabled people.

- **Lack of transport:** Specialist transport may be needed, e.g. for wheelchair users.
- **Few role models:** Lack of media coverage showing elite para-athletes.
- **Expense of equipment/participation charges:** Specialist equipment may come with high charges.
- **No suitable programmed sessions:** No provision for disabled activities; lack of suitable adaptations; no suitable clubs; no information available.
- **Lack of mobility/not physically able to do the sport:** The level of disability makes participation difficult.
- **Discrimination/views of others:** Some may feel that disabled sport is not a priority.
- **Lack of specialist staff:** To supervise or coach specialist club or activities.
- **Lack of confidence/lack of self-esteem:** Belief that they cannot take part.

## Unemployed/economically disadvantaged

Unemployed or economically disadvantaged people face many barriers to participation. These are listed below:

- **Lack of disposable income:** Low income due to unemployed or economically disadvantaged status. May not be able to afford membership/entrance fees.
- **Lack of transport:** May not have a car or money to pay for transport to facilities.
- **Other priorities for use of leisure time:** For example, time to find a suitable job or source of income.
- **Cost of equipment:** Many sports require specialist equipment, which comes at a cost.
- **Lack of awareness:** Unaware of activities or opportunities that are subsidised, cheap or free.

**Figure 1.7** Unemployed people may prioritise their time to find a job rather than participating in physical activity.

## Working singles and couples

Working singles or couples face many barriers to participation. These are listed below:

- **Work commitments:** May prioritise work commitments over leisure commitments.
- **Lack of time:** Mainly due to work and other 'essential needs', e.g. seeing family.
- **Too tired:** Due to excessive work hours.
- **Unsuitable timing of activities:** Activities cannot be attended as only available during work hours.
- **Lack of provision:** Local provision is limited or at unsuitable times.

**Figure 1.8** Working life can get in the way of leisure time, making participation in activities difficult to fit in.

- **Transport issues:** May work in the city and be unable to easily travel to facilities.
- **Appeal of alternative leisure activities:** For example, work events, corporate socialising.

## The solutions to barriers which affect participation in sport

Solutions to barriers faced by the various user groups are often very similar and can be solutions for many of the user groups. Some of the common solutions that could be put into action in an attempt to eradicate the barriers for the different user groups are listed below:

- Promoting positive role models to aspire to.
- Increased media coverage of the user group.
- Improved accessibility to be able to access the activity.
- Increased provision of suitable activities.
- Subsidised cost to gain access, use transport or join as a member.
- Targeted campaigns to engage the user group.

Details of specific strategies to eradicate barriers to participation of different user groups are shown in Table 1.1 below.

**Table 1.1** Common solutions to address barriers to participation of different user groups.

| User group | Solutions to the barriers | | | | | |
| | Targeted promotion | Role models | Access | Provision | Cost | Specialist strategy |
|---|---|---|---|---|---|---|
| Ethnic minorities | Campaign targeted specifically at ethnic minorities | Promote multi-cultural role models | Subsidised transport links | Provision of sports that appeal to a diverse range of people | Free or subsidised sessions for minority ethnic groups | Encourage integration amongst cultures |
| Retired people/ people over 50 | Campaigns aimed at older people and the sports they could enjoy | Promote elderly role models | Arrange sessions during the day when public transport is more readily available | Activities for the elderly, e.g. walking football, senior-only sessions | Subsidised rates for retired people | Gym sessions for a certain age only, positive representation of this age group in promotions |
| Families with young children | Better promotion of available activities for families | Promote role models who balance a young family with sports commitments | Availability of free/affordable crèche in leisure centre  Organise activity sessions at the weekend/after school/suitable times | Provision of parent/toddler sessions | Subsidised cost/free kids/ family discount  Provide (cheap) transport | Offer free or subsidised equipment  Provide a soft play area |

**Table 1.1** (*Continued*)

| User group | Solutions to the barriers | | | | | |
|---|---|---|---|---|---|---|
| | **Targeted promotion** | **Role models** | **Access** | **Provision** | **Cost** | **Specialist strategy** |
| Single parents | Better promotion of available activities | Promote role models who balance raising a child with sports commitments | Availability of crèche in leisure centre<br><br>Half-term sessions for children at the same time as adult sessions | Provision of parent/toddler sessions | Subsidised cost/free kids/family discount<br><br>Provide (cheap) transport | Free public facilities for parent/child, e.g. 'trim trail' in the park |
| Children | Better promotion of available activities for children | Promote positive role models for children | Reduced restrictions on when children can attend | Children-only clubs | Free/cost effective sessions for children | Free public facilities for parent/child, e.g. 'trim trail' in the park |
| Teenagers | Better promotion of available activities for teenagers/ taster sessions/ targeted marketing via social media | Promote positive role models for teenagers | Subsidised or free transport | Programming of times to suit teenagers<br><br>Competitive and non-competitive provision | Free/ concessionary prices for sessions for teenagers | Incentives or rewards for sustained involvement, e.g. through apps |
| Disabled people | Promotion of disabled only events<br><br>Media coverage of disabled sport | Promote disabled role models | Wheelchair access, disabled parking bays | Provision of transport for disabled users, separate disabled sessions, e.g. wheelchair basketball, specialist equipment – e.g. ball with bell inside<br><br>More specialist coaches | Subsidised sessions, subsidised specialist equipment | Signs written in braille |
| Unemployed/ economically disadvantaged | Better promotion of available/ subsidised activities | Promote positive role models | Provide transport/ link up with local transport (subsidised) | Offer schemes/ activities specifically aimed at the unemployed | Offer free/ subsidised activities, offer free/discounted equipment | Link activities to 'job club' |
| Working singles and couples | Better promotion of available activities outside of working hours | Promote positive role models | Workplace gymnasiums<br><br>Access to work-based running clubs | Provision of singles 'clubs'<br><br>Twilight (out of work time) sessions | Subsidised membership through work or medical schemes | Medical cover with health and fitness incentives |

## The factors which can impact upon the popularity of sport in the UK

Sport is an extremely popular part of the culture within the UK. There are many factors which can impact upon the popularity of a sport. The section below also provides specific examples of how these factors have affected the popularity of sport in the UK.

### Participation/current trends/growth of new activities

As of March 2018, Sport England's Active Lives Survey figures showed that:

**Figure 1.9** Activities such as walking football help retired people to participate in physical activity.

- 61.8 per cent of the population within England are active (carrying out at least 150 minutes of moderate intensity exercise per week).
- 25.7 per cent are inactive – meaning they do less than 30 minutes of physical activity per week.

(**Source:** www.sportengland.org/news-and-features/news/2018/march/22/figures-show-nations-activity-levels/)

Walking for leisure was the most popular activity within the survey, with participation rates in rock climbing, bouldering and outdoor and adventurous activities increasing. Fitness based activities such as spinning, Zumba and gym sessions remained very popular.

Football has widespread mass participation due to strong infrastructure being in place and encouragement of team sports in schools. Somewhat surprisingly, participation rates in cycling and swimming were down in the 2018 Active Lives Survey.

Emerging sports are deemed to be new sports that have enjoyed increased participation in the UK in recent years. 'New or emerging' activities are showing some popularity – for example, parkour, ultimate frisbee and handball have shown increased participation rates.

### Provision

Provision of activities varies in the UK. Quite simply, people cannot participate if there is little or no provision available. Although there are many leisure centres and grass pitches, the provision of specialist facilities does vary. Tennis lacks easily accessible courts, impacting on base level participation, as indoor courts can be expensive and require membership. There are only six indoor velodromes for cycling in the UK, although there are many outdoor versions.

### Environment/climate

The inclement weather within the UK can impact upon how much participation takes place. For example, there are some indoor snow areas within the UK but regular involvement in snow sports

> **Classroom discussion**
>
> Discuss the provision for sporting activities in your local area. Are you lucky and have a lot of clubs and facilities or do you feel there is a lack of opportunities?

for some people requires either frequent trips abroad or the use of artificial slopes. The provision of all-weather pitches has improved for sports such as hockey, although versions also exist for football and rugby. However, Britain's inclement weather can pose a barrier to participation for some who do not like getting cold or wet.

## Spectatorship/media coverage

The number of spectators viewing sports and being inspired to take part affects participation rates. Some sports channels are available 24/7 and terrestrial and subscription channels allow sports to be easily watched. However, the availability of sports to watch is variable, with some no longer free to view:

● The BBC has a deal to show Wimbledon tennis for free until 2024.
● Sky and the BBC will share a five-year deal to show the Ashes (cricket) from 2020.
● The Masters golf tournament can only be watched live on subscription TV (Sky) with it holding a three-year deal which expires in 2021.

The number of spectators at home clearly correlates to the sports which receive media coverage. Sports such as netball and women's football now receive more media coverage, whereas sports such as badminton and squash receive very little coverage.

**Figure 1.10** Live coverage of the world's top golfers at the Masters can only be watched via subscription TV.

## Success for both teams and individuals

The expression 'success breeds success' can certainly be applied to sport and participation rates. As sporting success is achieved, people are generally inspired to take part. As Britain does well in major sporting events, there tends to be an increase in participation in the sports in which success has taken place. Netball success at the Commonwealth Games in 2018 resulted in an increase in netball participation throughout the rest of the year. The success of British cycling in recent Olympics has inspired many to take part, including inspiration from gold medal-winners such as Sir Chris Hoy and Sir Bradley Wiggins.

## Role models

Although many sports performers can be said to be positive role models for future generations, it can also be argued that certain sports or user groups lack role models. Many people would argue that there is a lack of role models in sports for user groups including women, ethnic groups and those with a disability. The success of England's women in the Cricket World Cup in 2017 inspired many girls to take up the sport for the first time.

**Figure 1.11** Sir Chris Hoy's success has inspired many to take up cycling.

**Figure 1.12** England's netball players have proved to be positive role models for young girls.

## Acceptability

Culture tends to dictate what is deemed to be an acceptable or unacceptable sport. Certain sports within the UK have resulted in some people voicing concerns. For example:

- Many believe that horse racing is cruel to the animals involved, due to the use of a whip.
- Many believe that boxing should be banned due to the potential for injury and the history (albeit limited) of fatalities.
- Many believe that heading should be banned in football due to some research about potential brain injuries.

 **Classroom discussion**

Have a discussion in class about what the most popular activities are. Does anyone do a new or emerging activity which is not that popular? Why do they like it?

**Group activity**

Conduct a survey of the activities in which people take part. Aim to produce a bar chart that shows how popular each activity is within the class.

## Stretch activity

Look at page 16 of the Active Lives Adult Survey and compare your area to other areas. Can you think of any particular reasons why activity rates are lower or higher in your area than others?

Link: www.sportengland.org/media/13217/v-mass-markets-digital-content-editorial-team-active-lives-march-2018-active-lives-adult-survey-nov-16-17-final.pdf

## Links to other units

You can find further information on the synoptic links to this unit in **Units R052, 53, 54, 55** and **56.**

## Know it!

1 Name five 'user groups' who face barriers to their participation.
2 For each user group, state a particular barrier to participation that is faced.
3 Describe the value of role models to a particular user group.
4 State five factors that can affect participation rates.
5 Suggest three strategies to engage disabled people in sport.
6 Suggest three strategies to engage unemployed people in sport.

## Assessment preparation

Think about the paper that OCR will set you to assess your knowledge of contemporary issues in sport. Make sure:

● You have visited **www.ocr.org.uk/qualifications/cambridge-nationals/sport-studies-level-1-2-j803-j813/assessment/** to look at sample and past papers.
● You are clear about examples of:
  ○ who the user groups are
  ○ barriers that affect these user groups
  ○ potential strategies to eradicate the barriers
  ○ factors that affect participation.

## LO2 Know about the role of sport in promoting values

### Values which can be promoted through sport

There are clearly many positives to be gained by participating in sport. Some of these benefits are given below:

- **Team spirit**: Sport can allow performers to gain the feeling of pride and loyalty that exists among the members of a team which makes them want their team to do well or to be the best. For example: having extreme pride in each other's performance that contributes to the overall team performance.

- **Fair play**: Sport can allow performers to show fair play. This is appropriate, polite behaviour which involves respect for fellow competitors and adhering to the rules and does not involve illegal doping. For example: respecting an opponent's right to take their time when putting in golf.

- **Citizenship**: Sport can allow performers to act as good citizens. In other words, they act in a way that citizens of a country should. This can involve getting involved in the local community through sport.

- **Tolerance and respect**: Sport can help performers to tolerate and understand others and to show respect to opponents. This can involve a willingness to respect the differences of others. For example: respecting different cultures and countries through international sport; respecting their national anthem.

- **Inclusion**: Sport can allow people to be included within teams, competitions or structures. This can include campaigns to encourage under-represented social groups to get involved in sport.

- **National pride**: Sport can help to develop a sense of pride in the name, culture and practices of a country. Such national pride can be shown when supporters and performers unite behind their country in international events, e.g. during the national anthem or wearing certain colours.

- **Excellence**: Sport can help to encourage and develop excellence – in other words, striving to be the best that you can. For example: aiming to constantly improve in your favourite sport.

### The Olympic and Paralympic movements

The Paralympics are games for people with a disability which run in parallel with the Olympic Games. They are both held once every four years in the same host city. Both Olympic and Paralympic movements aim to represent similar core values (shown opposite).

**Key terms**

**Team spirit** The feeling of pride and loyalty that exists among the members of a team that makes them want their team to do well or to be the best

**Fair play** Appropriate, polite behaviour, which involves respecting fellow competitors and adhering to the rules and does not involve illegal doping

**Citizenship** Acting in a way that citizens of a country should

**Tolerance and respect** Willingness to accept others' differences

**Inclusion** Being included in a team, competition or structure

**National pride** A sense of pride in the name, culture and practices of a country

**Excellence** Striving to be the best that you can

**Classroom discussion**

Can you think of any other values or benefits that sport can provide?

## The creed

The **Olympic creed** (or message) has appeared on the scoreboard at every Modern Olympic Games. The message, which was written by the founder of the Modern Olympics, Baron Pierre de Coubertin, reads:

> 'The most important thing in the Olympic Games is not to win but to take part, just as the most important thing in life is not the triumph, but the struggle. The essential thing is not to have conquered, but to have fought well.'

The Olympic creed is designed to provide a moral message about taking part, emphasising that life is similar to sport in that there will be struggles, but what is important is that you try your best to deal with these struggles.

## The symbol

The **Olympic symbol** includes five interlocking rings to represent the union of the five continents of the world which take part. The symbol is synonymous with all aspects of the Olympics and Paralympics and reminds everyone that the brand logo for the sporting event involves all areas of the world.

**Figure 1.13** National pride can often be seen when the national anthem is sung.

**Figure 1.14** The Olympic creed emphasises the importance of trying your hardest when taking part.

**Figure 1.15** The Olympic symbol of five interlocking rings.

## The Olympic and Paralympic values

The **Olympic and Paralympic values** have subtle differences, but similar underlying meanings. They can, however, be seen as one set of Olympic values which include both the Olympic and Paralympic values.

There are three Olympic values:

- friendship
- respect
- excellence

**Key terms**

**Olympic creed** The Olympic message

**Olympic symbol** Five interlocking rings to represent the union of the five continents of the world that take part

**Olympic and Paralympic values** Friendship, respect and excellence – along with the four Paralympic values – determination, inspiration, courage and equality

along with the four Paralympic values:

- determination
- inspiration
- courage
- equality.

The values can be seen as universal in that they apply to the Games as a whole, as well as to aspects of education and life.

## Other initiatives and events which promote values through sport

Initiatives and campaigns can be used to instil certain values for those taking part. Often the campaigns try to accentuate the overall good that can be gained by taking part. Some examples are given below:

- **FIFA's 'Football for Hope' campaign:** This programme started in 2005 as a collaboration between FIFA and 'street football world'. The programme funds 'not for profit' organisations to encourage social projects for disadvantaged people, using football as a focal point.
- **ECB's 'Chance to Shine' programme:** Since 2005, this programme has aimed to ensure that cricket continues to be played in state schools. However, this charity-run programme also aims to bring cricket to thousands of inner city children who may not have been given the chance to play it. It is intended that the initiative will help develop social cohesion, teamwork and respect and reduce anti-social behaviour.
- **Sport Relief:** This is an annual public campaign that encourages people to get active and raise money for vulnerable people across the UK and overseas. It is intended that the money is used to help those people live happier, healthier, safer lives. Many people take part in active events in order to raise sponsorship and funds for the Sport Relief campaign. This can include sponsored runs, fitness classes or even following a designated programme like 'Couch to 5K'.
- The Premier League's **'Creating Chances' initiative** works within English communities to address five key areas:
  1 Education – including initiatives such as the Premier League Reading Stars and the Premier League Enterprise Academy.
  2 International initiatives – including Sport Relief and Premier Skills.
  3 Health – including the Premier League Health initiative.
  4 Community cohesion – including the Premier League Into Work initiative and collaborations with the Prince's Trust.
  5 Participation – including the Premier League Schools Tournament.

**Figure 1.16** Sport Relief aims to help people get active and raise money.

**Figure 1.17** The 'This Girl Can' programme aims to encourage women to take part in activity, irrespective of their circumstances.

The Premier League and its clubs work in partnership with an array of professional, political, business and charitable organisations with the aim to enhance the lives of people all over England.

- **£10m Sport England scheme to increase participation in sport by women:** One main focus of Sport England is to increase the participation rates of women. The Active Lives Survey clearly pinpoints that more men than women participate in physical activity. The 'This Girl Can' programme is funded by the National Lottery and is developed by Sport England. It aims to get women active, through normalising the idea that women sweat, go red and do wobble at times! It aims to allow women to overcome the fear of being judged and make the choice to take part in physical activity, irrespective of shape, size or ability.

### Sports initiatives to break down barriers

There are many initiatives in place to break down barriers. Examples are shown below:

| Initiative | Barrier to be broken |
| --- | --- |
| Kick It Out | Racism |
| Respect campaign | Abuse of referees in football |
| Transforming British Tennis Together | Cost and accessibility of tennis |
| Back to Netball | Age |

## The importance of etiquette and sporting behaviour of both performers and spectators

**Etiquette** is a major part of sports performance. Etiquette includes the unwritten rules concerning player behaviour. Examples of etiquette in sport include:

- Kicking the ball out of play in football when someone is injured. The ball is then returned to that team.
- Not walking across the 'line' of someone else's putt in golf.

**Sporting behaviour** is behaving in a way that shows sportsmanship. This involves appropriate, polite and fair behaviour while participating in a sporting event. The vast majority of people involved in sport encourage positive sporting behaviour as being the acceptable norm.

### Reasons for observing etiquette and sporting behaviour

Performers who follow etiquette and adopt positive sporting behaviour can be seen to be:

- performing in a fair way
- promoting positive values
- ensuring the safety of themselves and other performers
- being respectful to those in their own team and the opposition
- acting as a positive role model for children.

**Group activity**

Read more about the This Girl Can campaign and take some notes:
www.theguardian.com/sport/video/2017/feb/25/this-girl-can-campaign-launches-new-ad-video
www.thisgirlcan.co.uk/

Read more about Sport England's campaign to encourage women to take part in physical activity:
www.sportengland.org/our-work/women/

**Key terms**

**Etiquette** The unwritten rules concerning player behaviour

**Sporting behaviour** Behaving in a way that shows sportsmanship – involves appropriate, polite and fair behaviour while participating in a sporting event

## Sportsmanship

Appropriate, fair and polite behaviour, also known as sportsmanship, can be seen in many sporting examples:

- being gracious and respectful when winning or losing
- clapping an opposition's goal in netball
- 'giving' a small putt to your opponent in match play golf
- shaking hands before and after a game.

## Gamesmanship

Performers who do not show sporting behaviour sometimes make use of **gamesmanship**. This is when the performer bends the rules. They make use of dubious methods that are not strictly outside the rules to gain an advantage. Examples of gamesmanship include:

- taking a long time to collect the ball to waste time in football
- re-tying shoe laces when an opponent is about to serve in tennis, with the intention of putting them off
- grunting when playing a tennis shot (may put the opponent off).

## Spectator etiquette

In a similar way that performers should show etiquette, it can be argued that spectators also have unwritten rules to follow that mean they behave in an appropriately sporting way. For example:

- being quiet during rallies at tennis tournaments
- remaining quiet during play in snooker
- respecting an opponent's national anthem
- staying quiet when a rugby player kicks a conversion
- staying quiet for the start of an athletics race.

It is very difficult to control spectator behaviour and many spectators do not follow sporting etiquette. It is common for NBA basketball spectators to deliberately put opposition players off when shooting free throws and partisan crowds at football can be very unsporting towards the opposition team. However, there are many examples of spectator etiquette that can be seen in different sports. Golf crowds tend to be very respectful and quiet when players are taking their shots and crowds at tennis tend to be quiet when the players are serving.

 **Classroom discussion**

Having watched a This Girl Can advert, do any of the girls in the class feel that the advert is a success, inspirational or motivating?

The adverts can be seen via these links:

www.youtube.com/watch?v=jsP0W7-tEOc

www.youtube.com/watch?v=ilSKDZvjaSs

 **Key term**

**Gamesmanship** Bending the rules, making use of dubious methods that are not strictly outside of the rules to gain an advantage

 **Classroom discussion**

Do you feel that gamesmanship is a perfectly acceptable part of sport? Perhaps you believe that if it is not breaking the rules, there is nothing wrong with 'bending them'.

**Group activity**

In pairs, describe activities in your local area that you feel are only for those that can afford it. Do you know how much these activities/memberships cost? Share your findings with the rest of the group.

## The use of performance-enhancing drugs (PEDs) in sport

Sporting authorities continue their fight to eradicate the use of prohibited performance-enhancing drugs. Unfortunately, many **PEDs** are still in existence within the world of sport and performers still get caught on a regular basis.

**Key term**

**PEDs** Performance-enhancing drugs

### Group activity

Research the following prohibited performance-enhancing drugs and try to work out what types of sports performers would take each drug:

- stimulants
- diuretics
- EPO (erythropoietin)
- beta-blockers.

### Reasons why PEDs are used

Performers who choose to take prohibited performance-enhancing drugs do so for a variety of reasons. Many of these reasons are shown in Figure 1.18:

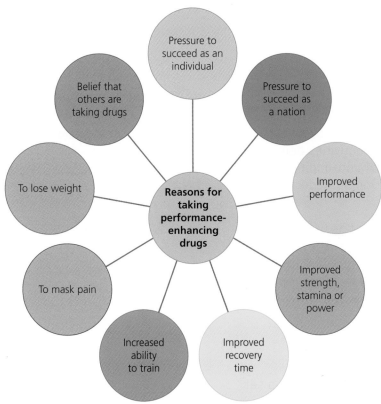

**Figure 1.18** Reasons for taking performance-enhancing drugs.

## Reasons against using PEDs

There are many obvious reasons why drug use is frowned upon. The main reasons against the use of prohibited PEDs are shown in Figure 1.19:

**Figure 1.19** Reasons against drug use.

## World Anti-Doping Agency (WADA)

**WADA** was founded in 1999 and it aims to ensure a drug-free sporting environment all over the world. It is funded by sports organisations and governments, with its main activities being scientific research, education, development of anti-doping methods, and monitoring of the World Anti-Doping Code.

### The whereabouts rule

The whereabouts rule involves information that has to be provided to the authorities by select groups of elite athletes. They must supply information to the International Sport Federation (IF) or the National Anti-Doping Organisation (NADO) that included them in their respective registered testing pool. These athletes must supply information about:

- their location
- accommodation being used
- 60-minute timeslot every day when the athlete must be in a set place for testing

**Classroom discussion**

When sport is still concerned about drug scandals, why do you think some performers knowingly break the rules and hope to get away with prohibited drug use? Do you feel it is worth the risk?

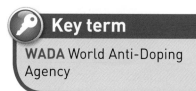
**Key term**

**WADA** World Anti-Doping Agency

- training schedule
- competition schedule.

*Testing methods*

Many testing methods are in use to try to catch those using prohibited performance-enhancing drugs. Athletes can be tested at any time and in any place. Athletes are often required to attend a special 'doping control station'. Testing methods include:

- Blood or urine samples: Urine samples are the most commonly used test, although blood samples are sometimes taken as well.
- Occasionally hair or nail samples are taken.

## Normal procedure for testing

The procedure for testing involves the following points:

- The athlete is notified by a doping control officer (**DCO**) or chaperone that they have been selected for testing.
- The athlete reports for testing at the stated time – they are accompanied at all times by the DCO or chaperone.
- A collection vessel is selected. Some athletes may be required to provide urine and blood.
- The sample is provided and witnessed – i.e. a same gender witness must have an unobstructed viewpoint of the urine being passed.
- The samples are divided, sealing the sample.
- The samples are tested in a laboratory.
- The result is recorded and certified and the athlete is told of any problems with the sample/s.

## Current initiatives

There is a constant fight to make sport doping-free. This involves cross-organisation work between WADA, governing bodies, sports organising bodies and other partners. This work has resulted in some high profile bans and sanctions. For example:

- The Russian Olympic Committee was suspended in December 2017 due to evidence of **state-sponsored doping**, resulting in 43 Russians being given life bans from the Olympics. State-sponsored doping is a wide-scale doping programme organised and supported by government agencies.

  However, in February 2018 the Court of Arbitration in Sport (CAS) ruled there was insufficient evidence to prove beyond doubt that 28 of the 43 Russians had committed an anti-doping rule violation, so their ban was dropped.

**Key terms**

**DCO** Doping control officer

**State-sponsored doping** Wide-scale doping programme organised and supported by government agencies

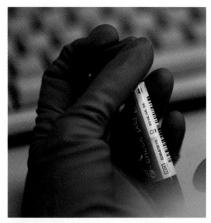

**Figure 1.20** An employee of Russia's national drug-testing laboratory holds a sample vial in Moscow, Russia.

## Drug offences by elite performers

There have been many high profile drug offences by elite performers. Some of the most publicised examples include the following:

| Year, performer, sport | Banned drugs |
| --- | --- |
| 1988 Ben Johnson (100m and 200m sprinter) | Anabolic steroids |
| 2001 and 2006 Justin Gatlin (100m and 200m sprinter) | Amphetamines |
| 2003 Dwain Chambers (100m and 200m sprinter) | Anabolic steroids |
| 2004 David Miller (cycling) | Kenacort, EPO |
| 2012 Alberto Contador (cycling) | Clenbutarol |
| 2016 Maria Sharapova (tennis) | Meldonium |
| 2017 Nesta Carter (100m and 200m sprinter) The IOC removed Usain Bolt's 2008 gold medal for the 4 x 100m, which no longer counted due to Nesta Carter's doping violation | Methylhexaneamine |

## Impact of drug taking on the reputation of sport

Clearly, doping scandals in sport are not positive for anyone involved. The damage can be significant and long lasting. For example:

- The reputation of the sport may be tarnished.
- Spectators may question whether they are viewing 'clean' and fair sport.
- There may be mistrust of results.
- When there are several cases, e.g. sprinting and the Tour de France, spectators become sceptical about the whole field of performers and the credibility of the sport.

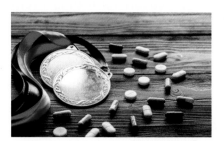

**Figure 1.21** It is a huge risk to take PEDs that can affect health and reputation.

## Ethical issues related to drug taking

**Ethics** are the moral principles that govern a person's behaviour. Taking prohibited performance-enhancing drugs is generally deemed immoral and unethical. There are many ethical variables to be considered:

- Should doping simply be classed as cheating?
- Is it fair that some performers appear to get away with doping whereas others don't?
- Is it fair that the illegal drugs list does not include all drugs and there are some grey areas about what is and what isn't acceptable?
- Should there be a stronger distinction between use of performance-enhancing drugs and recreational drugs?
- Should those that are caught be allowed to compete again?

 **Key term**

**Ethics** The moral principles that govern a person's behaviour

**Classroom discussion**

Discuss the final point here – should those that have been caught taking PEDs be allowed to compete again?

Also discuss whether the ban on doping should be lifted altogether so that performers can take whatever they want.

 **Group activity**

Design a poster for young athletes warning them about the dangers of prohibited performance-enhancing drugs in sport.

## Stretch activity

Watch the clip of Maria Sharapova's press conference following her failed drugs test: www.youtube.com/watch?v=80lfHwmkGNA

How does it make you feel? Do you think she cheated deliberately or was she just unlucky? Why do you think she took the drug? Do you think she is showing remorse? Do you feel any athlete in her position will be able to recover from the reputational damage?

## Links to other units

You can find further information on the synoptic links to this unit in **Units R052, 53, 54, 55** and **56**.

**Figure 1.22** Tennis star Maria Sharapova was found guilty of taking the illegal PED meldonium in 2016.

## Know it!

1  Describe three values that can be promoted through sport.
2  State what the Olympic rings represent.
3  State the four Paralympic values.
4  Give one example of sportsmanship and one of gamesmanship from the same sport.
5  Discuss the potential benefits and negative consequences of deciding to take prohibited performance-enhancing drugs.

## Assessment preparation

Think about the paper that OCR will set you to assess your knowledge of contemporary issues in sport. Make sure:

- You have visited www.ocr.org.uk/qualifications/cambridge-nationals/sport-studies-level-1-2-j803-j813/assessment/ to look at sample and past papers.
- You are clear about examples of:
  - values which can be promoted through sport
  - the Olympic and Paralympic movements
  - other initiatives and events which promote values through sport
  - the importance of etiquette and sporting behaviour of both performers and spectators
  - the use of performance-enhancing drugs in sport.

# L03 Understand the importance of hosting major sporting events

## The features of major sporting events

Major sporting events involve an incredible amount of organisation and follow certain protocols and traditions.

### Regularity/scheduling

Major sporting events are scheduled at a certain time and with a degree of regularity.

#### 'One-off' events

One-off events are simply held once in a certain place or at a certain time. For example, when a city hosts the Olympic or Paralympic Games it may be a one-off for that city or a once in a lifetime opportunity for a generation; for example, Sweden has only hosted the Olympics once, in 1912.

#### Regular events

Most major sporting events are regular, in that they are held **annually** (every year), **biennially** (every second year) or every four years. Examples include:

- Annual: the UEFA Champions League final is an annual event which a city could host more than once in a relatively short period of time, but as a rule it is shared around. The 2018 final in Kiev was the first time that Ukraine had hosted the event.
- Biennial: the Ryder Cup is a golf event between the United States and Europe that takes place every two years. The event alternates between a US and a European golf venue.
- Every four years: the Olympics, the Paralympics and the Football and Rugby World Cups are held every four years. The venues for all of these major events change each time.

#### Regular and recurring events

Many sporting events are **regular** and **recurring** – regular in that they happen often at set intervals, and recurring in that they are periodically repeated in the same place. Examples include the following:

- Many Formula 1 Grand Prix events are annual and contracted to be at the same venue for a period of years in the host country/city, e.g. Monaco.
- Wimbledon is an annual tennis tournament always held at the All England Club in Wimbledon, south London.
- The Masters Golf tournament is held every April at the Augusta National Golf Club in Georgia, United States.
- The FA Cup Final happens at Wembley every May.

**Key terms**

**Annually** Every year

**Biennially** Every second year

**Regular** Happens often at set intervals

**Recurring** Periodically repeated in the same place

**Figure 1.23** The championships at Wimbledon are regular and recurring.

## International element to the event

Many major sporting events have an international element, in that the performers involved come from different countries. As the competitors come from different countries, so do the spectators and the media attention. Truly international events are broadcast worldwide. Events with an international element include:

- the Olympic Games
- the Paralympic Games
- the FIFA World Cup
- the Rugby World Cup
- Wimbledon tennis
- the Netball World Cup
- the Rugby Union Heineken Cup
- the World Snooker championships.

## Level of investment in the event

Major sporting events require a significant amount of investment to be a success. The investment costs can be millions or even billions of dollars for the largest worldwide events.

**Figure 1.24** The French victory at the 2018 World Cup was estimated to be worth $38 million to the French Football Federation.

## Required investment in the event

The money that is required to put on a major sporting event does vary. For example:

- The FIFA World Cup involves significant costs. The 2018 World Cup saw Russia footing a $11.8bn bill for construction and preparation alone. Teams also received approximately $400bn in prize money with each team receiving $8 million and the winners, France, receiving $38 million.
- 2017 figures revealed that the average cost of a Formula 1 race is approximately $1bn.
- The cost of hosting the Olympic, Paralympic and Winter Olympic Games has gone up consistently since 1960. The 2012 Games in London was the most expensive Summer Olympics so far, with just under $15bn being spent. Sochi 2014 was the most expensive Winter Olympic Games so far, with just over $20bn being spent. The cost of hosting such events has meant that the number of cities vying to host the Games has reduced.

## Funding which may be attracted for the event

Up to 70 per cent of the funding for the Football World Cup comes from public revenue. This includes general taxation. **Sponsors** also play a huge role. Sponsorship can be deemed as the act of supporting an event, activity, person or organisation through the

**Key term**

**Sponsors** The act of supporting an event, activity, person or organisation through the provision of finance, products or merchandise

provision of finance, products or merchandise. Approximate costs for sponsors to act as an official partner of the World Cup vary from $10 to $25 million. There are currently seven official 'partners', including Coca Cola, Adidas and Visa.

For the 2012 London Olympics, taxpayers from all over the UK were responsible for covering $4.4bn of the costs.

In 2016 Heineken signed a $227 million deal to be the official beer partner of Formula 1. Sponsorship is a crucial element of funding, to ensure that major sporting events are financially viable. Companies such as Slazenger, Robinsons, Ralph Lauren and Stella Artois pay significant funds to Wimbledon to be an official sponsor of the tennis.

**Figure 1.25** Sponsors' logos are likely to be highly visible during major sporting events.

## Potential 'legacy' of the event

The Olympic Games is an example of an event for which the **legacy** is extremely important. A legacy deals with the long-term effects and positive impact of having hosted the Games for the country, its people and its provision of sporting activities. The International Olympic Committee (IOC) states:

> 'Olympic legacy is the result of a vision. It encompasses all the tangible and intangible long-term benefits initiated or accelerated by the hosting of the Olympic Games/sport events for people, cities/territories and the Olympic Movement.'

**Source:** Page 2 of www.olympic.org/-/media/Document%20Library/OlympicOrg/Documents/Olympic-Legacy/IOC_Legacy_Strategy_Executive_Summary.pdf?la=en&hash=783C018C6DDC9F56B7A3B428BE0A33334C47E343

### Key term

**Legacy** The long-term effects and positive impact of having hosted a major sporting event for the country, its people and its provision of sporting activities

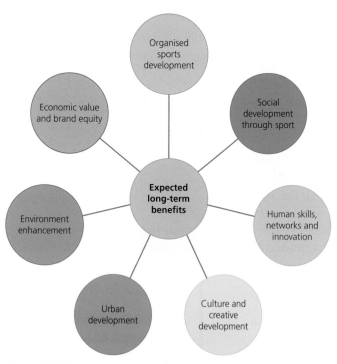

**Figure 1.26** The expected long-term legacy benefits of the Olympic Games.

## Social legacy of the event

One of the seven main legacy expectations of the Olympic Games is 'social development through sport'. Social development can be deemed to be improving the well-being and interaction of those in society so they can feel safe and secure, reach their potential and communicate effectively with others.

Social development as part of a legacy tends to involve encouraging grassroots participation projects and engagement programmes. For example, in Barcelona after the Olympics, there have been city-wide sports activities for children who have suffered economic hardship or social exclusion.

The IOC specifically states that social development through sport should include:

- health and well-being benefits from the practice of recreational sport and physical activity
- Olympic values and sport as a tool for education
- peace-building and international co-operation
- gender and other inclusiveness (minorities, people with disabilities, LGBT, etc.).

## Economic legacy of the event

The expectations of the International Olympic Committee (IOC) include an economic legacy, in that there should be an economic benefit for the host country, host city and its people. This can be achieved in many ways. For example:

- increased awareness about the city around the world
- increased tourism as a result of the Games and their legacy
- long-term investments in the city
- business and economic development within the city and country.

# The potential benefits and drawbacks of cities/ countries hosting major sporting events

Although it may simply seem like 'an expensive way to advertise your city', there are a number of benefits and drawbacks of a city or country hosting a major sporting event.

## Benefits

Many benefits can be gained from winning a bid to become the host city or country for a major sporting event:

- Investment will be used to develop and/or improve the transport system within the city. The city must be able to deal with the influx of tourists and spectators who will visit before, during and after the major sporting event.

**Key term**

**Social development**
Improving the well-being and interaction of those in society so they can feel safe and secure, reach their potential and communicate effectively with others

- There will be an increase in *tourism*. This is likely to be **direct** and/or **indirect tourism**. Direct tourism is when visitors visit the host city as a result of attending the major sporting event. Indirect tourism is when visitors visit the host city after the event, as they have been made aware of the city when following the event via the media.

- There will be some *commercial benefits*. For example, the city will receive money from sponsors.

- *External investment* which would not otherwise have been attracted will come into the city. For example, the investment in the city's infrastructure, transport and sporting stadia.

- *Participation* may increase in some sports as a result of the population being inspired by elite athletes.

- *Jobs* will be created to build, manage and administer the new infrastructure, stadia and social facilities.

- *Sports facilities* will be improved or new facilities will be built, which can also be used for the residents of the city as part of the legacy.

- The major sporting event will *raise the status for the country* as people will hear about and see images of the city and the country. This is known as the '**shop window effect**' as the city and country are advertised to the world.

- The *morale* of the country is often raised as the population shows pride in their city, country and athletes.

There are also many drawbacks which can result from hosting the Games:

- The bidding process to host a major sporting event can be very *expensive* and there are no guarantees that the event will be awarded to your city or country. Tokyo reputedly spent in excess of $150 million on its failed bid for the 2016 Olympic Games. It was, however, successful in its bid for the 2020 Games.

- Event-hosting costs may be *more than the event raises* in revenue. Thus the city makes a loss. It is reported that the Montreal Olympics of 1976 resulted in such a big loss that tax payers took 30 years to pay off the debt.

- Sometimes facilities can end up not being used after the event if the legacy is not planned properly.

- If the event is run poorly, it can have a *negative impact on the status of the country*. Equally, controversy can affect public perception of the event, e.g. the terrorist attacks in Munich 1972, the bomb in Atlanta in 1996 and the over-spend which affected the Greek economy in 2004.

- Hosting the event may only help to *promote one or few areas of sport*.

- *Arguments* may focus on how funding should be spent.

 **Key terms**

**Direct tourism** Visitors visit the host city as a result of attending a major sporting event

**Indirect tourism** Visitors visit the host city after the event, as they have been made aware of the city when following the event via the media

**Shop window effect** The city and country are advertised to the world

**Figure 1.27** The 2012 Olympics in London allowed the city to be showcased around the world.

- *Legacy demands* may be hard to meet.
- The public may resent the use of taxation, feeling that their individual part of the country is not gaining from an event that might be located hundreds of miles away from their homes.

## The links between potential benefits and drawbacks and legacy

There are some clear links between the potential benefits and drawbacks of hosting a major sporting event and the legacy it should provide. Some of these benefits are relevant to more than one area of the legacy requirements:

- **Developing facilities:** although this can be very costly, it can allow future generations to make use of the facilities (sports development) and enhance opportunities for people to take part in social activities (social development).
- **Infrastructure:** although the cost of improving transport can be costly, it can be built and run in a more environmentally friendly way (environment enhancement) and allow the population to travel to take part in sport (sport development/social development).
- **Tourism:** it is costly to cater for the number of direct and indirect tourists but there will be an increase in income to the city (economic value) and the shop window effect will help others to appreciate the cultural value that the city offers (cultural development).

## Classroom discussion

As a class, discuss whether or not you feel that your city (or nearest city) could host a major sporting event. What would it need to develop to be ready for such an event? Would it be a good idea to bid?

## Stretch activity

Read the article entitled: Why (almost) no-one wants to host the Olympics anymore: www.vox.com/world/2018/2/23/17008910/2018-winter-olympics-host-stadiums-cost-pyeongchang

What can the IOC do to encourage more bids or to support cities that have won the bid?

## Links to other units

You can find further information on the synoptic links to this unit in **Units R052, 53, 54, 55** and **56**.

## Know it!

1 State three features of a major sporting event.
2 Describe why sponsorship is so important when financing a sporting event.
3 Describe three aspects of the 'legacy' requirements when bidding to host an Olympic Games.
4 State three main benefits of hosting a major sporting event.
5 State three main drawbacks of hosting a major sporting event.

## Assessment preparation

Think about the paper that OCR will set you to assess your knowledge of contemporary issues in sport. Make sure:

● You have visited: www.ocr.org.uk/qualifications/cambridge-nationals/sport-studies-level-1-2-j803-j813/assessment/ to look at sample and past papers.
● You are clear about examples of:
  ○ the features of major sporting events
  ○ the potential benefits and drawbacks of cities/countries hosting major sporting events
  ○ the links between potential benefits and drawbacks and legacy.

## Group activity

Design a poster for the IOC to send to cities around the world advertising the benefits of applying to host the Olympic Games. Remember, you are trying to persuade cities to bid to be the host so you should accentuate the benefits only.

# LO4 Know about the role of national governing bodies in sport

## What national governing bodies in sport do

**National governing bodies** (NGBs) are independent bodies that have responsibility to govern and manage their sport within a country. There is generally an NGB for each and every sport. Recognising an NGB is the role of all five **Sports Councils** (Sport England, Sport Scotland, Sport Wales, Sport Northern Ireland and UK Sport). Collectively they can decide if an NGB is viable. The five Sports Councils need to decide if the NGB applying to them even represents a sport, as the application will come from an independent body. If the independent body applying only represents those playing the sport in one country, then they need only apply to the Sports Council within that country.

For any NGB to be recognised, it must first be established if they have a reasonable level of importance or pre-eminence in that sport, that is, they appear to be the recognised body for that sport. If their application is robust enough they will be recognised as a fully fledged national governing body.

## Promotion

One major role of any recognised NGB is to promote their sport. **Promotion** involves any type of marketing used to persuade a targeted audience. To satisfy all of their targets and aspirations, an NGB must first of all promote the sport and ensure that it is gaining publicity. It is only when people know and understand the sport that knowledge of and participation in that sport will increase.

### Promoting participation

One major role of any NGB is to increase **participation**. Participation in its most basic form is simply taking part. A drive to increase participation affects all levels of performance, from grassroots through to an elite standard. NGBs must try to persuade people to play that particular sport so that they can progress through to higher standards.

Some examples of how NGBs try to get people participating include the following:

- Providing equal opportunities policies, whereby all genders, religions, cultures and ages are invited and made welcome to take part. The intention is that there are no obvious barriers to any user group taking part.
- Increasing the popularity of the sport through the provision of further media attention, publicity campaigns and schemes for schools, e.g. working in partnership with the Youth Sports Trust.

### Getting started

Search online for some national governing bodies in sport to read about what they do and how they present themselves on their website. There are many different ones but as a starting point, you could try:

- The Football Association: **www.thefa.com/**
- The Rugby Football Union: **www.englandrugby.com/**
- England Netball: **www.englandnetball.co.uk/**
- England Hockey: **www.englandhockey.co.uk/**
- British Gymnastics: **www.british-gymnastics.org/**

### Key terms

**Sports Council** There are five: Sport England, Sport Scotland, Sport Wales, Sport Northern Ireland and UK Sport

**Promotion** Promotion involves any type of marketing used to persuade a targeted audience

**Participation** Taking part

- Increasing exposure in the **media** (television, radio, newspaper, internet, social media) so that more people are aware of the sport and what is happening in relation to the sport. This can be done through:
  - press releases about recent or upcoming events
  - public relations
  - community engagement projects, e.g. elite athletes visiting schools
  - social media profiles, e.g. looking for 'Instagram moments'.

## Development

Another major role of any NGB is to enable performers to develop, showing clear and targeted **pathways** or structured routes for performers to progress through. However, the role of an NGB is also to help to develop coaches and officials, as well as performers. This is done in many ways:

- **Training and development for elite performers.** Clearly there has to be a designated programme for performers to follow to reach the top and to stay there. This includes national performance squads and national teams in most sports.

  An example is shown below for England Hockey:
  - Development Centres – Local entry point for Player Pathway. Players are U13s through to U17s.
  - Academy Centres – 49 different counties provide a high quality talent programme for players identified in the U13–U17 age groups.
  - Performance Centres – Based in different parts of the country, they provide high quality training with high quality coaches for U15 and U17 players.
  - Futures Cup – To encourage player development where the 'best play the best'.
  - Diploma in Sporting Excellence (DiSE) – Additional training and education for U17 players selected from Performance Centres. The education is sports-related.
  - National Age Group Squads (NAGS) – The first taste of international competition is provided to those selected at U16 and U18 age groups for girls and boys.
  - U21/Development Programme – Elite training and development for those aiming to make the senior squad.
  - Full England squad – The international senior men and women's teams.
- **Coaching awards.** Most NGBs have a level-based system of coaching awards for prospective coaches to work their way through. For example, England Netball uses the United Kingdom

**Key terms**

**Media** Television, radio, newspaper, internet, social media

**Pathways** Structured routes for performers to progress through

**Figure 1.28** Former Manchester United player Paul Scholes working with children in a school.

Coaching Certificate (**UKCC**) scheme whereby coaches of 16 years and over can progress through:

○ Level 1 Coaching certificate

○ Level 2 Coaching certificate

○ Level 3 Coaching certificate.

Level 3 costs in excess of £1000 to complete and must be completed in a minimum of 15 months or maximum of 3 years.

- **Training of officials.** Most NGBs have a designated set of courses that officials can work their way through to become a top class official. The Rugby Football Union (RFU) has a Young Officials Award which can be used as a starting point to becoming an official for those aged 14 to 24. The RFU has a set of level-based awards that officials can work their way through, as well as more specific courses aimed at helping officials to officiate particular laws of the game.

**Key term**

**UKCC** United Kingdom Coaching Certificate

## Infrastructure

NGBs are responsible for the **infrastructure** of their sport. Infrastructure refers to:

- how competitions are organised
- how leagues are administered
- how rules are made, changed and administered
- how disciplinary procedures are administered
- how a strategy and direction for the sport are delivered
- providing guidelines for all stakeholders and members
- running and assisting with the development of facilities.

### Competitions and tournaments

NGBs organise competitions and leagues for different levels of competitions. However, they predominantly organise or have a say in elite level leagues and administer the scheduling and officiating.

One example is the FA. They organise the FA Cup competition but act as 'special shareholder' for the Premier League. The Premier League is privately owned. The FA has the ability to vote on specific issues relevant to the Premier League, but has no role in the day-to-day running of that league.

England Basketball organises national competitions for over 500 teams from under-13 level to senior level.

### Rule-making and disciplinary procedures

The administration and decision making behind any rule changes varies from sport to sport. However, NGBs tend to have some role in the process within the country in which they operate.

Football involves an eight-seat committee called the International Football Association Board. As four of the seats are held by FIFA, no rules can be changed without FIFA's approval. However, the English, Scottish, Welsh and Northern Irish FAs hold the other four seats. The committee meets once per year. Individual FAs can make certain judgements which affect their own clubs, e.g. to use VAR (video assistant referee).

Similarly the World Rugby Executive Committee decides any rule changes to rugby. The individual rugby NGBs ensure these rules are followed in their country.

The varying NGBs administer any breaches of discipline or rule breaking and can result in fines or bans if necessary. For example, England Hockey provides detailed advice on their website about disciplinary procedures and ways that players can appeal against any disciplinary action.

## Providing a national directive and vision

All governing bodies provide direction and vision for their sport in their country. Many use a strapline or branding logo. Some are given below:

- England Hockey – Governing body of the year
- England Table Tennis – Building better experiences
- Lawn Tennis Association – Here to help as many people as possible enjoy and get involved with tennis, across the whole of Great Britain.

Most NGB websites provide details about the national team, development teams, national campaigns and areas for development and **vision**. Vision refers to what the NGBs feel they are constantly focused on achieving.

## Providing guidelines, support and insurance to members

NGBs tend to have an area on their website for official members. Within this area, members can access guidelines, support and information regarding insurance. Most NGBs have a partnership with insurance firms, endorsing their insurance products for their members. Many NGBs give advice as to what insurance is required for clubs, coaches, officials and players so that in the event of an injury occurring, legal protection is in place.

## Assisting with facility developments

NGBs generally play some part in facility developments, whether that is at international level or grassroots clubs. As an example, the RFU owns Twickenham Stadium and is responsible for the maintenance and upkeep of the 82,000-seater facility. However, Twickenham also generates a lot of income for the RFU.

**Classroom discussion**

Discuss what rule changes you feel would be beneficial in your own sports. How easy would it be to get these rules changed?

**Key term**

**Vision** What an NGB feels they are focused on achieving

On a smaller scale, NGBs such as the RFU often play a part in helping clubs around the country to apply for funding to develop their facilities. Many sports require clubs to apply to Sport England through their 'Inspired Facilities' fund. However, it is generally the case that the facility development project needs to be endorsed by the NGB to be successful. The Rugby Football Foundation (RFF) allows clubs to apply for small grants and loans up to £100,000. If successful, the club will manage the project themselves. Since 2003, the RFF has granted nearly £20 million to clubs in England.

## Policies and initiatives

NGBs operate many policies and procedures which set the direction and vision of that sport in the country. For example, on the England Table Tennis website there is a full section displaying its **anti-doping** policy. However, the website also provides information and the following additional policies and procedures:

- customer care and complaints policy
- disability awareness policy
- disability plan policy
- equality and diversity policy
- equal opportunities policy
- social media guidelines
- whistle-blowing policy
- diversity action plan
- safeguarding guidelines
- transgender guidelines.

### Anti-doping policies

NGBs will all have a section on their websites devoted to anti-doping procedures and guidance. Anti-doping refers to procedures taken to prevent the use of prohibited performance-enhancing drugs. For example, the England and Wales Cricket Board website has an anti-doping policy and a list of all substances that are permitted and those that are banned. The British Gymnastics website has a section which details banned drugs, doping procedures for testing, advice on nutrition and supplements and what is acceptable as a therapeutic use exemption (**TUE**).

### Promoting etiquette and fair play

All NGBs aim to promote appropriate etiquette, sporting behaviour and fair play. For example, the Football Association's 'Respect' campaign started in 2008. The intention was to improve the behaviour of coaches and parents to act as positive role models for those playing. The FA then also introduced 'We Only Do Positive', which aims to promote and educate coaches and parents on their important role in creating a fun, safe and inclusive environment for all the players.

**Figure 1.29** Twickenham Stadium – the home of England Rugby.

> ### Key terms
>
> **Anti-doping** Preventing the use of prohibited performance-enhancing drugs
>
> **TUE** Therapeutic use exemption (for a drug) – the process by which an athlete can obtain approval to use a prescribed prohibited substance or method for the treatment of a legitimate medical condition

## Community programmes

NGBs tend to involve themselves in and promote community engagement programmes. This comprises trying to engage the community with their sport, to encourage participation, fun and learning. For example, the Amateur Swimming Association's 'Swim fit' programme aims to engage members of the community to use an online coach to help them use swimming to shape up, get fit and complete a series of challenges. The 'Swim fit' programme also includes an area on the website to sign up for the 'swim buddy' newsletter to learn about how other members of the community are doing.

The Football Association takes part in many community projects. One such example sees the FA team up with fast-food chain McDonald's in a programme called 'Community Football Days'. These days are hosted by a county football association or club coach and create opportunities for those at a 'grassroots' level to take part in football.

As communities get more involved in a sport, so participation rates increase and the health and fitness of the community improves. This then has the knock-on effect of a more productive, healthy and happy nation, which reduces the strain on the National Health Service.

**Figure 1.30** NGBs try to engage communities with their sport and encourage grassroots participation.

## Information and guidance on safeguarding

**Safeguarding** is the action taken to protect the welfare of children and protect them from harm. With many high profile cases of abuse emerging from different sports, NGBs have a large role to play in ensuring appropriate advice is given to ensure the safeguarding of children.

 **Key term**

**Safeguarding** The action taken to protect the welfare of children and protect them from harm

As an example, British Rowing has stated guiding principles for safeguarding:

- Everyone who participates in rowing is entitled to do so in a safe and enjoyable environment.
- All British Rowing clubs, competitions and associated individuals must follow the policies defined in our policy documents.
- British Rowing is committed to helping everyone in rowing accept their responsibility to safeguard children and vulnerable adults from harm and abuse.
- There are procedures in place that show the steps to be followed to ensure that children and vulnerable adults are protected, that concerns are reported, listened to and acted on appropriately.

## Funding

As well as the main considerations such as overseeing rules, working with clubs and coaches and organising competitions, NGBs also decide how to spend income generated.

### Lobby for, and receive, funding

NGBs have to lobby for funding from the Department of Digital, Culture, Media and Sport. **Lobbying** refers to presenting an argument that seeks to influence another's decision. Government funding levels are not guaranteed and the Department of Digital, Culture, Media and Sport can alter the amount of funding that NGBs receive. NGBs have to present their arguments to the government of the need for funding and how it will be spent.

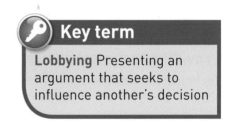

**Key term**

**Lobbying** Presenting an argument that seeks to influence another's decision

### Distribution of funds

Although government funds provide a large amount of NGBs' income, they are also funded through different sources. For example:

- money from grants
- membership fees from NGB members
- lottery funding
- money from TV rights and private partnerships
- money from sponsorship
- money from private donations
- money from merchandise sold
- money from admission costs/tickets sold
- fund-raising activities.

Having received this money, the NGB then has to decide how to distribute the funds. This is done in a variety of ways. See Figure 1.31.

**Figure 1.31** NGB distribution of funds.

## Provide members with advice about funding

NGB websites tend to include advice to performers in that particular sport on how to apply for funding. As an example, the Lawn Tennis Association (LTA) provides members with details about the various funding sources available. The very highest level players who play internationally can apply to receive a 12-month funding agreement which includes access to high quality coaches and the use of the National Tennis Centre. The LTA also provides information about other funding streams for players which include:

- 2019 pro scholarship funding
- 2018 national age group funding
- LTA sports science and medicine funding
- player grants for official trips.

## Support

NGBs provide other forms of support via their website and administration teams. Information can be given over the phone via NGB helplines, but is also available online.

## Providing technical advice

**Technical advice** refers to advice on equipment, venues and surfaces. NGBs provide technical support in many forms. This can include:

- advice on playing equipment, e.g. clothing, footwear, safety equipment
- advice on what is and what is not allowed, e.g. any banned or restricted equipment
- advice on playing surfaces, e.g. England Hockey provides information about artificial playing surfaces.

## Other advice

NGBs generally provide location and contact details for local clubs to help those attending or playing to find out how to get there. This is often in a directory and sub-divided into regions or counties.

NGBs play a large part in encouraging participation. One major aspect of this is providing information on how to get started in the sport. For example:

- where your local club is
- what age ranges are catered for
- when starter events are being held.

**Key term**

**Technical advice** Advice on equipment, venues and surfaces

**Figure 1.32** England Hockey provides technical information about appropriate playing surfaces for hockey.

**Group activity**

Design an information booklet to advertise all of the local sports clubs in your area. You may decide to include a map to help people find those facilities.

**Classroom discussion**

Do you feel that NGBs do enough? Have their forms of marketing and advertising been accessible or obvious in your day-to-day life? If not, what do you feel they could do to increase their profile?

## Links to other units

You can find further information on the synoptic links to this unit in **Units R052, 53, 54, 55** and **56**.

## Stretch activity

Spend some time looking at the following web page to see how Sport England works in partnership with NGBs to offer a co-ordinated approach to engaging the public and encouraging participation: **www.sportengland.org/our-work/national-governing-bodies/**

## Know it!

1 State three major roles of sporting national governing bodies.
2 Describe how NGBs are generally funded.
3 What is meant by the term '*safeguarding*'?
4 Give one example of a community engagement project offered by a national governing body.
5 Describe how the rules of football are decided and administered.

## Assessment preparation

Think about the paper that OCR will set you to assess your knowledge of contemporary issues in sport. Make sure:

● You have visited: **www.ocr.org.uk/qualifications/cambridge-nationals/sport-studies-level-1-2-j803-j813/assessment/** to look at sample and past papers.
● You are clear about examples of:
  ○ what governing bodies in sport do
  ○ governing body promotion, development, infrastructure, policies and initiatives, funding and support.

## Read about it

Read about the 'This Girl Can' campaign to encourage female participation: www.sportengland.org/our-work/women/this-girl-can/

Read about the Sport England strategy – Towards an Active Nation: www.sportengland.org/media/10629/sport-england-towards-an-active-nation.pdf

Visit www.sportengland.org/media/13217/v-mass-markets-digital-content-editorial-team-active-lives-march-2018-active-lives-adult-survey-nov-16-17-final.pdf to read the Active Lives Adult Survey, published March 2018.

Read about the ECB's 'Chance to Shine' programme: www.chancetoshine.org

Visit www.sportrelief.com

Read about what WADA do in their fight against PEDs: www.wada-ama.org/en

Read UK Anti-Doping's advice regarding the testing procedure: https://ukad.org.uk/education/athletes/performance/drug-test/

Read about Maria Sharapova and her reasons for taking meldonium: www.theguardian.com/sport/2016/mar/08/meldonium-maria-sharapova-failed-drugs-test

Read about partners and sponsors of the Netball World Cup, being held in 2019 in Liverpool: www.nwc2019.co.uk/sponsorship/

Read about the partner sponsors of the tennis at Wimbledon: www.compelo.com/wimbledon-2018-sponsors/

Read about the expectations of an Olympic legacy: https://bit.ly/2Q99lUW

Read about the economic legacy of the London 2012 Olympic Games: www.olympic.org/news/six-years-on-london-2012-is-still-delivering-a-positive-economic-legacy

A list of recognised governing bodies can be found at: www.sportengland.org/our-work/national-governing-bodies/sports-that-we-recognise/

Read more about England Netball's coaching awards: www.englandnetball.co.uk/coaching/ukcc-coaching-courses/

Details of the RFU courses for officials can be found in this document: www.englandrugby.com/mm/Document/General/General/01/32/64/75/RFUTrainingCourseBooklet2017-18_English.pdf

Read more about England Hockey's disciplinary procedures: www.englandhockey.co.uk/page.asp?section=1165

Read about how the RFU makes money from owning Twickenham Stadium: www.telegraph.co.uk/rugby-union/2016/11/03/rugby-is-a-business-and-twickenham-delivers-the-cash/

Have a look at the doping advice page on the British Gymnastics website: www.british-gymnastics.org/technical-information/performance-gymnastics/ anti-doping

Read more about the FA's Respect campaign: www.thefa.com/get-involved/coach/respect

Read about the FA's Community Football Days: www.thefa.com/get-involved/community/mcdonalds-fa-community-football-days

Look at the England Handball Association document, which highlights advice on safeguarding for children: www.englandhandball.com/uploads/EHA%20Safeguarding%20Policy%202016-17.pdf

NGBs lobbying government for funding: www.telegraph.co.uk/sport/football/11983022/Sports-bodies-last-ditch-effort-to-protect-grass-roots-funding.html

## Assessment preparation: Extended questions

1 Identify four different 'user groups' and suggest barriers to sporting participation that each group faces. [8]

To gain the top marks for this answer you will need to:

- Identify four different user groups from the specification – any from:
  - ethnic minorities
  - retired people/people over 50
  - families with young children
  - single parents
  - children

  - teenagers
  - disabled people
  - unemployed/economically disadvantaged
  - working singles and couples.

- Suggest barriers that each group faces.
- Ensure your answer is well structured.
- Include appropriate terminology and technical terms.
- Carefully check for spelling, grammar and punctuation.

2 Explain four factors which can impact upon the popularity of sport in the UK. [8]

To gain the top marks for this answer you will need to:

- State four factors from the specification which can impact upon the popularity of sport in the UK.
- Provide an explanation of these factors and how they impact the popularity.
- Ensure your answer is well structured.
- Include appropriate terminology and technical terms.
- Carefully check for spelling, grammar and punctuation.

3 Explain, using examples, how four different values can be promoted through sport. [8]

To gain the top marks for this answer you will need to:

- Name four values that can be promoted through sport.
- Explain the values.
- Give examples of how these values can be promoted through sport, e.g. team spirit (value) – learning how to work together with and support others by playing as part of a team (explanation).
- Ensure your answer is well structured.
- Include appropriate terminology and technical terms.
- Carefully check for spelling, grammar and punctuation.

4 Discuss reasons for and against taking prohibited performance-enhancing drugs (PEDs). [8]

To gain the top marks for this answer you will need to:

- Provide a range of reasons for and against taking prohibited performance-enhancing drugs.
- Develop some discussion of these points, showing a relatively balanced argument.
- Ensure your answer is well structured.
- Include appropriate terminology and technical terms.
- Carefully check for spelling, grammar and punctuation.

5 Explain four features which characterise a major sporting event. [8]

To gain the top marks for this answer you will need to:

- Identify four features from the specification which characterise a major sporting event.
- Develop an explanation of these points.
- Ensure your answer is well structured.
- Include appropriate terminology and technical terms.
- Carefully check for spelling, grammar and punctuation.

6 Evaluate four potential benefits for any country hoping to host a major sporting event. [8]

To gain the top marks for this answer you will need to:

- Identify four benefits for a country aiming to host a major sporting event.
- Develop an explanation of these points.
- Ensure your answer is well structured.
- Include appropriate terminology and technical terms.
- Carefully check for spelling, grammar and punctuation.

7 Explain, using examples, four key areas of involvement of national governing bodies in sport. [8]

To gain the top marks for this answer you will need to:

- Identify four key areas of involvement of national governing bodies from the specification.
- Develop an explanation of these points, using a wide range of examples.
- Ensure your answer is well structured.
- Include appropriate terminology and technical terms.
- Carefully check for spelling, grammar and punctuation.

# R052 Developing sports skills

## About this unit

There are many other ways of being involved in sport and the sports and leisure industries apart from being an elite performer; for example: physical education teachers, sports officials, roles within national governing bodies, sports facility management. People enter these roles because they developed an interest in sport and physical activity through performing. Participation in sport and physical activity provides young people with a range of transferable skills. They can learn to work both independently and as part of a team; to communicate with team mates or to an audience through performance; to perform under pressure; to use initiative to solve problems and to make decisions, considering rapidly changing conditions around them.

## Learning outcomes

**LO1** Be able to use skills, techniques and tactics/strategies/compositional ideas as an individual performer in a sporting activity

**LO2** Be able to use skills, techniques and tactics/strategies/compositional ideas as a team performer in a sporting activity

**LO3** Be able to officiate in a sporting activity

**LO4** Be able to apply practice methods to support improvement in a sporting activity

## How will I be assessed?

This mandatory unit is internally assessed through a written assignment, set and marked by your centre, which is worth 50 per cent of the overall mark for the OCR Level 1/2 Cambridge National Award in Sport Studies or 25 per cent of the overall mark for the OCR Level 1/2 Cambridge National Certificate in Sport Studies. It is estimated that the assignment will take about 10 hours to complete and is worth 60 marks.

### For LO1

Learners need to understand:

● the key components of performance for an individual performer in a sporting activity.

### For LO2

Learners need to understand:

● the key components of performance for a team performer in a sporting activity.

### For LO3

Learners need to understand:

● how to apply rules and regulations relevant to the activity (e.g. reference to NGB rule books)

● the importance of consistency (e.g. making sure rules are applied consistently in a variety of situations)

● the importance of accuracy (e.g. applying rules correctly)

● the use of signals (e.g. whistles/flags/gestures – how, when, why)

● how to communicate decisions (e.g. with other officials, performers and the audience)

● the importance of positioning.

### For LO4

Learners need to understand:

● how to identify areas of improvement in their own performance in a sporting activity

● types of skills

● types of practice

● methods to improve own performance

● how to measure improvements in skills, techniques and strategies developed.

# LO1 Be able to use skills, techniques and tactics/strategies/compositional ideas as an individual performer in a sporting activity

## Performance of skills and techniques

**Individual sports** are those involving a single performer competing against other performers or another single performer. Examples include various athletic and swimming events, cycling, tennis, badminton, gymnastics, trampolining, golf, boccia and rock climbing.

**Skills** are a learned combination of movements using muscles and joints to produce a co-ordinated action. One definition of skill is 'the learned ability to bring about predetermined results with maximum certainty with the minimum outlay of time or energy or both' (Knapp, 1963). For example, a badminton player needs to be able to use certain skills while completing the activity, such as serving, drop shots, smashing, net play and clearing.

A **technique** is the way a participant performs a skill. Different performers may use different techniques to perform the same skill. For example, Rafa Nadal uses a different technique when performing the skill of serving in tennis to the serving technique used by Andy Murray. The gymnast Claudia Fragapane uses a different technique to complete a walk-over to the technique used by Ellie Downie.

**Figure 2.1** Rafa Nadal's serve.　　**Figure 2.2** Andy Murray's serve.

Individual sporting activities require the participant to **perform skills and techniques**. For example, in trampolining a participant may wish to perform a front somersault. In table tennis, a participant may wish to perform a forehand smash.

Different sporting activities have different technical demands. In some individual activities, the range of techniques required is relatively small; for example, in long-jumping, at a simplistic level, there is only the run-up and the jump. But at a more sophisticated level, long-jumping can be broken down into the preparation for the skill, the run-up, the approach towards the board, the take-off, the flight and the landing. For each of these skills, the technique used needs to be perfected.

Other individual activities such as table tennis have a very large range of skills that the participant needs to become competent at performing; for example, long and short serves, forehand and backhand drives, topspin and backspin, etc.

## Creativity

Creativity is the ability to create or react to a situation in a unique or unusual way. It involves using your own ideas to solve a problem.

The benefits of creativity vary depending on the individual activity concerned. For example, in gymnastics creativity helps the performer score high marks. This is because creativity looks different and usually looks good. Creativity is the idea of communicating a theme to the audience through performance. For example, in ballet, the use of gestures and expression can convey mood.

In many individual activities, being creative involves doing something different or unexpected. This should be done not to show how clever or skilful you are, but as a means of outsmarting your opponent, possibly creating a scoring opportunity and potentially allowing you to win the point.

For example, in 1968, a high jumper used some creativity to invent a new way of clearing the high jump bar. He won the gold medal at the Olympic Games, using his 'Fosbury flop' method that has since become the standard way of high jumping.

In much the same way, the traditional way of shot putting involved a sort of shuffle across the throwing circle. Recently, many shot putters have created a different technique where they turn around in the circle, more like a discus thrower, before releasing the shot.

Creativity has not got to be as far reaching as inventing new athletics techniques. Creativity also occurs in a more instinctive way than the planning of the high jumper or shot putter. For example, the golfer may be able to create a shot which involves hitting the ball with some side-spin so the ball bends around a tree that is preventing a straight-line shot to the green. Trying a new move in a trampolining routine is being creative. Finding a different way down a snowboarding piste that is quicker than the usual route is also being creative. Changing your usual favourite table tennis serve that goes to your opponent's forehand and instead serving to

**Figure 2.3** Long-jumping.

### Stretch activity

1 Choose an individual sport and make a list of the more advanced skills and techniques needed for that sport.

2 Which skill is the most difficult to demonstrate and which is the easiest? Rearrange the list, placing the skills in order of difficulty from easiest to hardest.

**Figure 2.4** Ballet dancing involves creativity.

their backhand side, because you have noticed a weakness in their backhand returns, is being creative.

## Appropriate use of tactics/strategies/compositional ideas

When performing in an individual sporting activity, the performer needs to **use appropriate tactics/strategies/compositional ideas**. The terms tactic and strategy are often used interchangeably, but they are slightly different. Tactics are more immediate and changeable than strategies.

**Tactics** are the plans a performer uses to play against their opponent's weaknesses and to their own strengths. For example, in tennis, if you see that your opponent prefers to play from the baseline, you may adopt the tactic of regularly playing a drop shot against them. In gymnastics, if thanks to your performance in the previous pieces of apparatus you find yourself well ahead of the other performers in the competition, you may adopt the tactic of changing your routine to make it slightly easier to complete and avoid the possibility of falling off balance during your floor tumbling sequence.

**Strategies** are bigger plans. For example, in trampolining, a strategy could be to perform a back somersault as the final move in a ten-bounce routine. The difference between a strategy and a tactic is that, with this trampolining strategy, if you landed awkwardly on the ninth bounce, you would change your strategy by adopting the new tactic of attempting the easier-to-perform back drop, instead of the planned difficult back somersault. As a badminton player, you may play with the strategy of playing lots of drop shots because you are very strong at playing net shots.

**Composition** is the art of creating and arranging something such as a series of planned situations, likened to dance arrangements. In dance, composition is also referred to as choreography. Composition involves the use of space and height, as well as the development of motifs in performance. It also involves using repetition, variation and contrast and interpreting stimuli in developing performance. Composition is generally limited to the artistic types of individual activities.

## Decision making during performance

**Decision making during performance** is very important in sporting activities and is one of the main differences between the good and the not-so-good performer. Performers make decisions based on what they can see, hear, touch and feel. The decisions they make affect what, where, when and how they respond to a situation. The more experienced the performer is, the easier it is to make a good decision, because they have used most of the skills needed in an

### Key terms

**Tactics** Plans used against opponents' weaknesses and for own strengths

**Strategies** Overall plan of how best to perform

**Composition** Art of creating and arranging

### Links to other units

You can find further information on Sportsmanship and Etiquette in Unit R051 LO2

activity in many different situations and know which specific skill works best in each different situation.

Decision making involves the performer selecting a suitable movement or skill from a range of possible responses that are stored in memory. The bigger the bank of skills stored in memory, the more choice the performer has of what to do in a particular situation. Usually, the more a performer practises, the more perfected the skill becomes and the more likely the performer is to make the correct choice about what skill to perform.

For example, in golf the performer has to decide which type of shot to play next and which golf club to use to execute the intended shot. This decision would take into account things such as the wind direction and strength, the way the ball is laying and the position of any obstructions or hazards. The golfer takes their time before making a decision about how to play the shot.

**Figure 2.5** The golfer has to decide which club to use.

In most other sporting activities, decision making has to take place very quickly. For example, the gymnast who is in the middle of a floor routine may feel themselves landing awkwardly from a move. They then have to make a very rapid decision as regards what to do next. Do they decide to continue and attempt the next planned move, such as a handspring, or do they make a decision that, because of the landing position, they will not manage the handspring, and instead go for the much easier forward roll in order to regain some control of their sequence? This decision has to be done in a fraction of a second, and this is the more usual amount of time that decision making takes.

Think of an amateur boxer. Their decision making has to be really quick to counteract any moves made by their opponent. The amateur boxer must also be able to capitalise quickly on any mistakes made by their opponent. In fact, in many individual activities the ability to make instantaneous decisions is a requirement of the activity, and the better the decision is, the more likely it is that the performer will win.

## Ability to manage/maintain own performance

The performer needs to have the **ability to manage/maintain their own performance**. When competing in a sporting activity, performance does not always go perfectly, and this can cause a change in levels of arousal. **Arousal** is a physical and mental state of alertness/excitement varying from deep sleep to intense excitement.

Deep sleep ⟶ Intense excitement

Low level of arousal ⟶ High level of arousal

Arousal affects both the physical and mental state of a performer. Physically, increases in arousal may cause a rise in heart rate or cause a performer to sweat more. Mentally, increased arousal leads to increased anxiety. Anxiety is a negative emotional state

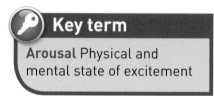

**Key term**

**Arousal** Physical and mental state of excitement

with feelings of worry, nervousness and apprehension that are associated with arousal. In general, arousal has two kinds of effects on performance. First, it increases muscle tension and affects co-ordination. Too much tension is damaging to performance. Second, arousal affects attention or focus. Therefore, attention can become too narrow – with too much arousal, you are unable to focus on everything that is happening around you; you cannot take in all the information needed to perform skills. Attention can also be too broad with too little arousal, which makes the performer pay too much attention to their surroundings and not pick out the important signals that inform them of what to do next.

As arousal increases, performers must use specific strategies to control their level of arousal, because if arousal is not at the correct level, performance may suffer. For all performances, there is an **optimal level of arousal** where performance will be good. Too much (and too little) arousal hinders levels of performance. What a performer wants to achieve is the optimal level of arousal for every different skill they perform, because different skills require different levels of arousal. For example, when putting in golf, the fine, precise movements involved require a low level of arousal, whereas performing the shot putt requires high levels of arousal.

In many activities, arousal levels need to change to be at their optimal level for the different skills involved. A smash in badminton may require a different level of arousal than a delicate drop shot.

When performance does not go as expected and arousal levels change, the performer must be able to get their level of arousal back to the correct level needed for that skill in the activity.

For example, platform divers need to control their arousal in order to make sure their performance is the best it can be. An incorrect level of arousal may result in mistakes being made as a result of under- or over-arousal. This can work both ways. If the previous dive was really good, the diver may get over-excited and their arousal levels may increase above the optimal level that the diver actually needs. When they perform their next dive, because they are over-aroused, performance is not as good as it should be and they will get a lower score from the judges.

In much the same way, a poor dive may deflate the performer and cause their levels of arousal to drop below the optimal level. Low levels of arousal will also cause a drop in performance and corresponding lower scores from the judges.

The difficult thing for many performers is trying to make sure that levels of arousal are kept at the correct level throughout performance. Think about an individual sport such as tennis. Think about a player such as Andy Murray. He had lost the 2012 Wimbledon final to Roger Federer, but made the final again in 2013 to face Novak Djokovic. Wimbledon is the British tennis

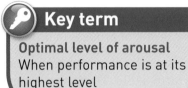

**Key term**

**Optimal level of arousal**
When performance is at its highest level

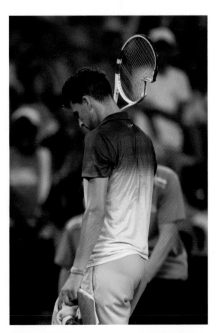

**Figure 2.6** Over-arousal could lead a tennis player to smash their racket.

championships, Murray is British. The vast majority of the 15,000 Centre Court crowd are British, wanting Murray to win. The TV audience is over 17 million, nearly all of them wanting Murray to win. How do you think the circumstances of that Wimbledon final affected his level of arousal, his level of excitement?

Murray's levels of arousal just before that 2013 final must have been astronomical. In order to play well, he had to find some way of controlling his arousal and bringing it down to his optimal level.

Most performers suffer from over-arousal. Usually the more important the occasion, the higher the level of arousal. Waiting at the start of the Olympic Games 100-metre final must cause massive increases in arousal and the athletes must find ways of controlling their levels of arousal in order to be able to perform at their best.

Arousal affects everybody, but especially those who are about to perform skills. Think about performing in front of the camera, as you will have to do as part of this learning objective. Knowing you are being filmed, and that how well you perform will result in a good or bad mark being awarded for your performance, invariably causes an increase in arousal levels.

Increases in arousal can occur before performance but may also occur during performance. For example, the triple jumper will get over-aroused if they have already had two illegal jumps and they will need to make sure they are composed, at the correct level of arousal and able to perform at their best before they make their third and final attempt.

You can often observe elite performers trying to control their arousal levels. Many will practise deep or controlled breathing techniques to lower their levels of arousal. Others may talk to themselves, telling themselves how well they are doing in the hope they may relax, and their levels of arousal may drop. Another common method for controlling arousal is **mental rehearsal**.

This can be done in several ways. One method involves the performer picturing themselves performing the skill perfectly before attempting it. This relaxes and focuses the mind on the task in hand and can be used before and during performance to control arousal levels.

Another mental rehearsal method is to picture themselves doing the skill before they actually attempt it. They perform the skill in their head without moving. You can often see athletes such as high jumpers moving their body slightly as they rehearse the skill in their heads.

The final way of mentally rehearsing is to think of a calming situation that you have previously experienced, where everything is relaxing; the sounds, the scenery, the circumstances. The idea with this method is to get the performer to think of a relaxing place and so reduce levels of arousal to the optimal level for best performance.

**Figure 2.7** Mental rehearsal before a pole vault attempt.

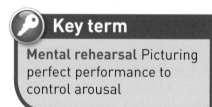

**Key term**

**Mental rehearsal** Picturing perfect performance to control arousal

## Know it!

1 Explain, using examples from an individual sport, the difference between a skill and a technique.

2 Explain, using examples from an individual sport, the difference between tactics and strategies.

3 Describe, using examples from an individual sport, how decision-making may affect performance.

4 Suggest how a performer in an individual sport could achieve an appropriate level of arousal.

5 Identify the key components of performance for an individual performer in a sporting activity.

 **Classroom discussion**

Watch a YouTube clip of a Grand Slam tennis match. What do the players involved do to control their arousal? Do both players do exactly the same thing?

## Stretch activity

Make a list of those skills, techniques and strategies where you feel improvements could be made in your chosen individual activity. For each skill, technique and strategy you have listed, devise a practice to improve that skill, technique or strategy. Use your time before you are being assessed to implement those practices and improve your individual performance.

## Assessment preparation

Think about the task/s that your teacher may set you to assess the key components of performance for an individual performer in a sporting activity.

Make sure you:

● Know the key components of performance for an individual performer in a sporting activity:
  ○ performance of skills and techniques
  ○ creativity
  ○ appropriate use of tactics/strategies/compositional ideas
  ○ decision making during performance
  ○ ability to manage/maintain own performance.

## Mark scheme

| LO1 Be able to use skills, techniques and tactics/strategies/compositional ideas as an individual performer in a sporting activity | | |
|---|---|---|
| **Mark band 1** | **Mark band 2** | **Mark band 3** |
| Demonstrates **limited** application of skills and techniques as an individual performer in a sporting activity. | Demonstrates **effective** application of skills and techniques as an individual performer in a sporting activity. | Demonstrates **advanced** application of skills and techniques as an individual performer in a sporting activity. |
| Creativity, use of tactics/strategies/ compositional ideas and decision making often **lacks accuracy** and **fluency**. | Creativity, use of tactics/strategies/ compositional ideas and decision making shows **some accuracy** and **fluency**. | Creativity, use of tactics/strategies/ compositional ideas and decision making shows **accuracy** and **fluency** on **most occasions**. |
| Ability to maintain performance is **inconsistent**. | Ability to maintain performance is **consistent**. | Ability to maintain performance is **consistent** and **confident**. |

# LO2 Be able to use skills, techniques and tactics/strategies/compositional ideas as a team performer in a sporting activity

## Performance of skills and techniques

Team sports involve two or more players working together towards a shared goal of winning. Examples of team sports include basketball, volleyball, rugby, handball, football, cricket and hockey.

The majority of team sports require a large range of **skills and techniques to be performed**. For example, in basketball, at a simplistic level, the basic skills are just running, jumping, passing, dribbling and shooting. But the more you think about it, the more you realise that there is more to it than that.

Basketball players need to start, stop and change direction quickly and efficiently; they need to be agile. Being able to run forwards as well as backwards at a fast pace is also important. There is also a lot of side to side movement and other activities such as jumping, turning and stretching. Basketball players must also know how to dribble a basketball and the range of dribbling skills includes using either hand and alternating between the two. Other dribbling skills include the crossover dribble, the cross-behind dribble and dribbling between the legs. Basketball players must have a repertoire of shooting skills, including the standard jump shot, the three-point shot, the lay-up and the free throw shot. Passing skills such as the chest pass, a one-handed pass, a javelin pass and the bounce pass are all equally important and basketball players must develop a range of catching skills because the ball will come to them from a variety of angles and heights.

**Getting started**

There are many skills and techniques that a sports performer needs to develop. Working in small groups, choose a team sport and discuss what some of those skills and techniques are. Make a list of the skills needed for that activity.

**Stretch activity**

Chose a team sport and make a list of the more advanced skills and techniques needed for that sport.

Which skill is most difficult to perform and which is easiest? Rearrange the list, placing the skills in order of difficulty from easiest to hardest.

**Figure 2.8** Basketball dribble.

## Creativity

Showing **creativity** in a team sport is concerned with using your own ideas to solve a problem by creating or reacting to a situation in a unique/unusual way.

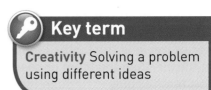

**Key term**

**Creativity** Solving a problem using different ideas

In a team game, the objective is to win. This is achieved by scoring more goals, points, runs or some other means of measurement than the other team manages. In most team games, there are two aspects to winning: defence and attack. Defending is about preventing the other team from scoring, while attack is concerned with scoring goals, points, etc. for your own team.

Generally, creativity is associated with attacking. That is not to say that defenders cannot be creative, but they are more inclined to be responding to a situation rather than inventing a solution to a situation. We tend to think of the creative players in a team as the more skilful players. This is because these players must have the necessary high levels of skill to show their creativity. A player could be highly creative but unable to display their creativity because they lack the necessary skill to do so. Creative players solve problems by doing the unexpected, doing things that others haven't done before or sometimes haven't even seen before.

The team player who thinks of a different way of doing something is being creative. For example, the basketball player who pretends to pass the ball to a team mate, but instead feints or dummies and starts dribbling to drive towards the basket is being creative. The player who thinks of a new line-out move in rugby is being creative. The volleyball player who sees that the opposition blocker has stumbled and sets the ball to where there is a gap in the defence is being creative. The hockey player who flicks the ball over an opponent's head and runs around to collect their own flick is being creative.

Creativity may not work every time. The basketball player who feints and then drives towards the basket may actually miss the lay-up and not score. But the effect that has on their team mates and the opposition may affect the outcome of the match. The team mates begin to expect the unexpected and give the creative player more of the ball in order that they can be creative more frequently. The opposition will be more wary of the player when they are in possession of the ball, and in doing so, give the creative player more space rather than marking them tightly. Or alternatively, they may mark the creative player really closely, which then frees up the other members of the team. Either way, the creative team will find attacking easier.

## Appropriate use of tactics/strategies/ compositional ideas

Using **appropriate tactics/strategies/compositional ideas** in a team sport is not necessarily based on decisions made by individual players, but often is a decision made by several people, or possibly the decision of somebody who doesn't even play, such as the coach.

Usually, the strategies put in place before taking part in a team sport are designed to suit the needs of the team or the situation. For example, if the football team has a very tall striker who is good in the air, then the team or coach may decide that the best way for this team to play is through the use of high balls up to this striker and to play off the glancing headers that they can produce. The rugby team which has a large and efficient set of forwards may employ the strategy of keeping the ball close to the forwards rather than running the ball through the backs, as they think this is the best way to win matches.

Many tactics and strategies are decided during play rather than before play. For example, in cricket, the batsman may decide, because of the state of the match, or because of the ability of the bowler, to go on the attack and try to score runs quickly. In much the same way, the bowler may decide that the batsman is weak against the short-pitched ball and increase the number of bouncers that they bowl to try and get the batsman out. The rugby team may have the strategy to play through the forwards, but realise during the match that the opposition wing is weak in defence and so change their strategy to adopt the tactic of passing the ball out along the backs so that their fast wing can try to run around the weak opposition wing.

Composition is the art of creating and arranging something within a sport competition such as a series of planned situations. In team sports, there is opportunity for composition with set plays or set pieces. For example, in hockey, most teams have pre-arranged plays for penalty corners. In basketball, teams may use a pre-arranged attacking set piece such as a motion offence. In football, most teams have specific set plays for both attacking and defending at corners. Creating new, different, practised, successful set plays such as free kicks or throws and running them smoothly are good examples of the use of composition in team sports.

**Figure 2.9** Cricket bouncer.

## Decision making during performance

In team sports, **decision making during performance** is very common. Often the decision making is instantaneous, with the performer in rugby, for example, having to decide who to pass to as they are running and trying to avoid being tackled.

Most performers in team sports can pass. It's one of the basic requirements of being able to play the sport. What separates the better players from the weaker players is the ability to decide who to pass to and when to make that pass. Deciding which player is in the best position to receive the pass is an important aspect of skilled play.

Many team sports are played with the other team in direct opposition. Your opponents can interfere with your progress by intercepting passes or tackling you. The presence of this direct opposition often puts a time limit on your decision making. You may have to pass quickly, before you get tackled. In most team sports, decisions have to be made very quickly. Often TV commentators will point out that the good players seem to have more time to perform skills. What they mean is that the good players have decided what to do, how to do it and actually do it faster than other players.

For example, in netball the better centre is able to see, decide and pass much faster than the less effective centre. Added to that, the better centre's pass often creates the scoring opportunity, whereas the weaker centre's pass is simply to a team mate who then has to look for the pass into the shooting circle. In volleyball, the better setter is able to not only perform the necessary skill to set the ball to an appropriate hitter, but they are also able to decide whether to set the ball for the middle hitter or the outside hitter, and all this is done in a fraction of a second.

**Figure 2.10** Netball shooting.

Decision making in team sport is limited by how long it takes to decide. For example, a football goalkeeper watches an opponent shoot and prepares to save it. The decision of what type of save to make is more properly called the **reaction time**. Reaction time is the brief amount of time it takes for the player to determine how to move to save the shot before they begin to move.

A performer's ability to react shows how quickly and effectively they can make decisions and initiate actions. The decision-making process can be speeded up by using specific strategies that give an advantage in competitive situations.

The more choices that are available, the longer it takes to make a decision. Delays in decision making can make the difference between winning and losing. For example, if a cricket batsman is indecisive about how to handle an oncoming bowl, they could miss the ball completely and be bowled out.

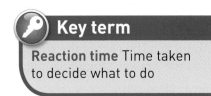

**Key term**

**Reaction time** Time taken to decide what to do

There are various ways that a performer can speed up their decision making. One way is to know the opposition's preferred options when it comes to being in possession. For example, in hockey, if the player you are marking always tries to push the ball past you and then tries to run around you, you can narrow the number of choices and appropriate responses to their move. Another way of speeding up your decision making is to spot the signs or signals of what your opponent is going to do next. In cricket, a good batsman should be able to see the grip that the bowler has on the ball and this should enable them to work out what type of bowl is going to come towards them.

Practice speeds up reaction time, but the practice needs to be specific to the needs of the performer. You need to practise deciding what to do in different situations. The amount and quality of practice can reduce the amount of time it takes for a performer to make an appropriate decision. For example, the hockey goalkeeper should practise making saves against different types of shots from different positions. This will speed up their decision-making time.

Performers should anticipate an opponent's actions. The ability to predict what an opponent will do in certain situations and when they will do it speeds up planning and decision making. Performers intending to deceive opponents can use anticipation to their advantage by making movements unpredictable. If opponents are unable to anticipate a move, deciding a response is slower.

## Awareness of role within/contribution to the team

Most team sports have specific roles for a number of players within the team, and players must be **aware of their role/contribution to the team**. For example, in volleyball the main positions are setter, outside hitter, libero, middle hitter and opposite. In handball, there is usually a goalkeeper, two full backs, two wingers, a circle runner and a centre player.

Team players need to know what their role is within the team and the expectations that other players have of them. For example, the rest of the football team have expectations of what the goalkeeper should do. The rest of the rugby team have an expectation about what the hooker should be doing during the match.

There is also the need to be adaptable during the match in case circumstances change. For example, who takes the hockey penalty flick if the person who usually takes them is injured? In football, who is going to cover for the central defender who has gone into the opponent's penalty area for an attacking corner? In rugby, who acts as the scrum half if the usual scrum half is at the bottom of a ruck?

**Figure 2.11** Volleyball.

### Stretch activity

Choose a team sport and list the main positions involved. Write down the main roles of the performers in each position.

## Know it!

1 Explain, using examples from a team sport, the difference between a skill and a technique.

2 Explain, using examples from a team sport, the difference between tactics and strategies.

3 Describe, using examples from a team sport, how creativity may affect performance.

4 Describe, using examples from a team sport, how decision-making may affect performance.

5 Describe, using examples from a team sport, the importance of knowing the different roles of the members of the team.

6 Identify the key components of performance for a team sport performer in a sporting activity.

## Stretch activity

Make a list of those skills, techniques and strategies where you feel improvements could be made in your chosen team activity. For each skill, technique and strategy you have listed, devise a practice to improve that skill, technique or strategy. Use your time before you are being assessed to implement those practices and improve your team performance.

## Assessment preparation

Think about the task/s that your teacher may set you to assess the key components of performance for an individual performer in a sporting activity.

Make sure you:

- Know the key components of performance for an individual performer in a sporting activity:
  - performance of skills and techniques
  - creativity
  - appropriate use of tactics/strategies/compositional ideas
  - decision making during performance
  - ability to manage/maintain own performance.

## Mark scheme

| LO2 Be able to use skills, techniques and tactics/strategies/compositional ideas as a team performer in a sporting activity | | |
|---|---|---|
| Mark band 1 | Mark band 2 | Mark band 3 |
| Demonstrates **limited** application of skills and techniques as a team performer in a sporting activity. | Demonstrates **effective** application of skills and techniques as a team performer in a sporting activity. | Demonstrates **advanced** application of skills and techniques as a team performer in a sporting activity. |
| Creativity, use of tactics/strategies/compositional ideas and decision making often **lacks accuracy** and **fluency**. | Creativity, use of tactics/strategies/compositional ideas and decision making shows **some accuracy** and **fluency**. | Creativity, use of tactics/strategies/compositional ideas and decision making shows **accuracy** and **fluency** on **most occasions**. |
| Awareness of role within/contribution to the team is **limited.** | Awareness of role within/contribution to the team is **clear**. | Awareness of role within/contribution to the team is **well developed**. |

## **L03** Be able to officiate in a sporting activity

### How to apply rules and regulations relevant to the activity

Officials must know **how to apply rules and regulations relevant to the activity**. The rules and regulations of sports are written and enforced by the national governing body of that sport. Often rule changes are actually set by the international sports federation of that sport.

The **rules** define how a team or individual can win and are designed to make sure that the sport is played fairly. The **regulations** define the area in which the sport can be played and, in some sports, also define the surface on which the sport is played. For example, tennis can be played on grass, clay or a hard surface and can also be played indoors or outdoors.

Rules are sometimes changed to improve the sport. For example, the rules of rugby (more properly called the laws) were altered in 2017 to allow a player in a scrum to pick the ball up from the feet of the players in front, instead of having to have the ball at their own feet. In 2016, the rules of netball were changed to allow the player taking a throw-in to only have one foot within 15 centimetres of the line rather than one or both feet immediately behind the line.

One of the jobs of a national governing body is to make sure that everybody involved in the sport, but especially the players and officials, are aware of these rule changes. The officials in a sport are responsible for ensuring that the rules or laws of the sport are correctly applied. If the rules are broken, then it is the officials who have to recognise the offence and apply the appropriate sanction. For example, in football some offences will

### Getting started

Choose three team sports. For each sport, write down the main rules of that sport.

### Key terms

**Rules** Define how to win fairly
**Regulations** Define the playing area

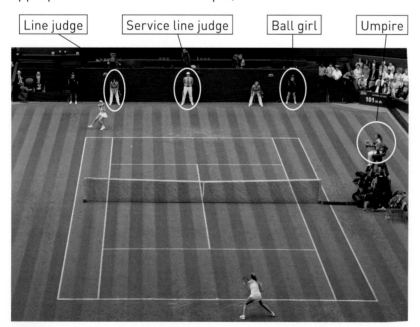

| Line judge | Service line judge | Ball girl | Umpire |

**Figure 2.12** Tennis court with officials.

be rule infringements, such as the ball going out of play and the awarding of a throw-in. Other offences include foul play, which may result in the awarding of free kicks or other more serious punishments.

The officials are responsible for making sure that the correct number of players are involved. This is especially important in sports where substitutions are allowed. In many sports the officials also have to keep score, which is not always easy in some sports, such as rugby where different ways of scoring result in different numbers of points being awarded.

Some sports are played with limits on the amount of time the activity takes and, again, it's the official's job to keep time. In sports such as basketball, the time-keeping is dealt with by a specific official, because the clock is stopped every time the ball is out of play. Elite football and rugby also have a running clock, as it is known, for situations such as injuries and substitutions.

Officials are also responsible for making sure that the facilities and equipment being used for the sport are correct and suitable. This also involves the safety of the performers. For example, in gymnastics the officials must make sure that the rings, bars, etc. are at the correct settings and are secure, with no dangerous projections. Many sports require the performers to wear protective equipment such as the gum shields and pads worn by hockey goalkeepers and it is the officials who check that such equipment is appropriate.

## The importance of consistency

It is **important that consistency** is shown by officials. Many officials, especially young officials, have more difficulty with consistency than any other quality. This is usually because they tend to lack the necessary experience to realise when their decisions are inconsistent.

All officials have a certain amount of difficulty with consistency, but the really good officials are always looking to maintain consistency in their judgements. Good officials can see what exactly is happening in front of them and will make decisions that are correct nearly all the time.

The key to consistency is to make the same decision in the same kind of situation, whether it's the first minute of a game or when the scores are level with one minute left to play. If coaches and players believe an official is being consistent, they will adjust accordingly. Inconsistent decisions in similar situations are a major cause of negative behaviour and poor sportsmanship among players and will invite criticism from coaches.

Good judgement in terms of decision making and consistency is a result of effort and experience. It goes beyond the rule book and includes an almost instinctive ability to apply the critical principle of 'advantage/disadvantage'. When you see a situation occurring during a match, in virtually every circumstance if there is an advantage being gained by the non-offending team, and if no player has been put at a disadvantage, there should be no whistle; allow play to continue. Put simply, think: 'no harm, no foul'.

## The importance of accuracy

Officials are expected to know the rules of their sport. They need to not only know the rules, but it is important that they apply the rules **accurately** and correctly. Officials are required to make accurate decisions according to both the 'letter' and the 'spirit' of the law. Because of the complexity of the many rules involved in sports and the difficulty of how to interpret those rules, errors are possible. In order to reduce the amount of errors made when officiating, it is important that officials try to be as accurate as possible.

The accuracy needed when officiating is at two levels. There is the accuracy required in terms of knowing the rules and the accuracy in seeing what is happening. Knowledge of rules should not be limited in any way. Officials must know all the rules and apply them correctly. It's no good knowing just how to keep score; there are other rules that occasionally crop up and you must be able to interpret these rarer ones as well.

For example, in badminton, if the shuttlecock touches the net during a serve, is that a service fault? Or if the shuttlecock lands on the service line, is that in or out? These and others are the more difficult rules that you will have to know for accuracy of knowledge. (To answer the previous questions, in badminton, if the serve clips the net you play on and if the shuttlecock touches the line, it's in!)

The accuracy in seeing what is going on is developed through experience – the experience of being able to concentrate for long periods on what is happening so that you never have to say 'I didn't see that!' Similarly, with experience officials will anticipate what might happen next and be in the correct position to see it happen. This links with the idea of positioning (see page 65).

## The use of signals

When the referee starts waving their arms about after blowing the whistle, do you know what they are indicating? They may look like they are involved in a medieval dance, but more likely they will be indicating that an infringement has occurred and are **using signals** to indicate to the players and spectators what infringement or foul has occurred and, in some sports, why the player has been penalised.

**Figure 2.13** A tennis line judge signalling.

For example, in football, referees indicate a direct free kick by pointing with a raised arm in the direction that the free kick has been given. There is no need for the referee to make any other signal. In practice, players often wait before taking a free kick to check with the referee whether the free kick is direct or indirect.

Indirect free kicks are signalled by the referee showing the positioning and direction of the indirect free kick in the same way as any other free kick. However, to show that the kick is indirect, the referee keeps one arm outstretched above their head until after the kick is taken. This avoids any confusion when a goal is scored directly from a free kick.

When a football referee books or sends a player off, the signal is the same – it's just the colour of the card that is different. When booking or sending a player off, the referee notes down the name or number of the player and then holds the appropriate coloured card high above their head with an outstretched arm. If the player is sent off for two bookable offences, the referee should show the second yellow card before holding up the red card.

Even after a foul, a referee may allow play to continue. This is about playing the advantage law. They should look to see if the team that would have been awarded the free kick has an advantage in playing on. To signal that they are waving play on, the referee will extend both arms out in front of their body.

Arm signals, sometimes helped with flags to highlight their use, are used in many sports. For example, in tennis and badminton, line judges use arm signals to indicate whether the ball or shuttlecock was in or out. Similarly in basketball, the referee's decisions are supported by hand signals that indicate the reasons for the infringement or foul, and the number of the player causing the foul, so the scorers can keep track of the number of fouls a player has committed.

**Figure 2.14** Referee signals in basketball.

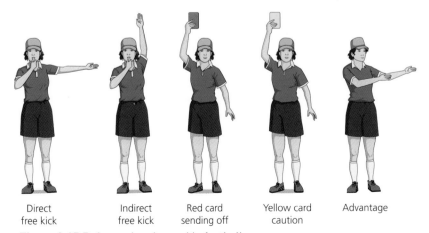

Direct free kick  Indirect free kick  Red card sending off  Yellow card caution  Advantage

**Figure 2.15** Referee signals used in football.

Other signals in other sports vary considerably and you need to study in detail the appropriate national governing body website to discover and practise the signals used by officials.

## How to communicate decisions

Basically, communication means, 'Can you deal with people?' Can you deal with coaches and players during the game? Can you **communicate your decisions** to the players, other officials and possibly the spectators?

Communication can be accomplished in many ways and in most cases, the situation will dictate your appropriate response. Sometimes a simple response to a question, a one-word answer or a look can communicate what is needed at a particular time. Saying the right thing to the right person at the right time can help avoid potential problems in a game. Communication is also the knowledge of when it's best not to say anything. It is important that an official communicates at an appropriate level, with the authority that they are correct in their decision.

In many team games, the referee communicates through the use of a whistle, which is used to signify the beginning of the game and any stoppages. The referee can often use their whistle as a communication tool, by adjusting the use of whistle. Most good whistles are designed to offer a range of sounds depending on how much air is used to blow the whistle. This enables the referee to 'talk' with their whistle. A gentle blow of the whistle can be given to signal to the players, 'I've seen that, no more now!' Alternatively, a strong, furious blow can say, 'That is a serious offence, do that again and you'll be sent off'.

In many other sports such as golf, tennis and athletics, where there is little if any contact between the performers, officials are more passive and there is no need for a whistle to be used. This is because instructions can be given verbally during breaks in play in the form of scores or explanations of decisions and rules.

When officiating, not everyone is going to like you, and while you are not there to make friends, that doesn't mean that you can't be respectful. Good communication helps keep the sport flowing and helps the players, coaches and other officials to be clear on what's going on. Treat everyone with courtesy and respect, but keep some distance. Don't become over-friendly. Be open to questions, complaints and attempts to communicate with you, and make sure that you clearly communicate with the players, whether through the sport's approved signals or through other means.

**Figure 2.16** Communication.

## The importance of positioning

In order to make the correct decision, it is important that officials are in the best **position** to make that decision. In many sports, the officials are placed in the right position. For example, in tennis and badminton, the line judges stand or sit in exactly the right position to be able to see clearly whether the ball or shuttlecock is in or out. In long and triple jumping, the judges sit in exactly the right place to see whether the athlete's foot crossed the edge of the take-off board. In gymnastics and trampolining, the judges sit with a clear view of the action taking place.

However, in many sports it is up to the official as to where they are positioned to see the activity. For example, in football and rugby, the referee and the assistant referee or touch judge are able to freely move around to get into a good position to see what is happening during the match. The referee tries to get close to the action in order to see what is going on, but not get so close that they are in the way or cannot see what is happening 'off the ball'. There is nothing worse for a referee than being so close to the ball that it actually hits them, or the players and referee collide.

The assistant referees and touch judges will keep near the side lines to make judgements on the ball being in or out of play but will also be acting as a second pair of eyes for the referee for decisions such as off-sides and what is happening in general play.

Because many team games are played at a fast pace, and in order to keep relatively close to the action, a referee needs to be fit. Every good official moves efficiently to be in the right place at the right time. It's the only way to see the entire play and make the correct decision. This means that, for team games at least, officiating becomes a game of angles and positioning, with the referee trying to be in a position where they can see what is happening and anticipate what might happen next.

## Know it!

1 Describe, using examples form a sport of your choice, the importance of consistency when officiating a sporting activity.

2 Describe, using examples form a sport of your choice, the importance of accuracy when officiating a sporting activity.

3 Describe, using examples form a sport of your choice, the importance of using signals when officiating a sporting activity.

4 Describe, using examples form a sport of your choice, the importance of communication when officiating a sporting activity.

## Stretch activity

Work with a partner who is learning to officiate the same activity as you. Ask your partner to suggest areas of weakness in your officiating that they feel could be improved. Use the time before your assessment to try and improve your officiating.

## Assessment preparation

Think about the task/s that your teacher may set you to assess your ability to officiate in a sporting activity.

Make sure you:

- Know how to apply rules and regulations relevant to the activity:
  - the importance of consistency
  - the importance of accuracy
  - the use of signals
  - how to communicate decisions
  - the importance of positioning.

## Mark scheme

| LO3 Be able to officiate in a sporting activity | | |
|---|---|---|
| Mark band 1 | Mark band 2 | Mark band 3 |
| Demonstrates **limited** officiating skills in the sporting activity selected. | Demonstrates **effective** officiating skills in the sporting activity selected. | Demonstrates **advanced** officiating skills in the sporting activity selected. |
| Rules and regulations are applied in **simple** situations with **limited** accuracy and consistency. | Rules and regulations are applied in **common** situations with **some** accuracy and consistency. | Rules and regulations are applied in **complex** situations, **most** of which are accurate and consistent |
| Communication and use of signals is often **hesitant**. | Communication and use of signals is **clear**. | Communication and use of signals is **clear and confident**. |

## LO4 Be able to apply practice methods to support improvement in a sporting activity

### How to identify areas of improvement in own performance in a sporting activity

All performers want to improve because no performer is perfect. The difficulty is **identifying areas to improve upon in your own sporting activity**. It is too easy to suggest that performance would improve if you were fitter, because most sports do not just depend on fitness; they also depend on performing skills. You could be the fittest cricket player in the team, but if you cannot bat, bowl or field, your contribution to the team will be minimal. The same goes for other team sports. You may be really fit, but if you cannot perform the skills needed, you may be of little value to the team.

#### What are the key skills in the activity?

One certain way of improving performance in a sport is to improve the skills required for that activity. The difficulty here then becomes **identifying the key skills in the activity**.

#### Which key skills are strengths?

Most people are able to perform some of the skills needed for an activity quite well, while they may struggle with some of the more difficult skills. For example, a trampolinist may be able to perform a really good back drop, but they may struggle with a back somersault, which limits the level of difficulty of their routines. The volleyball player may be brilliant at blocking when defending, but if they cannot spike (smash) or retrieve effectively, they have limited benefits as a team player. In other words, most performers have some **key skills that are strengths** and some key skills where their performance is weaker.

Being able to occasionally perform a skill is not a strength. Skilled performers can perform a skill consistently. For example, if you can only occasionally land a bunker shot near the flag in golf, you are not skilful at bunker shots and bunker shots are not a strength. If you are taking a penalty in rugby and going for the posts, but you miss as often as you score, then you are not a skilful penalty-taker.

#### Which key skills are weaknesses?

If you cannot perform a skill regularly and accurately, it is a weakness. Many performers cannot see that occasional success when attempting **key skills** is a **weakness**, not a strength.

### Types of skills

Skills are learned and, when mastered, are consistently done in a way that looks easy and uses the correct technique. Although some skills such as playing chess can be mental (thinking skills), we tend to think of sporting skills as physical, for example, passing a netball, tackling in football or shooting in basketball.

Most sports involve performing a variety of **types of skills**. Some are easy to learn and master, others are difficult to perform. Some are performed in the same way, each and every time you perform them, while others need to be slightly adjusted every time you perform them.

You are not able to perform sporting skills immediately when you are born; they must be learned. In learning how to perform skills in sport, such as a pass or a dribble in hockey, performers tend to learn the basic skill first followed by more advanced versions. For example, you may learn how to simply hit the hockey ball with a hockey stick first. Then you may learn how to tap the ball along the ground using the normal and reverse stick, before learning how to carefully control the ball in a fully fledged dribble around defenders.

## Simple skill

A **simple skill** is one that needs limited decisions to be made while doing the skill. The performer does not have much to think about because they find it so easy to perform. Few decisions actually affect the success of the movement.

Simple skills tend to be taught while the performer may be regarded as a beginner and are learned fairly quickly. Simple skills include things like walking, running and jumping. Such skills are used in lots of different sports activities. Simple skills are said to be transferable between a number of sports; for example, because you run during long-jumping, you run during rugby and you run during tennis. Similarly, you jump during netball, you jump during volleyball and you jump during football.

**Figure 2.17** A forward roll is a simple skill.

## Complex skill

A **complex skill** tends to be specific to a sport. It is non-transferable. For example, a tennis serve is a complex skill. It only works in tennis, it cannot be used in other sports such as hockey or

## Group activity

Working with the list of key skills made earlier, place a tick alongside a skill if you think it is one of your strengths.

## Group activity

Working with the list of key skills made earlier, place a cross alongside a skill if you think it is one of your weaknesses.

## Key terms

**Simple skill** Skill made with few decisions

**Complex skill** Skill made with many decisions

trampolining. Team sports tend to have a large number of complex skills that need to be learned and if possible perfected.

Complex skills require a lot of decision making to be made in order to be successfully completed. Complex skills tend to be taught after experiencing success in simple skills and can take a considerable time to master. For example, the jump shot in basketball is a complex skill requiring co-ordinated jumping while in possession of the ball, followed by a correctly timed shot. The complex skill of basketball shooting takes a long time to perfect.

A dribble in hockey is another example of a complex skill, because the player has to take into account the position of both the attackers and defenders, as well as concentrating on the ball and the control of the stick.

## Open skill

An **open skill** is one that is performed slightly differently each time it is attempted, because the environment in which it is performed is unpredictable and frequently changes. An unpredictable environment simply means all the things that the performer has to think about when playing the sport, such as the position on the pitch, the position of the opposition and the position of team mates, are all slightly different each time they attempt the skill.

For example, in netball the goal attack may have possession of the ball and is looking to pass, but who they pass to and when they pass and what type of pass they use depends on the circumstances they find themselves in. This is the environment. The goal attack must make decisions while the skill is in progress. Passing in netball is an open skill, and a skill such as passing is best practised in a variety of situations, so the performer gets used to adjusting the skill because of the slight differences in situations.

An unpredictable environment does not necessarily refer to the weather but will include the changing positions of players on the pitch and the unexpected bounce of a ball. The way you 'do' the skill is affected by what is going on around you. You may decide to do the skill differently to 'normal' because of a change in the environment, such as what your opponents are doing.

For example, a football pass may be carried out in a certain way to avoid an oncoming opponent. It may be passed round the player or passed faster so it goes before they can be in a position to intercept, or it could be chipped over them. A rugby tackle may need to be performed in a certain way to catch and stop a moving opponent, such as if they get past you, the tackle becomes a rear tackle rather than a front tackle. Both skills have been performed in a certain way because of opposition players. They may well be performed differently next time. Passing and tackling tend to be open skills.

**Figure 2.18** A double somersault is more complex than a forward roll.

### Key term

**Open skill** Skill made within a changing environment

### Stretch activity

Refer to your list of skills in your chosen team sport. Write down which of the skills are complex skills and which are simple skills.

**Figure 2.19** Rugby pass – an open skill.

## Closed skill

A **closed skill** is one that is performed in a predictable environment when, rather than having to adapt actions during the performance of the skill, the player can repeat the actions consistently and there are fewer decisions to be made. For example, the penalty flick in hockey is usually a repeated action in which the player uses the same technique to put the ball in the same part of the goal each time. Closed skills are best performed by repeating the same action time and time again. They are also best practised by performing the same technique over and over again.

For example, in basketball the free throw should be performed in exactly the same way each time it is attempted, because the environment is stable and unchanging. It's always from the same position on the court. It is a closed skill.

Closed skills are performed in a stable environment. The way you perform the skill is not affected by the people around you. You do not change how you do the skill because of your opponents, or the score, or because of the weather. If you were playing basketball outside and it was raining, you would still shoot the ball with the same technique. It is done the same way every time because there are no factors within the environment to affect how you do it.

For example, a somersault in gymnastics is done the same way each time you attempt it. You would try to replicate the skill in the same way each time as you do not need to change how you do it. Similarly, a javelin throw is replicated each time. There is nothing to affect the direction of throw. The way you carry out these skills is not affected by the environment. You aim to carry these out the same way each time.

**Key term**

**Closed skill** Skill made within an unchanging/ stable environment

**Figure 2.20** Javelin throw – a closed skill.

## Types of practice

In order to improve skill performance, you need to practise and there are various **types of practice** that can be used to improve skills. The best type of practice to use depends on the type of skill that needs to be practised.

### Whole

**Whole practice** involves performing the skill in its entirety without breaking it up into parts. For example, repeatedly performing a basketball free throw is whole practice. A hockey goalkeeper repeatedly practising diving to their left to save balls hit to their left is involved in whole practice. Whole practice works well with closed skills.

The coach might decide to use whole practice when the skill is performed very fast and cannot easily be broken down into parts. For example, a golf stroke is very difficult to break down into its parts and the whole skill should be practised. Whole practice is also good for simple skills that do not require much thought so that fewer demands are placed on the performer.

**Key term**

**Whole practice** Skill performed in its entirety

**Links to other units**

You can find information about how you might apply these methods in Unit R053.

You should use whole practice when the feel of the skill is important or when the links between the parts of the skill need to be performed in a specific order. For example, serving in volleyball is best developed through whole practice, because it contains the approach towards the service line, the ball toss, the jump into position, the striking of the ball and the landing.

The advantages of using whole practice are that it gives a feel for the whole skill and the links between the different parts of the skill are maintained. The performance of the skill may therefore be more fluent, and by using whole practice, it may take only a short amount of time to perfect the performance.

The disadvantage of whole practice is that it may place unnecessary demands on the performer, who may not be able to cope with all the aspects of the skill at once, especially if they are a beginner. For example, asking a gymnast to perform a floor sequence will only work if the gymnast can perform each of the individual skills involved. There may be too much decision making for the performer to cope with in an activity such as a basketball motion offence. There could be the possibility of fatigue if the performer tries to do a whole task such as a javelin throw repeatedly without a break.

## Part

**Part practice** is where the skill is broken down into its constituent parts, which are then practised separately. This method of practice is useful for complicated skills such as triple jumping where, if appropriate, the jump phase could be practised separately to try to improve the leg drive off the landing leg.

Part practice is also good for skills that are part of a sequence, such as realising that one part of your gymnastics beam routine is not very good, so you practise that part of the routine separately. Part practice is also good for maintaining motivation because you successfully complete that part. It is also good for focusing on specific aspects of the skill. Part practice tends to be less fatiguing than whole practice and so works well with skills that are very strenuous, because there is time to rest between each skill practice.

## Variable

**Variable practice** is where practices are varied. This is best used for open skills where the environment is unpredictable and changes. This would involve repeating a skill, but in various situations. For example, shooting practice in football could involve the coach setting up drills where shooting is practised from a range of different positions around the goal, and could involve defenders being present, as is normally the case during a match.

**Key terms**

**Part practice** Skill broken down and only part of it practised

**Variable practice** Changing the practice – best for open skills

The advantage of variable practice is that it allows the performers to adapt their skills to changing environments, which makes it very appropriate for open skills. The variety of practice prevents the players from becoming bored and can make practices more fun, which increases the motivation of the players.

The disadvantage of variable practice is that it is time consuming. You don't get as many goes with variable practice as you do with other types of practice. Another problem with variable practice is that it can put unnecessary demands on the players if they are given too many things to focus on. There is also a danger of fatigue if the variable practice is strenuous.

### Fixed

**Fixed practices** are sometimes also known as drills and involve repeatedly practising a skill in the same way each time, in order to develop it. This type of practice is best done with closed skills. For example, in badminton the short serve could be practised repeatedly to improve the skill. In rugby, the hooker could practise their line-out throwing using fixed practice.

The advantage of fixed practice is that the skill becomes ingrained and perfected. The handball winger could practise their shooting using fixed practice. The disadvantage of fixed practice is that it can become boring because you are repeatedly doing the same skill over and over again. Because of this repetition, fixed practices can often lead to fatigue.

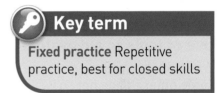

**Key term**

**Fixed practice** Repetitive practice, best for closed skills

## Methods to improve own performance

There are different methods of **improving your own performance**. These include changing the type of practice being used, altering the context of performance and using tools to assist evaluation of performance.

### Different types of practice

One way of improving your own performance of a skill is by using a **different type of practice**. Varying how you practise a skill may give you a better idea of how the skill may be performed and will also help with motivation. For example, practising serving in table tennis using fixed practice could be altered by putting a target on the table, or by changing the position of the server, or by making the serve a game, such as how long it will take to achieve 20 accurate serves. A swimmer might separate practices from using the full stroke, using the arm action only, or using the leg action only, or doing dry land-based strengthening practices using pulleys.

## Altering context of performance

Another way of improving performance is by **altering the context of a performance.** This means changing the circumstances in which a performer is playing. For example, as a cyclist you could practise with other, more proficient cyclists. This would benefit you in that you would probably travel at a faster pace than you normally do and have to make decisions faster than you would normally do. You could also observe the other cyclists and learn some different techniques.

Similarly, playing with and against netball players who are slightly better than you can improve your performance. This is because you will be forced to play at a slightly faster pace than you are used to. You will be practising making quicker decisions. You will also see how better players do things and learn from the experience.

## Use of tools to aid evaluation

When you perform a sport, you will do some things well and some other things not so well. The aim of most performers is to maximise the number of things they do well and minimise the number of things they do not do so well. The problem then becomes working out what you did do well. Deciding what things you did well is called **evaluation** and you can **use a variety of tools to aid evaluation**.

Some performers are able to evaluate their own performance and suggest ways to improve it. This is done by making a judgement about the appropriateness and effectiveness of what you've seen in your own performance. To do this, you have to use your knowledge to make decisions about the good and bad points of your own performance and decide on what improvements are needed.

But for many performers, this is a very difficult skill because they are so heavily involved in the actual performance. Many performers rely on others, especially their teacher or their coach, to observe and make an evaluation of their performance. In fact, that is one of the main functions of a coach – to observe and evaluate performances.

Many coaches use video, DVD or digital technology to analyse individual technique, as well as team performances. Performances are recorded and then watched through on playback. At an individual level, **video analysis** can also be used to analyse techniques and skills. There are a number of software programs that enable direct comparisons between performers. For example, a performer's shot-put technique can be analysed to see whether the shot is being released at the correct angle.

At the team level, **match analysis** can be used to record individual and team performance. For example, in basketball, the ratio of

### Key terms

**Evaluation** Judging something's worth, appropriateness and level of success

**Video analysis** Use of motion recording to analyse individual techniques

**Match analysis** Use of motion recording to analyse tactics and team performances

shots taken to baskets scored; in netball, the identification of strengths and weaknesses of an individual player to provide a focus for future practice sessions; in rugby, the positioning of the full back in defence. These can all be done following recording of performance, but in some elite sports, such as rugby, such analysis is often done during the match to allow for tactical changes during the match.

**Classroom discussion**

Watch a YouTube clip of somebody performing a popular sporting activity. Evaluate their performance.

## How to measure improvement in skills, techniques and strategies developed

Having decided that a performer or team has weaknesses that need improving, the problem then becomes **how to measure improvement in skills, techniques and strategies**.

### Completion of proficiency awards

Many sports such as gymnastics, trampolining and swimming have **proficiency awards** that can be completed to show improvements in ability. Many of these proficiency awards are designed to act as a form of motivation to attract and keep young people interested in the activity.

In golf, improvement and understanding of the sport are indicated through the handicap system, with a low handicap (number) indicating a performer who has attained a certain level of competence.

### Keeping individual logs of performance

Another way of showing improvements in performance is to **keep individual logs of performance**. For example, you could keep a record of the score of any team sport matches you play, or keep a record of the scores you achieved in any individual sports that you take part in.

By keeping a record of performances, you may begin to see a pattern of improvement. For example, the ratio of the number of hockey wins compared to the number of defeats may increase, which indicates improvement in performances. Similarly, the scores given for your performances by the judges in gymnastics may show improvements over time. A more obvious sign of improvement if you keep a log of performance is if you recently defeated a tennis player that you lost to on a previous occasion.

## Keeping video diaries

For many sports, the **recording and collection of performance may be done by video** or DVD or, for ease of accessibility, using a mobile phone. This is especially easy with sports that only involve a limited amount of time and the focus is on the individual performer, such as trampolining, table tennis or high jumping. Team performances are also easy to record and evaluate, but the performances of individuals within the team are much harder to measure because many skills are less obvious than others. For example, video recordings may show how many goals a football striker scores, but may not show how well a defender closed down the player they were marking.

You cannot perform and record at the same time, so you will need help with the actual recording. This is possibly the easiest way to see improvements in the performance of individual skills. The video diaries can be shown to coaches to get help as to what needs improving. Most coaches can easily spot the difference between your performance and what should happen and can suggest ways of improving performance.

## Peer observation

Getting your **peers to observe** your performances can also help improve performances. This is especially true if the peer in question has suitable technical knowledge to spot mistakes and offer advice. It also helps if you have confidence in their ability to observe and evaluate.

## Monitoring competition results over time

As mentioned previously, keeping records of performances by **monitoring competition results over time** can provide performers with information about progression. For example, records could show that your team has recently beaten the netball team who defeated your team last season.

### Know it!

1 Describe how to identify areas for improvement in a named sporting activity.
2 Using examples from a named sporting activity, distinguish between simple and complex, and open and closed skills.
3 Using examples from a named sporting activity, distinguish between whole and part, and variable and fixed practices.
4 Suggest how to improve your performance in a named sporting activity.
5 Describe, using examples from a named sporting activity, how to measure improvements in performance.

### Stretch activity

Arrange to have your sporting activity filmed. Analyse your own performance and identify several weaknesses. Construct a plan to improve the weaknesses you have identified.

## Read about it

Find out more about reaction time and decision-making in sport:
https://www.sports-training-adviser.com/reactiontime.html

Watch a presentation about arousal in sport: https://prezi.com/kgpjntyfe6tr/arousal-in-sport

Read about how to become a basketball official:
www.basketballengland.co.uk/get-involved/officiate/?aid=31&pid=66

Read about how to become a netball official: www.englandnetball.co.uk/make-the-game/officiating

The 25 most important things to know about officiating: https://phillyref.com/articles/top25.html

Different types of skill: https://www.brianmac.co.uk/continuum.htm

Different types and methods of practice: https://www.teachpe.com/sports_psychology/teaching.php

Sports specific evaluation tests: www.brianmac.co.uk/evalsports.htm

Proficiency awards: www.gymnasticsforschools.co.uk/british-gymnastics-badges

## Assessment preparation

Think about the task/s that your teacher may set you to assess your ability to apply practice methods to support improvement in a sporting activity.

Make sure you:

- Are able to identify areas of improvement in your own performance in a sporting activity:
  - What are the key skills in the activity?
  - Which of the key skills are strengths?
  - Which of the key skills are weaknesses?
- Know different types of skill:
  - simple skill
  - complex skill
  - open skill
  - closed skill.
- Know different types of practice:
  - whole
  - part
  - variable
  - fixed.
- Know methods to improve own performance:
  - different types of practice
  - altering context of performance
  - use of tools to aid evaluation.
- Know how to measure improvements in skills, techniques and strategies developed:
  - completion of proficiency awards
  - keeping individual logs of performance
  - keeping video diaries
  - peer observation
  - monitoring competition results over time.

### Mark scheme

| LO4 Be able to apply practice methods to support improvement in a sporting activity | | |
| --- | --- | --- |
| Mark band 1 | Mark band 2 | Mark band 3 |
| The review of their performance is **basic**. | The review of their performance is **detailed** in **some aspects**. | The review of their performance is **detailed** in **most aspects**. |
| The application of practice methods is **basic** and addresses **few** of the areas and skills where improvement is needed. | The application of practice methods is **simple** and addresses **many** of the areas and skills where improvement is needed. | The application of practice methods is **considered** and addresses **most** of the areas and skills where improvement is needed. |
| Understanding of how to measure improvement is **limited**. | Understanding of how to measure improvement is **detailed**. | Understanding of how to measure improvement is **comprehensive**. |

# R053 Sports leadership

## About this unit

Within this unit, learners will begin to understand the important role that sports leaders have in influencing those around them. This unit will give learners the opportunity to experience, first hand, the knowledge, understanding and practical skills required to be an effective leader in sport. Learners are encouraged to consider and evaluate delivery of sporting activity sessions, focusing on their leadership styles, effective communication and personal behaviour conducive to being an effective leader. Learners will be given the opportunity to practically demonstrate and be adaptive in situations to enable them to meet the needs of the performers they are leading. This chapter will provide valuable knowledge and information which will assist in the practical processes that students will undertake.

## Learning outcomes

**LO1** Know the personal qualities, styles, roles and responsibilities associated with effective sports leadership

**LO2** Be able to plan sports activity sessions

**LO3** Be able to deliver sports activity sessions

**LO4** Be able to evaluate own performance in delivering a sports activity session

## How will I be assessed?

This is assessed over 30 Guided Learning Hours. Approximately 10 hours of internal assessment will be worth 60 marks (60 UMS). This is centre assessed and OCR moderated.

### For LO1

Learners need to have knowledge and understanding of:

- the different leadership roles and responsibilities in sport
- role-related responsibilities
- personal qualities which relate to leadership roles
- leadership styles.

### For LO2

Learners need to have knowledge and understanding of:

- key considerations when planning sports activity sessions

- safety considerations when planning sports activity sessions.

### For LO3

Learners need to have knowledge and understanding of:

- safe practice
- delivery style
- communication skills
- motivation techniques
- activity-specific knowledge
- adaptability.

### For LO4

Learners need to have knowledge and understanding of:

- aspects to consider in evaluating planning and delivery of a sports activity session, including what went well, what did not go well and what could be improved for the future.

## LO1 Know the personal qualities, styles, roles and responsibilities associated with effective sports leadership

**Leadership** can be defined as the action of leading a group of people. However, being a **leader** has distinctive requirements. Leaders hold responsibility and respect and have followers who they can influence.

### Different leadership roles and opportunities in sport

Sport in its nature provides opportunities for people to lead. Although not all sport is team-based, many activities include the need to work with others and to command respect and influence. In a sporting context, there are many examples of how leaders can influence others:

- **Captains**: Help to make decisions for their team and influence and motivate those around them. A good captain will listen to the viewpoints of others but be willing to make decisions when required. In a sport such as rugby, the captain is responsible for speaking to the referee about the conduct of his/her team and can make decisions such as whether to kick for goal or to kick to touch. Ama Agbeze captained the England Roses Netball team to victory at the 2018 Commonwealth Games.

### Getting started

As a class, list as many sporting leaders as you can. What attributes and characteristics do you feel these people have, e.g. good communication skills?

### Key terms

**Leadership** The action of leading a group of people

**Leader** Person who holds responsibility and respect and has followers they can influence

- **Managers**: Help to manage the processes and procedures, tactics and strategies that a team or sports performer uses. Managers can make decisions such as to substitute performers or to change how people are playing. However, it is generally accepted that managers should be fair to all of their players. In a sport such as football, managers play a key role and have many media duties to fulfil, both before and after their fixtures. Under Michael O'Neill, Northern Ireland qualified for their first ever European Championship in 2016.

- **Teachers**: Are in a position of authority and subsequently have the opportunity to lead and guide those they are teaching. Teachers of physical education may well lead sports teams in extracurricular activities and can influence who plays or the manner in which play takes place. However, PE teachers also teach core PE lessons and are responsible for planning and leading sessions, ensuring that all children progress in their learning. PE teachers are responsible for safety and tracking the progress of their students. They must also lead sessions in a way that helps children to develop their physical skills. PE teachers generally have a relevant university degree that entitles them to work with children in this capacity.

- **Coaches**: Influence those who they coach. Coaches can work on a one-to-one basis but equally may be coaching a large group of performers. Their leadership role is to guide and help performers in order to eradicate weaknesses and maximise strengths. Coaches usually have official coaching qualifications – often administered by the governing body for that sport. Whilst leading those that they coach, coaches have to ensure safety, progression and the learning of skills, and provide appropriate feedback. Tracey Neville led the England netball team to a gold medal in the 2018 Commonwealth Games.

- **Expedition leaders**: Influence those in the expedition. They may well hold significant responsibilities for the group they are leading, such as guiding them down a mountain or through dangerous terrain on a walk. Expedition leaders often need to help others to lead and to take on responsibility. An example of an expedition leader would be someone leading an activity for the Duke of Edinburgh's Award Scheme.

- **Role models**: Can be positive or negative. However, there is a general belief that sportspeople should act as positive role models to the general public, leading and guiding other sports performers in how to conduct themselves. This does not always happen, as their sporting influence can, of course, be negative as well as positive. PE teachers can act as positive role models for those they teach. National sports coaches and managers can act as positive role models on a wider scale. Gareth Southgate was praised for his conduct and demeanour whilst leading the England football team during the 2018 World Cup.

 **Group activity**

Try to name as many positive sporting role models as you can. What is it about them that makes their influence positive?

**Figure 3.1** A sports coach has the ability to act as a positive role model when leading their team.

## Role-related responsibilities

A major element of being an effective leader is having knowledge about the activity in which you are leading. This knowledge has to cover many aspects of the leadership role.

### Knowledge of activity

Any sporting leader must fully understand the activity and know the rules so that they can plan to play within the rules. Equally, if they are questioned about the rules they should know the answer and provide appropriate advice.

Sports leaders should be able to plan appropriate training and development activities for their group. This involves a thorough knowledge of the skills that are used when performing that activity and the correct technique that should be used. When planning sessions, a sports leader needs to understand how skill progressions can take place so that people of different abilities can improve and continue to develop their skills. In an activity such as trampolining, this may include specific examples and ways to learn more complex skills, e.g. learning how to bounce before learning how to do a seat drop. The sports leader needs to know and understand how to encourage the correct sporting behaviour, etiquette and tactics.

**Figure 3.2** A sports coach must have suitable knowledge in the activity they are leading.

### Enthusiasm for activity

A sports leader has to show an appropriate amount of motivation and enthusiasm for the activity they are leading. It is often advocated that 'enthusiasm is infectious' and can lead to others being enthusiastic. An uninterested sports leader is unlikely to get the best out of their group. Sports leaders must show the same drive and commitment that they expect from their performers.

**Figure 3.3** Sports leaders must show enthusiasm and drive for their activity.

## Knowledge of safety

The prime concern of anyone in a position of responsibility should be the safety of those involved. Teachers, coaches and managers hold a specific responsibility to maintain the safety of those they are leading and must take this role seriously at all times. In order to perform this role, sports leaders tend to need to have knowledge in the following areas:

- the techniques to be used in that activity
- what equipment is deemed safe in that activity
- what clothing and footwear is required for that activity
- how to carry out risk assessments for that activity
- how to reduce risks for that activity
- how to treat injuries.

**Figure 3.4** Injuries will occur in sporting activities but sports leaders should try to reduce the chances of these injuries occurring.

## Knowledge of child protection issues

Safeguarding, or protecting children from harm, is a major consideration for any sporting leader. Children should feel safe and supported when playing sport and the leader must do everything within their power to allow this to happen. Coaches and teachers, for example, have to be DBS (Disclosure and Barring Service) checked before being allowed to attend a coaching course or to instruct children.

## Knowledge of basic first aid

Sports leaders have often attended first aid awareness training to enable them to use basic first aid in the event of someone getting injured. Although serious injuries require the help of emergency services, many sports leaders are proficient in knowing how to treat minor injuries and how to help to prevent them from happening in the first place.

## Personal qualities that relate to leadership roles

There are a multitude of qualities that are common amongst good leaders. Some of these are shown in Figure 3.5.

**Figure 3.5** Leadership qualities.

Sports leaders must be punctual for training and reliable in attendance. They must be able to communicate with the people they are leading and be fair to everyone. They must have the confidence to instruct and the charisma or charm to persuade and motivate. Sports leaders must be creative when designing sessions for their group and knowledgeable about the activity, its skills, techniques and specific requirements.

## Leadership styles

**Leadership styles** can be seen to be the manner and approach in providing direction for those that you are leading. This involves the personality and attitude of the leader towards the activity being performed.

Kurt Lewin identified three main styles of leadership. These are:

- democratic
- autocratic
- laissez-faire.

Each style has its advantages and disadvantages depending upon the situation in which it is being used. The key is to realise that the style should be chosen to maximise performance in that given moment and situation. No one leadership style is necessarily the best; sometimes it has to be adapted to suit the situation.

**Democratic** leaders consult the group when making decisions. They look for consensus and are willing to listen to the viewpoint of others. They are not hasty in decision making, take the time to talk to group members and respect others' opinions. A team captain may take a democratic approach when discussing tactics before a major event. Elite-level performers may well have some informed ideas and suggestions for their coach or leader and so a democratic approach may prove to be fruitful. Democratic leadership can be very important when there is team unrest and people want their opinions to be heard.

| Democratic leadership style | |
| --- | --- |
| Advantages | Disadvantages |
| Makes people feel part of the decision-making process | Can be very slow to come to a decision |
| Lets others feel that their opinion is valued | Confusion as to who the leader is |
| Makes use of potentially good ideas from others | Can undermine the authority of the leader |

**Autocratic** leaders do not value the opinion of others. They do not ask for opinions or welcome suggestions. They are the sole leader and therefore make all of the decisions. This can be particularly useful when there are safety concerns if the activity is dangerous. For example, when a PE teacher leads a lesson on throwing the javelin, it is often in a very autocratic style to ensure the safety of all involved. It prevents students from messing about and simply provides them with prescriptive guidelines to follow. Although an autocratic leader may appear bossy, they sometimes have no choice in order to keep control of the group.

| Autocratic leadership style | |
| --- | --- |
| Advantages | Disadvantages |
| Quick decisions can be made | Can cause others to resent the leader |
| Everyone knows who is in charge | Others do not feel that their opinion matters |
| Leadership is clear | Can lead to unrest and mutiny against the leader as they are perceived to be bossy |

**Laissez-faire** is a leadership style in which the leader does not intervene and allows the activity to follow its own, natural course. When using this style, the leader may do nothing at all and feel relaxed about what is happening at that specific time. It can be very useful when a group is working really well, and when intervention

## Key terms

**Democratic** Leadership style in which the leader consults the group when making decisions

**Autocratic** Leadership style in which the leader does not value the opinion of others. They do not ask for opinions or welcome suggestions

**Laissez-faire** Leadership style in which the leader does not intervene and allows an activity to follow its own natural course

## Group activity

Are there any sports leaders in the class? If so, have they had to be autocratic with a group and if so, why?

may disrupt or distract them. When a team is highly motivated and skilled, this style may allow the leader to be told what to do by his or her performers. It can allow the leader to develop communication, thinking and leadership skills within the team. It can actually be a catalyst for helping others to succeed as leaders.

| Laissez-faire leadership style | |
| --- | --- |
| **Advantages** | **Disadvantages** |
| Creates an atmosphere of no stress or pressure | Can be very slow to come to a decision or none is made |
| Gives opportunities for those who want to lead | No-one really knows who is in charge |
| Can be good to simply let performers 'get on with it' without interruption | Can result in a lack of direction or purpose |

**Figure 3.6** Laissez-faire leadership may allow team performers to make their own decisions without input from the leader.

 **Classroom discussion**

As a class, discuss what leadership style or styles your sports coaches use. Do you feel that a particular style of leadership suits you when being led? If you have the consent of your classroom teacher, what style or styles would you say they use and why?

 **Group activity**

Produce a PowerPoint or Prezi presentation for the class that outlines the main advantages and disadvantages of using autocratic, democratic and laissez-faire leadership styles.

**Stretch activity**

Search on YouTube for footage of sports leaders. What styles do you see them using and why do you think that is? Can you come up with examples of leaders who use different styles but are often successful?

**Links to other units**

information on the synoptic links to this unit in **Units R051, 52, 54, 55** and **56**.

## Know it!

1 What is meant by the term *leader*?
2 State three different leadership roles and responsibilities which are possible in sport.
3 Describe what a leader must have knowledge of when leading a sporting activity.
4 State four key characteristics of an effective leader.
5 Describe sporting situations when the best leadership style to use is:
   ○ autocratic
   ○ democratic
   ○ laissez-faire.

## Assessment preparation

Think about the task/s that your teacher may set you to assess your knowledge of personal qualities, style, roles and responsibilities associated with effective sports leadership. Make sure you:

● Know what a leader is.
● Are clear about examples of:
   ○ the different leadership roles and responsibilities in sport
   ○ role-related responsibilities
   ○ personal qualities which relate to leadership roles
   ○ leadership styles.

How will you demonstrate that you can make clear and accurate links between different roles and the personal qualities and leadership styles of those who undertake them?

### Mark scheme

| LO1 Know the personal qualities, styles, roles and responsibilities associated with effective sports leadership | | |
| --- | --- | --- |
| **Mark band 1** | **Mark band 2** | **Mark band 3** |
| **Outlines** a range of different sports leadership roles and responsibilities associated with them. **Identifies** the styles and personal qualities which relate to leadership roles in sport. | **Describes** a range of sport leadership roles and related responsibilities. **Makes links** between different roles and the personal qualities and leadership styles of those who undertake them with some accuracy. | **Describes** a **wide range** of sports leadership roles and related responsibilities. **Makes clear and accurate links** between different roles and the personal qualities and leadership styles of those who undertake them. |

## LO2 Be able to plan sports activity sessions

### Key considerations when planning sports activity sessions

When planning any sports activity session, there are key components that must be considered and appropriately planned for. The success of the session will be down to appropriate planning as much as how it is delivered. If the planning is thorough and detailed, the session is easier to follow and often easier to deliver.

### Objectives for the session

In simple terms, the **objectives** are what you hope to achieve. When designing objectives, they must be about meeting the needs of the group. If the group has specific needs then these must be considered. Objectives cannot be too ambitious but equally should be challenging enough. If the group consists of beginners, do not expect to achieve a high level of performance in session one! Objectives can be kept simple, e.g. to improve a specific skill in a specific activity.

### Appropriate venue

The chosen venue for a sports session should be safe, suitably equipped and appropriate to meet the set objectives. For example, if the objective is to improve at basketball shooting, clearly there need to be basketballs, an appropriate surface to play basketball and a basketball hoop. The type and size of venue should be considered. Does it need to be indoors or would an outdoor venue equally allow the objectives to be met?

### Equipment needs

The **equipment** needs of the session should be considered. Equipment may include fixed equipment or portable equipment that can be moved. Does the equipment take a long time to prepare and set up and therefore need to be organised before the session? Will you need help in safely moving equipment at any point before, during or after the session? Is there enough equipment to cater for the size of the group, e.g. one ball between two participants?

Some age ranges can only use certain weights or sizes of equipment so this should be checked in advance via the particular sport's governing body or organisation website.

### Supervision needs

When deciding on the supervision needs of a session, several questions should be asked:

- Do I have any people in my session who will need additional help?
- Will anyone require one-to-one supervision?

**Key terms**

**Objectives** What you hope to achieve

**Equipment** Fixed equipment or portable equipment that can be moved

**Figure 3.7** You must consider whether the venue is suitable to allow the objectives to be met.

- Will I need additional leaders to assist me?
- What roles can I assign participants and will these roles require specialist support, e.g. support in gymnastics?
- Will they need to be taught how to support first?
- How many participants do I have? Is it acceptable to only have one leader with a group of that size?

Please note that recommended **ratios** differ for different activities. Ratio refers to the number of adult leaders required for the number of students. As an example, the Rugby Football Union recommends:

- 1:10 (1 adult to 10 children) for children aged at least 9
- 1:8 for children aged 7 and 8
- 1:6 for children under 7.

**Key term**

**Ratio** The number of leaders required for the number of students

## Timing of activities

When deciding how long to spend on each activity within the session, the leader must consider the following factors:

- An appropriate amount of time for the age range of the group. Older performers may not be able to sustain exercise for a long period of time.
- The experience level of the group. Experienced performers may be able to sustain exercise for longer periods.
- The fitness level of the group. Fitter performers are likely to be able to sustain exercise for longer.
- The weather and conditions, i.e. is it safe to work for a long period of time due to heat or cold etc.? If it is too hot, exercise can lead to heat exhaustion and dehydration, so rest periods may be required.

## Introduction and conclusion of session

Detail should be provided about the introduction and conclusion for the session. An introduction may include:

- who the group are
- when the activity will take place
- where the activity will take place
- how groups will be organised
- any equipment that needs to be set up
- how much space will be used
- where the performers will perform their warm-up (e.g. how, when, where?).

Conclusions tend to detail:

● the organisation of the group for the cool-down
● any equipment that will be used when the cool-down is taking place
● any particular points that need to be made to address the main objectives for the session.

## Basic warm-up/cool-down

Details of a **warm-up** should include:

● a pulse-raising activity, e.g. jogging
● stretches to stretch the main muscles that will be used
● familiarisation or skill-based activities, to familiarise the group with the skills and actions that will be needed in the session, e.g. passing a rugby ball.

**Mobility exercises** may also be used, e.g. moving a limb through its full range of movement, such as arm circles. A warm-up should prepare the performers both mentally and physically for the activity ahead.

**Cool-down** activities tend to gradually reduce the pulse and breathing rate of the participants, as well as incorporating some muscle stretches. This allows waste products to be removed and for the performers to reduce the chance of muscle soreness.

## Key terms

**Warm-up** To include a pulse-raising activity, stretches and familiarisation or skill-based activities

**Mobility exercises** Moving a limb through its full range of movement

**Cool-down** Gradually reducing the pulse and breathing rate whilst stretching muscles to remove waste products

**Figure 3.8** Stretching should form part of both a warm-up and a cool-down.

## Skills and technique development

Perhaps the main aspect of a session plan is the detail about how skills and techniques will be developed within the session. The activities chosen should be appropriate to allow the objectives to be met. For example, if a particular skill is to be improved, it would be common to:

● start with a basic version of the skill
● increase how dynamic the practices become
● progress the practices to add more challenge
● incorporate some competition into the practice, e.g. against an opponent or opponents.

The activities should follow a distinctive structure. The session plan may detail how they will be organised and how demonstrations, if any, are to be shown.

**Figure 3.9** If the objective of a session is to improve dribbling skills for basketball, the plan should detail appropriate progressive drills to develop that skill.

## Engagement

How **engaging** a session is means how well the session will hold the participants' attention. Will they find it fun and enjoyable and want to persevere? Will the session seem to flow smoothly from one section of the session to the next?

This may mean that the session needs to include some fun elements to keep the group motivated and happy, e.g. short competitive games.

**Figure 3.10** The leader should make a session engaging for the group.

**Group activity**

In small groups, share how your coaching session is designed to improve skills in training sessions. Can you think of any good progressions for your main sport?

**Key term**

**Engaging** How well the session will hold the participants' attention

## Organisation

When organising the session, many variables should be considered. These are shown in Figure 3.11.

**Figure 3.11** Variables to be considered when organising a session.

## Safety considerations when planning sports activity sessions

In all aspects of a session, the leader must take measures to ensure that safety procedures are in place. This includes appropriately risk assessing, taking the right control actions and following predetermined emergency procedures if necessary.

### Risk assessments (e.g. facilities, equipment/clothing checks, activity-specific risks)

**Risk assessments** are used to identify and eliminate risks where possible, protecting participants from harm. Not all risks can be eliminated completely and, in these instances, it is important that the risks are managed. Risks include those posed by the facilities, the equipment used, the clothing and footwear worn and any activity-specific risks.

There is a five-step procedure that can be used to carry out risk assessment. These steps are outlined below:

1 **Identify the hazard**: This may be something like equipment that could fall on top of someone.

 **Key term**

**Risk assessment** Used to identify and eliminate risks where possible, protecting participants from harm

2 **Who is at risk**: Identify who the risk could potentially affect.

3 **Severity and probability**: How severe is the risk, i.e. what are the chances of the hazard causing a problem? Would the outcome of the risk potentially be severe? The severity is often classed as 'low, medium or high'. For example, the probability of a basketball backboard collapsing in a sports hall is quite low, but the severity would be high as if it did collapse, it could cause serious harm.

4 **Control measures**: How can the risk be controlled? What 'control measures' can be taken to reduce the probability of the risk, e.g. mopping up any water on a court in advance of play taking place to prevent slipping? Sometimes these are known as '**corrective actions**', i.e. actions to correct or reduce the chances of the risk taking place.

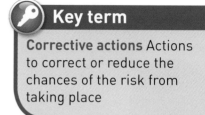

**Key term**

**Corrective actions** Actions to correct or reduce the chances of the risk from taking place

5 **Review and update of the risk assessment**: Risk assessments should be reviewed and altered as necessary on a regular basis.

**Table 3.1** The layout of a standard five-point risk assessment

| Hazard | Who is at risk? | Severity and probability (high, medium, low) | Control measures | Any further action required? |
|---|---|---|---|---|
| Leak from roof onto floor | Participants and staff | Medium | Clean up water Use wet floor signs | Keep mop and bucket nearby in case leak re-occurs |
| | | | | |
| | | | | |
| | | | | |
| | | | | |

## Emergency procedures

It is important that any risk assessment also has emergency procedures, i.e. what to do when or if an emergency were to occur. For example:

- procedures in the event of an accident – e.g. call 999
- procedures in the event of other emergencies – e.g. who to call when equipment breaks or when the venue appears to be unsafe
- how to summon qualified help – emergency services, emergency doctor, etc.
- how to complete relevant documents – e.g. emergency action sheet.

**Figure 3.12** Part of a risk assessment should include who to phone in an emergency.

**Classroom discussion**

Do you feel the sports hall or playing areas in your school are completely safe? What would need to be considered if you were to lead a session in this area?

**Group activity**

Take turns in pairs to lead each other through an appropriate warm-up. Remember to include:

- a pulse-raiser
- stretching exercises
- familiarisation/skill-based/mobility exercises.

## Stretch activity

Visit a local sporting venue and try to carry out a risk assessment using the five-step rule. Can you suggest corrective measures to try to reduce the risks?

## Links to other units

You can find further information on the synoptic links to this unit in **Units R051, 52, 54, 55** and **56**.

## Know it!

1 What is meant by 'session objectives'?
2 What are the five steps for risk assessing?
3 What is meant by the term 'corrective measures'?
4 What is meant by a supervision ratio?
5 What are the three components of a warm-up?

## Assessment preparation

Think about the task/s that your teacher may set you to plan a suitable sports activity session. Make sure you:

● Understand the key considerations when planning a sports activity session.

● Consider objectives, equipment needs, supervision needs, organisation and so on.

● Consider safety factors, including how to risk assess and take corrective measures to control the potential risk.

How will you demonstrate that your plan is **comprehensive** and has considered all of the key requirements for an effective and safe sporting activity session?

## Mark scheme

| LO2 Be able to plan sports activity sessions | | |
|---|---|---|
| Mark band 1 | Mark band 2 | Mark band 3 |
| Produces a **basic** session plan which demonstrates **limited** consideration of the key requirements for an effective and safe sporting activity session. Requires **some** prompting from the teacher in producing the session plan. Draws upon **limited** skills/knowledge/understanding from other units in the specification. | Produces an **effective** session plan which demonstrates **appropriate** consideration of the key requirements for an effective and safe sporting activity session. **Little** prompting from the teacher is required in producing the session plan. Draws upon **some relevant** skills/knowledge/understanding from other units in the specification. | Produces a **detailed** and **comprehensive** session plan which demonstrates **thorough** consideration of the key requirements for an effective and safe sporting activity session. The session plan is produced **independently**. **Clearly** draws upon **relevant** skills/knowledge/understanding from other units in the specification. |
| Mark band 1 | Mark band 2 | Mark band 3 |
| Shows a **limited awareness** of safety considerations. **Some** teacher support may be required in planning and setting up a suitable risk assessment. Corrective action of risks is **basic**. Provides a **brief outline** of emergency procedures related to the facility and equipment to be used in the session. | Shows **some understanding** of safety considerations, requiring **little** teacher support in planning and setting up a suitable risk assessment. Corrective action of risks is **effective**. Provides a **clear description** of emergency procedures related to the facility and equipment to be used in the session. | Shows **well developed understanding** of safety considerations, planning and setting up a suitable risk assessment **independently**. Corrective action of risks is **considered** and **effective**. Provides a **thorough explanation** of emergency procedures related to the facility and equipment to be used in the session. |

## LO3 Be able to deliver sports activity sessions

When delivering a sports activity session, it is important to realise how you will be assessed. The assessor will take several key considerations into account that can be prepared for in advance.

### Safe practice

The assessor will consider whether the session was safe for all involved. This must be of paramount concern throughout and a conscientious effort should be made to prevent any identified risks from occurring.

### Organisation of group/activity

The session must be organised in a manner that allows the objectives to be met. Here are some examples of things to be considered:

- Try to position yourself in an area whereby you can see the whole group. Where possible, do not have your back turned on group members.
- Ensure that equipment is ready to use prior to the session.
- Make sure group sizes for any activities are not too large so that the majority of the group are not standing around waiting for most of the session.
- Keep an eye on the time. You should have a good idea in advance of the session of how long different activities will take. Try to stick to your time plan.

### Safe supervision (e.g. as a leader, coach)

As the leader of the session, safety is your responsibility. Here are some key considerations to remember:

- If you see practice which is unsafe, stop the session immediately.
- It is suggested that you have a mobile phone to hand. If you don't, ensure you know where the nearest point is to place a call in the event of an emergency occurring.
- Rehearse the session in your head prior to actually starting the session. A detailed and well thought-out session plan is less likely to result in unforeseen safety problems.
- Expect the unexpected! Sometimes injuries happen as people can get hurt when least expected. Stay calm and follow your pre-determined safety procedures, e.g. call 999.

> **Getting started**
>
> Have you decided what you will do in your session? Discuss with a partner what your plan is and try to help each other to identify any potential problems that may arise during the session.

**Figure 3.13** Sports coaches should stop the session immediately if practice is seen which is deemed unsafe.

## Delivery style

Think about the **delivery style** and manner in which you will lead the session. For example:

- The session should not drag. It should move at an appropriate pace to keep the group interested, but not so fast that they don't have time to complete the tasks set.
- Try to be **proactive** and **reactive**. In other words, make decisions to eliminate any problems before they happen (proactive); but if anything does occur, be reactive to change what you are doing.
- Demonstrations given should be clear. You do not have to do all the demonstrations yourself, as you can use others in the group to demonstrate. **Demonstrations** are simply a visual way to show the group how to do something. These could be done via:
  - physical demonstration by the leader
  - physical demonstration by a group member
  - use of video footage
  - use of pictures or key cards
  - use of online material, e.g. YouTube.

Explanations given to the group must be clear and concise. Everyone must be able to see and hear all instructions and demonstrations. Sometimes a horse-shoe approach to demonstrating or explaining may be a good idea. This involves all members of the group forming a horse-shoe shape around the leader, so that nobody's view is obstructed.

### Key terms

**Delivery style** The style and manner in which you lead the session

**Proactive** Making decisions to eliminate any problems before they happen

**Reactive** Reacting to problems by changing what you are doing

**Demonstrations** A visual way to show the group how to do something

**Figure 3.14** Group members listening to their coach in a horse-shoe shape so that nobody's view is obstructed.

## Communication skills

The skills used to communicate effectively are vital to a good session. Communication must be clear, concise and unambiguous, i.e. easy to understand.

- **Verbal communication** will be used and should be loud and clear enough for the whole group. Pronounce your words properly and accentuate any words that need to be emphasised, e.g. aspects of technique.

- **Non-verbal communication** involves gestures, hand signals, facial expressions and movements. Non-verbal communication should match verbal communication, e.g. if a positive point is being made verbally, facial expressions and gestures should be positive as well.

- **Appropriate language** should be used at all times. Try to avoid patronising or demeaning the group and aim to increase their confidence and motivation. If you want to make a negative point within your feedback, it is often good to balance the comment with some positivity. For example:
  - 'That was a great effort, but next time try to ...'
  - 'I loved the way you dribbled the ball towards the basket, but look to aim for the top corner of the square when laying up.'
  - 'Fantastic attempt to pass to your partner but keep your eye on the ball.'

- **Technical terms** should be used where possible to help the group understand how to improve their technique. However, do not use words or expressions that they are unlikely to understand. If a technical term needs to be used, but it is difficult to understand, try to explain it as you communicate it. For example:
  - 'I want you to turn your hands and wrists to push and pull the ball across both sides of your body when dribbling. This is called an Indian dribble.'
  - 'I want you to do a seat drop, then a half twist to another seat drop. This is sometimes referred to as swivel hips.'

## Motivation techniques

**Motivation** is the desire or drive to accomplish something. A motivated group is a happy group that will persevere and work hard. If motivated, the group is more likely to follow your instructions and fulfil your expectations with a high degree of effort. There are many simple strategies that can be used to motivate a group:

- **Encouragement** is a simple way to motivate performers. Encourage them to do well and accentuate the positives with praise and positive feedback.

- **Extrinsic motivators** can be used as motivational tools. This simply means that something is offered to create motivation from an external source. **Tangible** extrinsic motivators are things that can be touched, e.g. rewards, prizes or certificates. **Intangible** extrinsic rewards are things that cannot be touched, e.g. praise from others, a smile, a nod, or acknowledgement from the group via clapping.

 **Key terms**

**Motivation** The desire or drive to accomplish something

**Extrinsic motivators** Something is offered to create motivation from an external source. This can be tangible or intangible

**Tangible** Rewards that can be touched, e.g. a certificate

**Intangible** Rewards that cannot be touched, e.g. praise from a coach

**Figure 3.15** Tangible rewards such as a trophy can act as an extrinsic motivator.

 **Classroom discussion**

Discuss within the group what you feel works best to motivate you. Do you prefer tangible or intangible rewards or are you happy with doing the best you can to gain personal satisfaction?

## Activity-specific knowledge

It is important that you fully understand the activity that is taking place prior to starting the session. This may require some research online to appreciate and understand current techniques and tactics that are appropriate to the requirements of the performers.

 **Group activity**

Research online to discover what current tactics and techniques are being used in the activity you are undertaking within your session.

## Adaptability

Although you are likely to meticulously plan your session, things can go wrong or take an unexpected turn. As sessions rarely go exactly as planned, a good skill to develop is the ability to be **adaptable**. This simply means being flexible with your plans and willing to make changes if necessary. It is important that you make adjustments in an activity that isn't working and address any issues you hadn't prepared for. Some examples are given below:

 **Key term**

**Adaptable** Being flexible with your plans and willing to make changes if necessary

- The group is getting too tired, so build in extra rest periods.
- The group is finding an activity too hard, so make the activity less challenging.
- The group does not understand instructions, so provide another demonstration or a more simplistic set of instructions.

 **Classroom discussion**

What are the most obvious things in an activity session that are likely to go wrong? Discuss how adaptability may need to be shown.

### Stretch activity

Read this article on what makes a good sports coaching session. Take note of how some of these points can be considered in your own session.

www.connectedcoaches.org/spaces/10/welcome-and-general/blogs/general/232/what-makes-up-a-good-coaching-session

### Links to other units

You can find further information on the synoptic links to this unit in **Units R052, 54, 55** and **56**.

## Know it!

1 What is meant by reactive and proactive in relation to a sports activity session?

2 Give an example of an extrinsic reward that could be used that is tangible.

3 Give an example of an extrinsic reward that could be used that is intangible.

4 Describe two ways that demonstrations could be given in a session.

5 Why is it important to be adaptable during a sports activity session?

## Assessment preparation

Think about how your teacher will assess the success of your sports activity session. Make sure you do the following:

● Deliver skills in a clear and progressive way.

● Demonstrate knowledge of the activity being used.

● Maintain safe practice at all times.

● Communicate instructions and delivery in a clear and concise manner.

How will you ensure that the group remains motivated throughout the session?

### Mark scheme

| LO3 Be able to deliver sports activity sessions | | |
|---|---|---|
| Mark band 1 | Mark band 2 | Mark band 3 |
| Demonstrates **limited** application of skills and knowledge in delivering a sports activity session. | Demonstrates **effective** application of skills and knowledge in delivering a sports activity session. | Demonstrates **advanced** application of skills and knowledge in delivering a sports activity session. |
| Delivery of the session shows **limited** application of activity-specific knowledge, with **little awareness** of adaptability as the session progresses. | Delivery of the session shows **effective** application of activity-specific knowledge, with **some awareness** of adaptability as the session progresses. | Delivery of the session shows **advanced** application of activity-specific knowledge. Adapts the session **efficiently** as it progresses to meet the needs of the participants. |
| Shows a **basic** appreciation of safe practice **at times** during the delivery of the session. | Shows a **clear** appreciation of safe practice on **most occasions** during the delivery of the session. | Appreciation of safe practice is **well developed** and evident **throughout** in both the organisation and supervision of the session. |
| Communication skills and motivation techniques are **hesitant**. | Communication skills and motivation techniques are **clear**. | Communication skills and motivation techniques are **clear and confident**. |

## LO4 Be able to evaluate own performance in delivering a sports activity session

### Key aspects to consider in evaluating planning and delivery of a sports activity session

Evaluation is to make a judgement about something's worth, appropriateness and level of success. Therefore, in evaluating a session, you are looking at how well it went and how successful particular aspects of the session were.

In order to evaluate all aspects of your session, it is important to consider how much detail you can provide about three key questions:

1 What went well?

2 What didn't go so well?

3 What could be improved in the future?

In answering the three questions above, it is clear that certain key characteristics should be evaluated. These include the following:

- Were the objectives met?
- Did you follow the plan?
- Was the order of activities appropriate?
- Was the group motivated?
- Was the organisation effective?
- Was the equipment appropriate and fit for purpose?
- How well was the session communicated to the group being led?
- How was my positioning during the session?
- Were there any safety concerns?
- Were there any other concerns?

### The objectives

The whole focus of the session is covered in the objectives, which are set out in advance of the session. Therefore, it is important to make a judgement about how well these were achieved, if at all. In considering how successful you were in meeting these, you may consider whether you were too **ambitious**, i.e. expected too much, or were not ambitious enough. This can be reflected in your suggested improvements for the future. As an example:

- If the objective was to help group members to achieve a successful basketball lay up in a session but they did not manage this, perhaps the initial objective should have been less ambitious, e.g. to learn to dribble first.

*As an example, your evaluation may include a statement such as: 'I need to be less ambitious with my objectives and perhaps only have one main objective to achieve such as...'

## The plan

You need to judge how well you stuck to the initial plan and how easy it was to follow. Remember that if you changed the plan and were adaptable to unforeseen circumstances, this is actually a good thing. When evaluating your plan, you may consider:

- Was the plan clear enough and easy to follow?
- Did the plan contain enough detail?
- Would you need to include more or less detail in the next session?
- Are there specific aspects that the plan lacked, e.g. do you need to consider your positioning more for future sessions?

*As an example, your evaluation may include a statement such as: 'I need to include some diagrams in my plan to show where I will stand when watching the group.'

## The activities

An evaluation of the activities included within the session could include elements such as:

- Were the activities too short, too long or just about right?
- Did the activities challenge the group without making them feel like they could not achieve them?
- Did the activities show suitable progression, so that the group was challenged? And then, were they further challenged and pushed to achieve more?
- Did the activities enable all members of the group to get suitably involved or did some people experience more involvement than others?

*As an example, your evaluation may include a statement such as: 'In future I will aim to ensure that I only have three progressive skill drills, as four or five is not possible in the time I have available.'

## Motivation

Your evaluation may pay some focus to how enthused and motivated the group appeared. It is relatively easy to gauge if the group seemed to be content and happy. If so, what do you feel caused them to be motivated? Questions to be considered could include:

- Did the entire group appear to be motivated, or were some participants more motivated than others?
- How did they react to any rewards that were provided?
- Were any of the motivational strategies used more successful than others?
- Would you consider trying out new motivational techniques in future? If so, what would you use?

- If the group was uninterested, how do you feel this could be addressed in the future? For example, do you need to provide more rewards, more praise or simply design more exciting activities?

*As an example, your evaluation may include a statement such as: 'In future I will make sure the group knows that they will receive a certificate of attendance at the end of the session. I will tell them this at the start to provide extrinsic motivation.'

## Organisation

Your evaluation may pay some focus to the organisation of the session. By means of a reminder, an evaluation of the organisation could include factors like:

- Was the size/make up of working groups suitable?
- Did you make changes to group sizes for practices and was this successful?
- How well did you organise the equipment?
- Did you use any additional support and, if so, was it successful?
- Did you feel the size of working area was appropriate, too small or possibly even too large?
- Did the warm-up prepare the group for exercise?
- Was the timing of different activities successful in preventing boredom?
- Did you manage to encourage progression?
- Were your instructions given from a position in which all participants could hear and understand?

Clearly if any of the points above were not addressed or successful, you are required to reflect on how these could be altered in the future.

*As an example, your evaluation may include a statement such as: 'I will aim to be more conscious of my positioning so that the whole group can see me when I am demonstrating.'

## Equipment

Having planned what equipment to use, how to move it and when and where to use it, was it successful in allowing you to meet your objectives? Did you have enough equipment to be shared throughout the group or would you plan to have more in future?

One particular consideration here will relate to the availability of equipment. If you cannot access more equipment in future, do you need to think about different group sizes so that the equipment is more suitably shared?

*As an example, your evaluation may include a statement such as: 'I will need to get more hockey balls for a similar session in the future, so that I can provide one ball for every two players.'

## Communication

Your evaluation may reflect on how well you communicated to the group throughout the session. Remember to consider both verbal and non-verbal communication. Questions you may ask yourself include:

- Did I project my voice?
- Did I speak clearly enough?
- Was I loud enough to be heard but not so loud that I was simply shouting?
- Did my non-verbal communication match my verbal communication?
- Did I use language appropriate to the knowledge of the group, i.e. technical but not too complex?

*As an example, your evaluation may include a statement such as: 'In future, I need to speak louder and clearer as some participants told me they couldn't hear me. I will try to project my voice more.'

## Positioning

In evaluating your positioning, you can consider many aspects such as:

- Were you able to keep an eye on all participants?
- How well did the group behave? If there was misbehaviour, was that due to the group knowing you couldn't see them?
- Did you move around to see the whole group equally?
- Did you position yourself and the group suitably so that all group members could see demonstrations?

*As an example, your evaluation may include a statement such as: 'In future, I will insist that the group stands in a semi-circle (horse-shoe shape) around me when I am demonstrating so that everyone can see.'

## Safety

In evaluating the safety of the session, hopefully no major injuries occurred. However, if you did have safety concerns or something unexpected happened, how will you re-assess and change the information in your risk assessment? Do you need to avoid using certain pieces of equipment or were there safety factors you had not considered?

*As an example, your evaluation may include a statement such as: 'I had not considered that the group would sweat so much and make areas of the hall slippery. In future I will ensure there is a mop available to mop up any sweat that I spot so that nobody slips over.'

**Group activity**

In small groups, compile a tick chart for the following safety areas. Record a tick if group members suggest that it was not a safety concern, and a cross (X) if it was:

- floor surface
- fixed, immovable equipment
- movable, portable equipment
- slip, trips or falls
- sudden twisting injuries
- cuts or bruises
- fatigue, i.e. being too tired or exhausted.

### Anything else

There may be other aspects that you feel could be evaluated. For example, timing may have been a major concern or perhaps you feel that the cool-down was neglected. You may feel that comments should be made about the clothing or footwear worn or you may decide that an alternative venue needs to be sourced. As with the points above, include how you will address these areas in the future.

 **Classroom discussion**

What were the most common areas in which people had concerns about their session? Was there a common area of concern within the group? Discuss the thoughts of the group.

**Stretch activity**

Take turns within the class to read out one consideration for the future from your evaluation. The rest of the class should feed back as to whether it is clear enough what you plan to do in the future.

### Read about it

Read about what one person believes sporting role models should be like:
www.i9sports.com/Blog/240663/What-a-Sports-Role-Model-Should-Be/

Read about risk assessments in sport:
www.sportenglandclubmatters.com/club-planning/governance/managing-risk-2/risk-assesment/

Read more about examples of warm-ups and cool-downs:
www.livestrong.com/article/370679-examples-of-warm-up-cool-down-exercises/

Read more about examples of how skill drills can progress in a session:

Trampoline drills: https://usagym.org/pages/home/publications/technique/1998/7/trampoline.pdf

Hockey passing and receiving drills: www.sportplan.net/drills/Hockey/Passing-Receiving/practiceIndex.jsp

Long passing in football: www.soccercoachweekly.net/soccer-drills-and-skills/long-passing-soccer-drill/

Read some tips on how to communicate effectively as a coach:
https://uk.humankinetics.com/blogs/excerpts/good-communication-skills-are-key-to-successful-coaching

Read about the types of motivation in sport:
https://appliedsportpsych.org/resources/resources-for-coaches/extrinsic-rewards-and-motivation/

Read some tips about evaluating a sports coaching session:
www.google.com/amp/s/coachingyoungathletes.com/2016/02/29/how-to-evaluate-your-own-coaching-performance/amp/

Read about the equipment used in volleyball:
https://volleycountry.com/training/volleyball-ball-everything-need-know-volleyball-balls

## Know it!

1  What is meant by the term *evaluation*?
2  State four aspects of safety you can evaluate.
3  Describe different types of motivation you could provide in the future.
4  State one reason why it is important to be able to see the group at all times.
5  What is meant by being 'too ambitious' in relation to session objectives?

### Links to other units

You can find further information on the synoptic links to this unit in **Units R052, 54, 55** and **56**.

## Assessment preparation

Think about the task that your teacher will undertake to assess your evaluation. Do you feel you have provided enough detail in your evaluation? In doing so, have you addressed the following in relation to aspects such as the plan, organisation, safety, etc.

● What went well?
● What didn't go so well?
● What could be improved in the future?

How can you ensure your ideas for improvement are insightful and address specific aspects of planning and delivery that have been identified?

### Mark scheme

| LO4 Be able to evaluate own performance in delivering a sports activity session | | |
|---|---|---|
| Mark band 1 | Mark band 2 | Mark band 3 |
| Evaluation of the session is **brief**. Some basic positives and/or negatives are **identified**. Consideration of the plan for the session, how it was delivered and its overall success is **minimal**. Ideas for improvement are **limited**. | Evaluation of the session is **detailed**. **Both** positive **and** negative aspects are identified. **Some consideration** is given to the plan for the session and how it was delivered in evaluating its overall success. Ideas for improvement are **clear** and **relevant** to the aspects identified. | Evaluation of performance is **comprehensive**. **Most** positive **and** most negative aspects are identified. The plan for the session and how it was delivered are **fully considered** in evaluating its overall success. Ideas for improvement are **insightful** and address **specific** aspects of planning and delivery which have been identified. |

# R054  Sport and the media

## About this unit

Media is defined by the Oxford Dictionary as 'the main means of mass communication (broadcasting, publishing, and the Internet) regarded collectively'.

The media has four main functions: to inform, educate, entertain and advertise. Sport uses the media to promote itself and, in turn, the media uses sport to promote and maintain people's interest in its products. In other words, the media uses sport to sell itself.

This unit requires learners to look at a range of different media and how they differ in their sports coverage. The unit also looks at the impact the media has on sport and how this

has changed over the years. The unit also investigates the effect the media has had on public interest and involvement in sport.

By completing this unit, learners will develop their knowledge and understanding of the relationship between sport and the media, as well as their ability to evaluate and interpret the different ways in which sports events may be represented by the media.

The skills developed would be relevant in a range of careers and roles within the sports industry, such as sports reporting/broadcasting, sports analysis or research and public relations or media work within a sports organisation.

## Learning outcomes

**LO1** Know how sport is covered across the media

**LO2** Understand positive effects that the media can have on sport

**LO3** Understand negative effects that the media can have on sport

**LO4** Understand the relationship between sport and the media

**LO5** Be able to evaluate media coverage of sport

## How will I be assessed?

This mandatory unit is internally assessed through a written assignment set and marked by your centre and is worth 50 per cent of the overall mark for the OCR Level 1/2 Cambridge National Award in Sport Studies or 25 per cent of the overall mark for the OCR Level 1/2 Cambridge National Certificate in Sport Studies. It is estimated that the assignment will take about 10 hours to complete and is worth 60 marks.

OCR provides a model assignment for this unit: http://ocr.org.uk/qualifications/cambridge-nationals/cambridge-nationals-sport-studies-level-1-2-j803-j813/assessment/

### For LO1

Learners need to know:

● how sport is covered by television, written press, radio, and the internet.

### For LO2

Learners need to understand:

● the positive effects that media can have on sport.

### For LO3

Learners need to understand:

● the negative effects that media can have on sport.

### For LO4

Learners need to understand:

● the relationship between sport and the media.

### For LO5

Learners need to be taught:

● aspects which may influence the coverage of a story/item

● features of the coverage which may vary from one media outlet to another.

## LO1 Know how sport is covered across the media

### Television

Sport is a fairly cheap form of entertainment for television companies to show. It costs less to show a 30-minute sporting event than write, cast and produce a drama or a soap opera. Sport also has most of the requirements of a 'good' programme. It is easy to follow, has lots of excitement and contains only a few periods when the action slows down. Television can show sport in various ways, but normally sporting events are shown on TV as

### Getting started

Think about three or four sports stories from the past week. How did you find out about them? How were they reported – were they detailed or with limited information? Were the stories about the sport itself, or the performers?

a form of entertainment. This is the most popular way that sport is used. People watch football, rugby, cricket, tennis and so on to be entertained.

Sport can also be used as the basis for documentaries on sport. Documentaries provide factual reports and most documentaries are about a single sport, a sports performer or a sports event. They tend to be watched by people who like that particular sport, sports performer or event, or who have a general interest in sport.

TV programmes can also be made to be instructive. There are programmes produced for schools about sport and programmes produced to help coaches develop their skills.

In terms of **media**, television is viewed as the 'best' form of media for sport, because it provides images and sound that can be transmitted live. Television, when providing live coverage, however, is sometimes unable to provide as much in-depth information as other forms of media.

## Terrestrial

**Terrestrial** (or broadcast) television is where images are sent by radio waves from the terrestrial transmitter of a television station to a TV receiver having an aerial or antenna. Terrestrial TV was initially provided by several channels, including BBC1, BBC2, ITV, Channel 4 and Channel 5. These channels are available to all television receivers. In order to watch the BBC, the household must have a TV licence, which pays for the cost of producing BBC programmes. The other channels do not require a licence; they receive an income to produce programmes from their advertising revenue. Companies pay to advertise their products during the commercial breaks.

### Group activity

Arrange for some members of the group to watch a sports programme on terrestrial television that has commercial breaks. Make a note of the products advertised during the commercial breaks. Repeat the activity where the rest of the group watches a non-sports programme. Discuss your findings with the group. Produce a list of the differences between the products advertised during sports and non-sports programmes.

A more up-to-date term for terrestrial television is **digital terrestrial television** (DTT), because the UK switched to a digital signal for television in 1985. Most DTT channels are free to view as they are part of the 'Freeview' package which also includes SC4, ITV 2 and 3, and FreeSports.

### Stretch activity

Watch one of the programmes at either of the following websites:

www.theguardian.com/culture/2015/nov/06/10-best-sports-documentaries-ronaldo-when-we-were-kings-class-of-92

or

www.esquire.com/uk/culture/film/a15963/best-sports-documentaries-of-all-time/

How did this programme fulfil the functions of the media, which is to inform, educate, entertain and advertise?

### Key terms

**Media** Forms of mass communication such as television, newspapers, magazines, radio and internet

**Terrestrial** Signals sent from a transmitter to an aerial or receiver

**Digital terrestrial television** Digital form of TV signal for terrestrial channels

Historically, the terrestrial channels were the only channels available for viewers. Satellite TV did not begin programming until the 1980s. Football and Wimbledon tennis were first screened live on television in the UK in 1937 by the BBC. The BBC also showed the 1948 London Olympics, but only to those living close to the transmitter in London. The first colour sports broadcast in the UK was the 1966 World Cup final.

The advent of satellite television has reduced the amount of sport shown on terrestrial TV. This is because the satellite companies are prepared to pay much more to show various sports events and the sports events are happy to take the money and sell the rights to the satellite companies.

In order to safeguard sport for millions of people, the government has **ring-fenced** certain events which must be made available free to the TV audience. In other words, they must be shown on terrestrial television.

**Figure 4.1** The BBC Sport logo.

> **Key term**
>
> **Ring-fenced** Sports events that the government prevents TV companies from charging to watch so that everyone can watch for free

| Sport | Ring-fenced events |
|-------|-------------------|
| Multi-sports | The Olympics and Paralympics (Summer and Winter) |
| Football | FIFA World Cup finals (all matches) |
| | FIFA Women's World Cup finals (all home nations and one semi-final and final) |
| | UEFA Euro Championships (all matches) |
| | UEFA Euro Women's Championships (all home nations and one semi-final and final) |
| | The FA Cup final |
| | The Scottish Cup final |
| Horse racing | The Derby<br>The Grand National |
| Rugby league | Challenge Cup Final |
| Rugby union | World Cup Final |
| Tennis | Wimbledon Championships |
| Motorsport | British Grand Prix |

The main reasons for ring-fencing certain major sporting events is because it allows the largest number of viewers to watch the event and avoids restricting coverage to subscription channels, which are only available to those who can afford them. It was and still is thought that the viewing of certain events is part of our sporting heritage and culture.

## Satellite

**Satellite** television is a service that delivers programmes to viewers from a communications satellite orbiting the Earth straight to the viewer's location. The signals are received by a satellite dish. In many parts of the UK, the satellite system is in competition with a similar system that is delivered by underground **cable**. Satellite and cable channels are available only as a subscription service. The household pays to receive the signals.

Started in 1989, Sky TV was the first satellite service in the UK. **Sky Sports** is a group of channels operated by Sky TV. Sky Sports is the dominant subscription television sports brand in the UK. It has played a major role in the increased commercialisation of British sport since 1991. Sky TV was the driving force behind the breakaway and establishment of the Premier League from the Football League in 1992.

The current package of Sky Sports channels is available for an additional subscription fee on top of the basic Sky package. They are available for nearly every satellite or cable broadcasting system in the UK.

**BT Sport** is a group of sports channels provided by BT (British Telecom). BT Sport is in competition with Sky Sports and holds exclusive rights to numerous sporting events. In other words, BT Sport pays to show different sports and different matches or events to Sky Sports.

Cable TV is a subscription service normally bundled with a phone line and broadband internet service. **Virgin Media** is the main provider of this type of service in the UK. Virgin Media buys and shows sports programmes from both Sky Sports and BT Sport.

Most channels are carried on both satellite and cable platforms. Cable television faces intense competition from Sky's service. However, cable often lacks 'interactive' features such as text services and extra video screens. The satellite system lacks services requiring high degrees of two-way communication, such as true video on demand (a programme starts immediately on cable; there can be a delay with satellite transmission).

**Figure 4.2** The Sky Sports logo.

 **Key terms**

**Satellite** TV images sent from a geo-stationary satellite

**Cable** TV images sent through an underground fibre-optic cable

**Sky Sports** Main subscription-based sports channel provider in UK

**BT Sport** Group of sports channels provided by BT

**Virgin Media** Main cable TV operator

Amazon Prime and Netflix are new entries into the satellite and cable market. Both require a subscription. Amazon Prime has already moved into sports broadcasting and we should expect Netflix to follow.

Eurosport is a television sports network that owns a range of rights across many sports but generally does not buy the big sports such as the major football leagues. However, in 2015 Eurosport was awarded rights to broadcast the Olympic Games for 2018 and 2022. It also has the rights to all four Grand Slam tennis events.

The development and rise of satellite and cable television in the UK has been largely based on the development of its sports programmes. Fewer and fewer of the main sporting events of interest to UK viewers are shown on terrestrial TV, because satellite companies offer more money to show the events than the terrestrial channels.

Sports events such as the Football League, Premiership rugby union, Super League rugby, Test Match cricket and Ryder Cup golf, which used to be available live through terrestrial television, are now only available live through subscription to satellite or cable television.

Since the start of the Premier League in 1992, Sky TV deals have been very profitable for the clubs. The current package (2018–21) involves Sky paying the Premier League £10.7 million for every match shown live. This money is split between the teams concerned. The actual amount given to each team depends on the clubs involved and their position in the League, but the average income from Sky is over £5 million per team per match. The top teams are shown on Sky nearly 30 times a season, giving them an income from Sky in excess of £150 million.

Sports now produce 'packages' that different TV companies bid for. For example, there are seven packages for the 2019–22 Premier League seasons. Sky Sports has purchased four of these packages and will show as many as five Premier League matches each weekend. BT Sport has bought two packages that entitle them to show one match a week at 12.30 on a Saturday, as well as matches played on Bank Holidays. The BBC has bought the rights to show the highlights package (*Match of the Day*). Amazon Prime has purchased the rights to 20 Premier League matches.

### Pay-per-view

**Pay-per-view** (PPV) is a system where a television service provider allows a subscriber to purchase events to view. The broadcaster shows the event at the same time to everyone ordering it.

In the UK, PPV is available through satellite, cable and internet television services, mainly for films such as Sky Box Office. Some sporting events are also available through PPV. These tend to be

**Group activity**

Working with the rest of the group, obtain a listing of the sports programmes available on subscription channels. Analyse the listings and identify the range of sporting events being shown over the course of the week on different subscription channels.

**Stretch activity**

Analyse the results of the group activity and calculate the amount of time each week dedicated by that channel to different sports. Suggest reasons why some sports get more TV coverage than others.

**Key term**

**Pay-per-view** Service provided by a broadcaster where the subscriber pays to watch an event mainly boxing events and mixed martial arts. In 2017, 1.5 million subscribers used PPV to watch the heavyweight world title boxing match between Anthony Joshua and Wladimir Klitschko.

## Written press

Before the development of television and radio, the **written press** was the main form of media available for communication. The chief form of written press was originally newspapers, but other forms such as magazines have developed. The advent of the internet has led to a decrease in the numbers of printed newspapers and magazines that are available, because more and more people surf the web to gain information by reading online newspapers and magazines.

**Figure 4.3** There are different types of newspapers.

### Newspapers

**Newspapers** tend to appear in one of two forms – **broadsheet** or **tabloid** – although some 'broadsheets' are now appearing in tabloid size. Both types must sell large numbers of newspapers to make a profit. To sell copies, the two different types of newspaper tend to adopt different ways to attract readers. Broadsheet newspapers tend to provide more information on a wide variety of sports, whereas tabloid newspapers tend to report sensational stories that cover relatively few sports.

Unlike many other countries, there are very few newspapers devoted to sport in the UK.

**Group activity**

Each person in the group chooses a different sport and researches it to find out which broadcaster shows this sport. You should be able to detail whether the broadcaster has 'sole rights' to that sport or if they share the broadcasting rights with other broadcasters. For example, in football, who shows Premier League matches, FA Cup football, Champions League, Europa League and so on?

**Key terms**

**Broadsheet** More informative type of newspaper

**Tabloid** More sensationalist type of newspaper

## Magazines

There are numerous sport-specific **magazines** available in the UK. Some of these are published weekly, some monthly. The majority are based on a single sport. The main sports magazines in print at the time of writing (2018) are *Autosport*, the weekly motor sport magazine; the boxing magazines *Boxing Monthly* and *Boxing News*; and three football magazines, *FourFourTwo*, *Match* and *World Soccer*. *Sport* was a free weekly sports magazine which was given to commuters outside London Underground stations. It ceased publication in 2016.

There are other magazines, with smaller circulations, catering to other sports such as athletics, cricket, cycling, golf and rugby (league and union).

The Press Gazette published the following figures in 2016:

| Title | Total circulation 2015 | Total circulation 2016 | Percentage change |
|-------|------------------------|------------------------|-------------------|
| *Sport* | 304,899 | 0 | −100 |
| *Men's Health* | 194,682 | 182,026 | −6.5 |
| *Forever Sports* | 104,974 | 0 | −100 |
| *Runner's World* | 78,429 | 78,496 | +0.1 |
| *FourFourTwo* | 64,972 | 60,227 | −7.3 |
| *English Club Golfer* | 50,356 | 50,545 | + 0.4 |
| *Today's Golfer* | 48,018 | 45,688 | −4.9 |
| *Golf Monthly* | 46,057 | 39,614 | −14 |
| *Cycling Plus* | 43,746 | 40,865 | −6.6 |
| *Match of the Day* | 43,016 | 38,116 | −11.4 |
| *Bike* | 37,084 | 37,106 | + 0.1 |
| *Rugby World* | 31,893 | 22,780 | −28.6 |
| *Mountain Biking UK* | 28,992 | 27,382 | −5.6 |
| *World Soccer* | 25,132 | 22,708 | −9.6 |
| *Match* | 25,064 | 18,803 | −25 |

 **Group activity**

Each person in the group provides a different newspaper. Measure the amount of sports coverage in each paper by counting the number of pages devoted to sport as a percentage of the total number of pages in the newspaper. Then for each newspaper, list the number of sports that are covered by the newspaper.

## Books

**Books** about sport are very popular. The WHSmith bookshop lists over 20,000 books under the heading 'sport'.

Books on sport involve a wide range of categories, in both fiction and non-fiction. Non-fiction books can include biographies and autobiographies about individuals; coaching and instructional guides and explanations of the rules of sports; the history of sports; and annuals detailing a year of news or statistics about a sport.

Some books have become famous. The cricketer's almanac, *Wisden*, is a monthly publication that is compiled into an annual full of stories, reports, scores and statistics about cricket.

## Fanzines

**Fanzines** are non-official publications produced by fans of sports, events or teams for people with similar interests. The first football fanzine was published in 1972 and now most Premier League and Football League clubs have at least one fanzine.

Fanzines exist in many other sports, especially those with a reasonably sized spectator following. Rugby league has several fanzines, as do many non-league football clubs, but the development of the internet has led to the demise of many fanzines. The traditional paper fanzine has given way to the online '**webzine**', which is easier and cheaper to produce and available to a wider audience.

## Radio

**Radio** broadcasting began experimentally in the early twentieth century and became a medium for communication to most households by 1920. The early signals involving sounds being sent by radio waves to a receiver (a radio) were analogue but were replaced by digital signals in the 2000s.

The BBC broadcast its first commentary on a football match in 1927 and was soon commentating on over 100 matches a year. During the 1930s, every FA Cup Final was broadcast by the BBC and by 1939 about two-thirds of households owned radios.

The development of television in the 1960s and 1970s reduced the impact of radio as a broadcast medium. Both television and radio can broadcast 'live', but television has the advantage of being visual – you can see for yourself what's happening. Radio, however, is often more easily accessible than television, for example, in cars, or rooms without television sets. Therefore, radio is still a popular medium for sport.

Radio readily provides information about sport and tends to do so in great detail. Radio programmes can provide commentaries from sports events. These are intended to 'paint a picture' for the listener. They also often provide in-depth interviews with performers or experts in sports, providing information and opinions.

> ### Key terms
>
> **Fanzines** Non-official publications produced by sports fans
>
> **Webzines** Online versions of fanzines

## Dedicated sports radio stations

There are only two **dedicated sports radio stations** in the UK – Radio 5 Live and talkSPORT.

The BBC dominates sport on the radio with BBC Radio 5 Live and its local radio stations. BBC Radio 5 Live is the principal radio station in the UK covering sport. It broadcasts virtually all major sports events staged in the UK or involving British competitors, although rights restrictions may mean that some events cannot be covered live.

BBC Radio 5 Live cannot broadcast all of the sports they have rights to. Some, especially cricket and tennis, are covered on the sister station, 5 Live Sports Extra. 5 Live Sports Extra often broadcasts full coverage of secondary Premier League and Home Nations football, while 5 Live carries the first-choice match.

The main commercial rival for radio sports rights is talkSPORT. TalkSPORT is the only national radio station broadcasting sporting debates, interviews and commentaries 24 hours a day. TalkSPORT, alongside its sister station, talkSPORT 2, is an official broadcaster for the Premier League, broadcasting live commentaries of the second choice Saturday afternoon Premier League match around the world in multiple languages. Radio 5 Live gets the first choice, because the BBC paid for the rights to broadcast. TalkSPORT also has exclusive rights to broadcast Premiership rugby union and broadcast commentary of the 2017 British Lions tour to New Zealand.

**Figure 4.4** The British and Irish Lions playing in New Zealand in 2017.

Absolute Radio (formerly Virgin Radio) is one of the UK's three independent national radio stations. The others are talkSPORT and Classic FM. Although primarily a music station, Absolute Radio used to have rights to broadcast live commentary of selected Premier League matches on Saturday afternoons.

## Local radio coverage

**Local radio coverage** of sport can be through the BBC or through commercial stations. The BBC has nearly 50 local radio stations, ranging in audience sizes from Radio London (population 8.8 million) to Radio Guernsey (population 62,000). Nearly all of these stations offer coverage of local sports news, selected commentaries on matches or events, phone-ins and interviews.

For example, on Saturday 25 August 2018, the following football matches were available live on BBC radio stations:

*Premier League*
- Wolves v Manchester City, 12:30 BST (BBC Radio 5 Live)
- Arsenal v West Ham, 15:00 BST (BBC Radio London)
- Liverpool v Brighton, 17:30 BST (BBC Radio 5 Live)

*National League*
- Maidenhead United v Maidstone United, 12:35 BST (BBC Radio Kent)
- Barrow v Braintree Town, 15:00 BST (BBC Radio Cumbria)
- Boreham Wood v Halifax, 15:00 BST (BBC Three Counties Radio)
- Dagenham & Redbridge v Hartlepool United, 15:00 BST (BBC Tees)
- Dover Athletic v Eastleigh, 15:00 BST (BBC Radio Kent and BBC Radio Solent)
- Ebbsfleet United v Aldershot Town, 15:00 BST (BBC Surrey)
- Gateshead v Leyton Orient, 15:00 BST (BBC Radio London)
- Harrogate Town v Solihull Moors, 15:00 BST (BBC Radio York)
- Havant & Waterlooville v Salford City, 15:00 BST (BBC Radio Solent)
- Wrexham v Bromley, 15:00 BST (BBC Radio Wales)

*National League North*
- AFC Telford United v Chester, 15:00 BST (BBC Radio Shropshire)
- Brackley Town v York City, 15:00 BST (BBC Radio York)
- Curzon Ashton v Kidderminster Harriers, 15:00 BST (BBC Hereford & Worcester)
- Hereford FC v Bradford (Park Avenue), 15:00 BST (BBC Hereford & Worcester)
- Woking v Truro City, 15:00 BST (BBC Surrey)

**Figure 4.5** Digital radio has increased the number of stations available.

As well as the three national commercial channels previously mentioned (Absolute Radio, Classic FM and talkSPORT), the change from analogue to digital radio has brought about the establishment of local stations such as Xfm (now Radio X), Kiss and Kerrang! Radio to various areas of the UK.

Most local commercial stations in the UK broadcast to a city or a region, such as Merseyside. The main format is pop music, but sport is also often broadcast, with the emphasis on local teams and events.

### National radio coverage

Both BBC Radio 5 Live and talkSPORT provide **national radio coverage**. Both stations broadcast a wide variety of sporting events, but their programming is dominated by football, as this sport gains the widest listening audience. Latest figures suggest that BBC Radio 5 Live gets just under 5 million listeners per week compared to talkSPORT's nearly 3 million.

### Internet radio stations

Internet radio is where radio waves are converted into digital signals that are then broadcast on the internet. It is more properly called **webcasting**. The first internet radio service was launched in 1993.

Over 350 radio stations in the UK stream their stations online. Internet radio stations tend to offer news, sports, talk and various types of music – the same formats that are available on traditional broadcast radio stations. But the low cost of starting and maintaining internet radio services has allowed a substantial explosion of independent internet-only radio stations.

As well as internet radio, there is also **DAB** (digital audio broadcasting) radio. DAB receives digitised radio signals that do not allow any of the static that can affect analogue radio signals and is therefore much clearer when listened to. The UK now has about 300 DAB radio stations and DAB is being heavily promoted as a better source for radio than analogue signals.

Both internet and DAB radio stations provide national and local radio. Sport features heavily on these stations as it attracts listeners and is relatively simple and cheap to provide. The more local the radio station, the more local the sports coverage.

## Internet

The **internet** is a global system of interconnected computer networks. It carries a huge range of information and services, such as documents that inter-link to other resources, the **world wide web** (www), email, telephone communication systems and file sharing.

### Key terms

**Webcasting** Radio broadcast on the internet

**DAB** Digital audio broadcasting – a type of digitised radio signal

**Internet** Global system of interconnected computer networks

**World wide web** Part of the internet used for interlinked information

Most traditional communications media, including telephone, radio, television, letter writing, and newspapers, have been altered, redefined, or even bypassed by the internet. There are now new ways of communicating, such as email, internet telephony, internet television, online music, digital newspapers and video-streaming websites.

The internet has accelerated the development of new forms of person-to-person communication through instant messaging, internet forums and social networking.

Watching sports online is relatively easy provided you pay for the subscription and avoid geographical limits.

**Figure 4.6** You can now watch sport online on a mobile phone

### Blogs

A **blog** is a website that provides an informal online journal that displays information in reverse order, with the latest information (posts) appearing first. Sometimes the blog is the work of a single author, but recently blogs have tended to become collaborations of several authors. These multi-author blogs (MABs) are often the work of newspapers, other media outlets, universities and similar organisations.

The rise of Twitter and other microblogging systems has helped MABs and single-author blogs fit into the news media. Blogs have developed because the need to have technical expertise to publish online has decreased. Posting blogs (blogging) is a form of social networking.

Many blogs provide commentary on sport. A typical blog combines text, images and links to other blogs, web pages and other media related to the subject. In 2008, new blogs were being created at a rate of one per second, every minute of every hour of every day.

> **🔑 Key term**
>
> **Blog** Informal journal provided online

Some popular sporting blogs include:

| Name | Content |
|------|---------|
| Anfield HQ | Contains previews of football matches, articles from fans and podcasts |
| Perfect Tennis | Covers tournaments from around the world and has features such as Fan Stories and live chat for visitors |
| Caught Offside | Professionally produced football blog, daily updates, replays and much more |
| Cricket with Balls | Known primarily for its witty commentary on cricket |
| Love Tennis | Features tennis news and results, and tips to improve your own technique |
| Blood and Mud | Has news, features, videos and a fun and games section all about rugby union |
| Inside Snooker | Has straightforward news coverage and developments in snooker |
| The Liver Bird | A long-standing blog for Liverpool football fans, offering in-depth looks at the games, with regular updates |
| King Cricket | A reviews and discussion hub. There are links to cricket ticket pages for fans |
| London Cyclist | A traditional blog for cycling enthusiasts, with tips and tricks for cycling in London, rather than following professional cycling |

## Video-sharing sites

**Video-sharing sites** are websites that allow users to distribute their video clips. Some user-generated sites charge a fee, but the majority are free. Users can upload video clips and share them with the masses. Many sites place restrictions on file size, duration, subject matter and format of the uploaded video file. Popular sites include Facebook, Myspace, Photobucket, Vimeo and YouTube. Sport is a popular category amongst the uploaded video clips.

## Social media

**Social media** embraces the interactive technologies that assist the creation and sharing of information and ideas through electronic equipment such as computers, tablets and phones.

Social media covers internet-based technology using text, photos or videos. Users create profiles for a particular computer program on a website or mobile platform (**app**) that is maintained by the social media organisation. Users who connect with other users on the platform form social networks, through which they share, discuss and modify content that has been posted online.

Social media differs from more traditional media such as magazines and newspapers in that it is interactive and immediate, rather than informative and delayed. Some of the most popular social media websites are Facebook, Instagram, LinkedIn, Pinterest, Snapchat, Tumblr, Twitter, and WhatsApp. These social media websites have more than 100,000,000 registered users.

By attracting fans through social media, the holders of sports rights can open new forms of communication with their audience that can, at the same time, open new commercial opportunities with sponsors. Sports clubs are only beginning to appreciate the potential that this offers.

Barcelona has become the world's largest sports club on social media, with 150 million followers. Their followers will then view the various advertisements on the Barcelona home page.

Mobile phones and tablets have allowed social media to flourish. For example, most football stadiums offer Wi-Fi to their fans, enabling not only more interactions at live events, but more commercial activity as well. Spectators now can make additional purchases of clothing or seat upgrades while at the venue.

**Key term**

**App** Application software designed to run on smartphones and other mobile devices

## Fansites

A **fansite** is a website created and maintained by a fan about a sporting celebrity, a sport, a team or an event.

Fansites may provide specialised information on the subject, with pictures taken from various sources, the latest news related to their subject, media downloads and the chance to talk to other fans via discussion boards. They often take the form of a blog, highlighting the latest news regarding the fansite subject. They often include galleries of photos or videos of the subject and are often linked to other similar fansites.

Most fansites are unofficial, but a few are officially endorsed, where the person or organisation involved will supply material and even help with the expense and bother of running the site. Many unofficial fansites put a disclaimer on a visible place on the website, which sometimes also includes the copyright of the site.

Many fans are motivated by the need to be part of a group and are able to attend sporting events in person. In the online world, fans fulfil this need by building or participating in online fansites.

## Live streams

**Live streaming** is the delivery of internet content as events happen. It is the same idea as live television in that its contents are shown via a television signal. Live internet streaming requires something to capture the event, such as a digital video camera, and a delivery network to distribute and deliver the content.

Live streaming services include a wide variety of topics, ranging from social media to video games, but often include sporting action. Apps such as Facebook Live and Periscope include the streaming of scheduled promotions and events, as well as streaming between users. User interaction via chatrooms forms a major component of live streaming. Facebook Live and Periscope also include the ability to talk to the broadcaster or participate in conversations in chat.

## P2P sharing

**P2P** sharing (peer-to-peer file sharing) is the distribution and sharing of digital media using P2P networking technology. The technology allows users to access and share any digitised files such as photos, video clips and text.

Websites such as www.sportp2p.com/ and www.p2p4u.biz/ stream live sports events.

## Podcasts

A **podcast** is a series of digital audio or video files that can be downloaded and watched or listened to. Many are based on a subscription format, so that new podcasts are automatically downloaded as they are made available to your designated platform – computer, tablet or phone. The majority of podcasts are in an audio format.

Podcasts are usually available from all the producers of digitised media as downloads. For example, SopCast is a simple, free way to broadcast video and audio, or watch video and listen to radio on the

**Key terms**

**P2P** Peer-to-peer file sharing
**Podcasts** Digital audio recording available to download

internet. Using P2P technology, it is very efficient and easy to use. Anybody can become a broadcaster without the costs of a powerful server and vast bandwidth.

## Know it!

1  Describe, using examples from a sport of your choice, how that sport is covered by television.
2  Describe, using examples from a sport of your choice, how that sport is covered by newspapers.
3  Describe, using examples from a sport of your choice, how that sport is covered by radio.
4  Describe, using examples from a sport of your choice, how that sport is covered by the Internet.

## Links to other units

You can find further information on this topic in **Units R051, 52, 53** and **55**.

## Stretch activity

Choose a sports performer from an activity you are involved with. Search various forms of media (TV, newspapers, internet, social media) to find out about that particular performer. How many different forms of media are talking about that performer?

## Assessment preparation

Think about the task/s that your teacher may set you to assess your knowledge of how sport is covered across the media.

Make sure you:

● Know how sport is covered by the following media:
   ○ television – terrestrial, satellite and pay-per-view
   ○ written press – newspapers, magazines, books and fanzines
   ○ radio – dedicated sports radio stations, national radio stations, internet radio stations
   ○ internet – blogs, video-sharing sites, social media, fansites, live streams, P2P sharing and podcasts.

### Mark scheme

| LO1 Know how sport is covered across the media | | |
|---|---|---|
| Mark band 1 | Mark band 2 | Mark band 3 |
| Identifies **most** different areas of the media which cover sport supported by a **limited range** of examples. | Identifies **most** different areas of the media which cover sport supported by a **range** of examples. | Identifies **all** different areas of the media which cover sport supported by a **wide range** of examples. |

## **L02 Understand positive effects that the media can have on sport**

### Increased exposure of minority sports

The media uses sport to gain viewers or readers and to increase their income/advertising revenue. For the majority of people, the information and knowledge gained about sport is the result of what they have seen or heard in the media.

Minority sports may not get the same amount of **media exposure** as more popular sports. Minority sports do not receive the same level of attention as football, cricket or rugby because millions of readers or viewers do not want to follow a minority sport such as basketball instead of football, because football is the sport that people largely want to read about in the papers and watch on TV.

It used to be that the only way minority sports could get onto TV or into the newspapers was if a GB performer won a gold medal at the Olympic Games. For example, cycling and rowing were heavily covered in the media as the Olympics brought success to British competitors, and they were interesting to watch while the events were taking place. But it was not what people wanted to read about the next day if it took coverage away from the more popular sports.

This state of affairs has changed recently as the media, led by television, looks to find alternative sports to show because more popular sports are becoming unavailable to show. In simple terms, if Sky Sports and BT Sport have a virtual monopoly on Premier League football, what do the other TV channels show? The obvious answer is to show other sports that are not limited by expensive TV rights.

### Greater range of sport covered in the media

The **range of sports covered by the media** has increased in the last decade as television seeks to fill the hours in the day of the ever-increasing dedicated sports channels.

Many minority sports have grown through their use as a fill-in between football, cricket and rugby. Darts is a good example. The sport has grown from a pub-based recreation to a worldwide spectacle with professional players, mainly because of television. The biggest darts events are shown live on Sky Sports in the UK, and the top players have become household names (in some households). The same influence has led to the development of snooker as a popular professional sport.

### Increased promotional opportunities

As sport has become a more dominant aspect of everyday life, there have also been **increased promotional opportunities**.

> **Getting started**
>
> The role of the media is to:
> - inform
> - educate
> - entertain
> - advertise.
>
> Discuss each of these roles with a partner and decide which of these roles is most important.

Sport can promote itself, but it has also become a vehicle for promoting all sorts of goods, from shaving products to shoes, from banks to cereals.

## Clubs/sports can promote themselves more through different media

Sports clubs, sports and events are able to **promote themselves through different forms of media**. The promotion of sports events and teams, as well as the promotion of other goods and services, is called **sports marketing**.

The aim of sports marketing is to promote a product through sport. This can be done through advertising, using TV and radio broadcasting, the written press, social media and other digital platforms. All these different media are available to be used by individuals or organisations and, in the modern world, most successful individuals and organisations use as many different forms of media as they can to promote themselves.

Some organisations even have dedicated TV channels, for example, Chelsea Football Club has Chelsea TV and Liverpool has LFCTV.

Many organisations, as previously mentioned, produce their own blogs.

## Unlimited access to information about a favourite team/ club/performer through different media

Various media platforms are available to provide information about sport. Via different media outlets, you can have almost **unlimited access to information about various aspects of many different teams, clubs and performers**.

## Education

One of the main functions of media is to **educate**. The media is able to provide knowledge to its readers, listeners and viewers through, for example, statistics about the event or the expert opinions of pundits and commentators.

### Developing a better understanding of sports through media coverage

The general public may **develop a better understanding of sports through media coverage**. You can become more informed about the rules of a sport by listening to various experts who explain situations that occur in sports. Similarly, you can better appreciate and often improve the techniques needed for a sport by watching, often in slow motion, how a skill is performed correctly. You can also develop a better understanding about the use of tactics in a sport by hearing how different individuals and teams approach the opposition tactics in a match.

**Key term**

**Sports marketing**
Promotion of sport and associated products

**Stretch activity**

Choose a sporting event from an activity you are involved with. Search various forms of media (TV, newspapers, internet, social media) to find out about that particular event. How many different forms of media are mentioning that event?

## Increased income

One of the four roles of the media is to publicise and advertise the sport, products and performers. In doing so, the media is able to charge money for advertising these products. At the same time, media companies pay for the rights to show a sporting event. This means that there is **increased income**, which benefits sport.

## Income generated by media rights goes to the sport or sports clubs

**Sport in the media generates money, which the sport can invest** to further develop the sport, the team or the individual. From the millions of pounds paid by Sky to Premier League football clubs to the smaller amounts paid by companies to advertise their products on a website concerned with sport, the money is reinvested into that sport.

Sports can spend this increased income at all levels of the sport. Individual sports could improve facilities for the sport for both performers and spectators. Clubs could improve the equipment their performers use, or employ a better coach, or transfer in a better player. Individual performers could buy better clothing or footwear, or they could free themselves from work commitments and spend more time training. The additional income going into a sport from the sale of media rights can be used at **grassroots level** to make participation easier, or at elite level to support performers at the top of their profession.

## Inspiring people to participate

Overall, participation in sport is falling and this is partly attributed to too much watching of sport. However, studies have suggested that watching sport on TV may actually positively influence people to take up a sport.

Listening, seeing or reading about sport in the media brings sport to people who may not normally get to experience it. This can encourage people to get involved and **inspire people to participate**.

## Exposure/coverage in media encourages people to take part

**Coverage in the media makes more people want to take part**. Television has influenced participation rates in certain sports. When Channel 4 first showed volleyball between 1980 and 1984, participation rates increased by 70 per cent; when table tennis stopped being covered on TV, participation dropped by a third.

When British teams do well in a sport at the Olympics, there is often an increase in grassroots participation. The success of GB cyclists at various Olympics and in professional road races has led to a huge increase in recreational cycling. Another example is the

> **Key term**
>
> **Grassroots level** For ordinary people, rather than those who are specialists

large increase in people's participation in tennis that occurs every summer during Wimbledon fortnight.

### Creation of positive role models

Sports performers, through being seen, heard or spoken about, often become **positive role models**. Although they may not win every time, and sometimes their behaviour should not be copied, many performers have the skills, charisma and resilience that fans find attractive. Media coverage has made these role models more visible to the general public.

Professional performers are assumed to provide a role model effect for sport at grassroots level, whether by motivating people to take up a sport or by encouraging continued participation.

For example, David Beckham was a positive role model for many young footballers during his playing career. Baroness Tanni Grey-Thompson DBE has become a prominent role model through coverage of her successes in the Paralympics.

## Competition between sports and clubs

The media has such an influence on sport that there has to be **competition between sports and sports clubs** to attract spectators and hence advertising and therefore money.

### Competition for supporters/viewers

Sports and sports clubs are in **competition for supporters/viewers**. The more people who attend live or tune in to watch a sport, the greater the potential income for that sport or that club. This increased income is not necessarily just from ticket sales. The more people who attend, the more money the club or sport can charge for allowing the advertising of products.

Sports and sports clubs have to think more about the needs of their customers – the spectators. They need new ways to attract new audiences; for example, by offering reduced prices for regular attendees by providing season tickets; reducing prices for younger people in the hope that they will continue to attend when they are older; and selling merchandise so that the wearer feels affiliated to the team.

Some sports are adapting the way the sport is played or staged to attract large audiences. For example, more spectators watch Twenty20 cricket than watch county matches. In rugby union, the Twickenham double-header allows spectators to watch two Premiership matches for the price of entry. Rugby league has gone as far as holding a 'Magic Weekend' where the ticket price entitles you to watch four matches during the day.

### Stretch activity

Choose either netball or basketball and research your chosen sport to discover the positive effects of television coverage on participation.

### Links to other units

You can find further information on this topic in **Units R051** and **55**.

## Know it!

1 Identify four minority sports that have become popular because of media coverage.

2 Give three examples of sports marketing.

3 Describe, using a sport of your choice, how you have become more knowledgeable about that sport through media coverage.

4 Make a list of five ways that a sport of your choice has benefitted from media coverage.

## Assessment preparation

Think about the task/s that your teacher may set you to assess your knowledge of the positive effects that the media can have on sport.

Make sure you:

- Know of the increased exposure of minority sports:
  - greater range of sports covered in the media
  - increased promotional opportunities
  - clubs/sports can promote themselves through different media
  - individuals can have almost unlimited access to information about their favourite team, club or performer.
- Know the value of increased education:
  - developing a better understanding of sports through media coverage.
- Know about the increased income which benefits sport:
  - income generated by media rights goes to the sport or sports clubs, which can be invested.
- Know how media coverage inspires people to participate:
  - exposure/coverage in media makes more people want to take part
  - creation of positive role models.
- Know about the competition between sports and clubs:
  - competition for supporters or viewers means that sports and clubs need to think more about the needs of their customers and how to attract new audiences.

### Mark scheme

| LO2 Understand positive effects that the media can have on sport | | |
|---|---|---|
| **Mark band 1** | **Mark band 2** | **Mark band 3** |
| Identifies **some** possible positive effects that the media can have on sport. | Describes **a range** of possible positive effects that the media can have on sport. | Explains **a wide range** of possible positive effects that the media can have on sport, clearly supported with **relevant** examples. |
| Provides a **brief description** of the positive effects identified and supports **some** of the descriptions with examples. | Provides some explanation as to why they are positive supported with mostly **relevant examples**. | **Clearly** draws upon **relevant** skills/knowledge/understanding from other units in the specification. |
| Draws upon **limited** skills/knowledge/understanding from other units in the specification. | Draws upon **some relevant** skills/knowledge/understanding from other units in the specification. | |

## LO3 Understand negative effects that the media can have on sport

### Decline in live spectatorship

Some sports have had to change to fit into media coverage. Sky TV has changed football from a Saturday afternoon game to an everyday event, with matches played at different kick-off times throughout a weekend.

Sky bought the exclusive TV rights to rugby league, and promptly changed the sport from a winter sport to a summer one. Sky then restructured the league system to create a Super League and then created clubs in under-represented areas such as London and South Wales. All the clubs then had to devise a non-geographical nickname in order to merchandise themselves. The London team became the 'Broncos'.

Attendance at live events, or **spectatorship**, **is in decline** because it is more comfortable to watch the event at home on TV. This is why the Premier League charges large fees to TV companies wanting to televise matches.

You can now watch a vast amount of different sports (or the same sport) without ever having to attend the actual events, thanks to the amount of TV and media coverage. During the 2018–19 season, Champions League fixtures are scheduled to be played at two different times – 6.00pm and 8.00pm on both Tuesdays and Wednesdays to provide more games for TV companies to show as a package. Also, as part of the need to make money, it is often the case that as a sport or club improves and begins to attract a larger spectator base, the ticket prices increase to make the most of this increase in popularity.

### Loss of traditional sporting values

Many millions of people participate in sporting activities where there is no media coverage. But at an elite level, in order to provide the funding needed to pay the players, the media needs to be involved.

There have even been examples of the creation of new forms of a sport simply because they were more attractive to TV audiences; for example, 'American' scoring in badminton; 'international' rules in netball; the tennis tie-break; the penalty shoot-out in football and hockey.

Many aspects of popular sports have been changed for television and this has sometimes resulted in the **loss of traditional sporting values**. For example, football introduced a no back-pass rule and hockey removed its offside law to make the game more entertaining for the TV spectator. Athletics now only allows a single false start

**Getting started**

Choose a sport. Make a list of the ways that the media could negatively affect that sport.

**Key term**

**Spectatorship** Attending an event as against watching on media

in track events and has reduced the number of jumps and throws a performer may take while competing.

The largest televised sporting events are the Football World Cup and the Olympic Games. The scheduling of these events is amended to suit media coverage. The organisation of the Football World Cup was changed in 1998 to generate more television income. The number of teams was increased from 24 to 32, resulting in more matches, but also extra interest for the supporters from those additional countries. There are plans to make the 2022 event a 48-team tournament.

Kick-off times at the World Cup (and other competitions) are scheduled to draw a maximum viewing audience. Football has its biggest TV audience in Europe, so wherever the finals are held, the European teams involved will kick off at a time that means they play at about 8pm in Europe, when maximum TV viewing figures can be guaranteed. Changes to the number of teams involved and kick-off times are designed to generate extra revenue.

The Olympics are becoming controlled by the American TV networks. They will then influence the scheduling of the 'big' events for themselves. This usually involves the men's and women's 100-metre finals being held at a local time that allows them to be shown live in the USA during the early evening.

One of the main sporting values is that of **sportsmanship** or fair play. The additional pressure that competitors feel when they know they need to win and perform well often works against sportsmanship. Performers are more likely to bend the rules to gain an advantage, or even break the rules to gain an advantage. Few now condemn the professional foul in sport, but this is directly against the ethics of sportsmanship.

## Media coverage of inappropriate behaviour of athletes

The media covers sport. Through the media, we see all that is good about sport and sports performance. But we also get **media coverage of inappropriate behaviour of athletes**. This unsuitable behaviour often happens on the pitch or the court or in the stadium, but sometimes, because of a performer's high profile, may also include behaviour outside of the sport.

Because they are role models, the way that performers conduct themselves has an effect on the image of individual sports and the expectations of behaviour by those involved in them.

Different sports have different expectations about player behaviour. For example, golfers are expected to own up to anything that they do wrong and even disqualify themselves. Diving by footballers to get a free kick is increasing and most people complain about it as

**Key term**

**Sportsmanship** Fair and generous behaviour or treatment of others in a sporting contest

being a form of cheating. But the same people are happy to accept the rewards it brings when this form of cheating benefits their team.

In cricket, opposition fans sit and stand together and there is usually a friendly atmosphere. There is a very limited police presence and stewarding is light. Video surveillance is almost unheard of. Yet in football, although most supporters enjoy the presence of the opposition's fans, they are segregated to avoid outbreaks of violence occurring due to a small minority. Groups of fans taunt each other with insults. The police presence is large and stewarding is very thorough. Video surveillance is used to identify troublemakers who may be banned from future matches. All-seater stadia are required for all Premier League and international matches.

In rugby union, players are penalised for arguing with the referee, but some acts of violence are seen as part of the game. Etiquette requires that the players always clap each other off the field and problems are left on the pitch. Yet in football, players often surround the referee to argue against their decisions. Acts of violence become worse, with other players becoming involved and the fans further inflame the situation by booing and insulting players. Some disagreements on the pitch are continued and fights have been known to break out in the tunnel after the game.

### On-field behaviour

The way performers behave at sporting events can affect the outcome of the event. The actual rules of the game are fixed, but there are certain unwritten rules that performers should stick to, known as etiquette.

For example, football players will usually kick the ball out of play if another player is injured so that the injured player can get treatment. The team that kicked the ball out then get it back from the throw-in when play restarts. In tennis, after the match, the players shake hands with each other and the umpire. This type of behaviour happens in lots of sports.

However, there appears to be an increase in poor on-field behaviour in many sports, and because these sports are in the media, we get to see and hear about this bad behaviour. Although you rarely see or hear about a fight between players of non-contact sports such as tennis or snooker, fights, or at least lots of pushing and shoving, are becoming common in sports such as football and rugby, where the nature of the game is aggressive, with frequent, hard contact.

Such forms of violent conduct, and others such as unsporting behaviour and swearing, are more likely to be seen and heard in sport because nowadays there are far more cameras and microphones at sports events.

> **Group activity**
>
> Discuss whether football fans encourage players to play well or behave badly. Do the players incite the fans to celebrate or abuse each other?

Unlike in many other major sports, Premier League referees do not wear microphones, so we cannot hear what is being said. One of the main reasons for this is because of the foul language that permeates that sport.

Many sports have produced a code of behaviour for its players (and spectators).

**Figure 4.7** Football players arguing with the referee.

## Off-field behaviour

The media has helped develop role models for many sports. Some of these role models have become celebrities and adopt a celebrity lifestyle that may conflict with what people see as a sportsperson's lifestyle.

There have been numerous examples of poor off-field behaviour of performers, such as rugby, cricket or football players who have behaved badly in nightclubs or have become involved in scandals, which produces negative reporting that may affect their professional performance.

## Creation of negative role models

A negative role model is any person who influences others in a negative way. **Negative role models can be created** when a sports performer's poor behaviour and decisions set a negative example for others that is all too easily copied.

For example, spectators see players surrounding and arguing with the referee over a decision, and then some time later the aggressive behaviour shown towards the officials in professional sport becomes the norm at grassroots level.

## Increased pressure on officials

Sport involves physical exertion and skill where individuals or teams compete against others. Because sport is competitive, it requires officials to make sure the rules of the sport are being adhered to. Because of the media, many forms of sport are now becoming a form of entertainment and involve considerable amounts of money that go to the sport, the teams and the performers.

That money is not evenly distributed. The majority of the money goes to the winners. There is therefore increased pressure on officials to make sure that the rules are applied correctly and correct decisions are made. People's livelihoods depend on officials' decisions.

### Scrutiny of decisions made

In most sports, officials' decisions are final and never questioned. In some sports, the official's decisions are debated on the pitch. Players can be seen or heard arguing with decisions. It is now fairly common to hear or see players making suggestions as to what they should do next: 'That's a foul'; 'Award a penalty'; 'Give a yellow card'; 'Send them off!'

Some sports even allow **scrutiny of decisions made**. In tennis and cricket, the players can refer an official's decision to a series of cameras that review and make a judgement on the original decision.

The post-match examination of the referee's decisions is now commonplace. With the benefit of various camera angles and slow-motion replays, the experts can immediately discuss what the referee has decided. Incorrect or poor decisions are often highlighted and extensively publicised and the ability of officials questioned. This even happens when the experts, having spent several minutes debating the rights and wrongs of the original decision, are still unable to agree.

### Hype can make officials' role much harder

The media needs to create interest in sporting events to get more people watching or listening and so increase their own revenue and increase the cost of advertising other products. One way they may do this is by increasing the **hype** around events. This increased **hype created by the media can make the officials' role much harder**.

In simple terms, the scrutiny of decisions becomes even more intense. This is especially the case when the event involves close or traditional rivals.

**Key term**

**Hype** Extravagant or intensive publicity or promotion

## Newspapers are dominated by a few sports

People's knowledge of sport is often based on what is in the media. The media including **newspapers is dominated by a few sports**. Previously (page 113) you investigated the types of sports that were found in different types of newspapers.

If you refer back to that list of sports covered by each newspaper, you will see that largely male-dominated sports such as football, rugby (league and union) and cricket predominate. Most of these male-dominated sports are also associated with gambling.

This is very different from the list of the most popular sports in terms of participation.

Coverage in newspapers of sportswomen and sports popular with ethnic minority groups tends to be restricted to those periods of time when there has been some female or ethnic minority success in 'traditional' sports such as cricket, rugby and football.

## Saturation

We may be getting close to the **saturation** point for sport and the media. There may simply be no more room for sport in the media. The public may be falling out of love with sport.

### Group activity

Refer back to the list you made for the group activity on page 110. How many dedicated sports channels are now available in the UK? How many sports are being shown on subscription?

Discuss the idea that the amount of sport on TV has reached saturation point.

### Links to other units

You can find further information on this topic in **Units R051, R052, R053** and **R055**.

## Know it!

1 Identify four minority sports that have become less popular because of media coverage.

2 Describe, using a sport of your choice, how some sporting values have been lost.

3 Discuss, using examples from a sport of your choice, whether levels of sportsmanship have declined.

4 Make a list of five negative effects that a sport of your choice has suffered from media coverage.

## Assessment preparation

Think about the task/s that your teacher may set you to assess your knowledge of the negative effects of the media on sport.

Make sure you:

- Know about the decline in live spectatorship.
- Know about the loss of traditional sporting values.
- Know about the media coverage of inappropriate behaviour of athletes:
  - ○ on-field behaviour
  - ○ off-field behaviour
  - ○ creation of negative role models.
- Know about increased pressure on officials:
  - ○ scrutiny of decisions made
  - ○ hype around events created by media can make officials' roles much harder.
- Know that newspapers are dominated by a few sports.
- Know about saturation.

### Mark scheme

| LO3 Understand negative effects that the media can have on sport | | |
| --- | --- | --- |
| Mark band 1 | Mark band 2 | Mark band 3 |
| Identifies **some** possible negative effects that the media can have on sport. Provides a **brief description** of the negative effects identified and supports **some** of the descriptions with examples. | Describes **a range** of possible negative effects that the media can have on sport. Provides some explanation as to why they are negative supported with mostly **relevant examples**. | Explains **a wide range** of possible negative effects that the media can have on sport, clearly supported with **relevant** examples. |

## LO4 Understand the relationship between sport and the media

### How media uses sport to promote itself

The **media uses sport to promote itself** by using itself as a form of entertainment. In this respect, up-to-date sports news is the best possible entertainment and watching sport on TV or online is the best possible way to witness the actual thing happening.

The media sticks to the needs of the general public who want to know what is happening in the world of sport. Even if the football match is taking place in Russia, or the tennis match is in New York, media brings the tennis game and the football match straight to your living room, without the need to get up from the sofa and buy the ticket to Russia. Media brings coverage of sports into our homes and shows it to us whenever we want.

The leader of the pack, as far as bringing sport to the masses, is Sky Sports, which is the flagship of the satellite and cable TV market.

### How sport uses the media to promote itself

**Sport uses the media to promote itself** by regularly advertising upcoming events in the media. In simple terms, to find out about a team or sport, whether at a professional or local level, we use the media.

The big teams and the major sports use television to promote their matches and the sport itself, while social media has become the main platform for advertising sports and sports teams that play at a slightly lower level.

Most sports and teams now have websites and can therefore be searched for on the internet. Other ways of promoting a presence include newsletters sent via email or using a platform such as Facebook, YouTube or Twitter to promote the team or sport.

Some of the bigger football clubs, such as Liverpool, Chelsea and Manchester United, have their own TV channels.

### Sport as a commodity

A **commodity** is a product that can be sold or traded. **Sport is a commodity** to be bought and sold at a profit. Sport teams and players are used as commodities.

Sport is not just a hobby – it is also a career path for professional performers. Professionals are paid. In order to generate the money to pay the professionals, sport, like any other business, relies on consumers. **Consumers** are the people who pay for the commodity.

 **Key terms**

**Commodity** A product that can be sold

**Consumers** People who buy commodities

## Many sports more dependent on media as a source of revenue

**Sport is much more dependent on media as a source of revenue**. Sport is a big business; sport provides thousands of jobs. A football club such as Manchester United has close to 1,000 full-time employees.

Sport relies on consumers to build income for the sport and make a profit. The consumers (me and you) use the media to find out what is happening in sport. Without the media, you will not know what is happening with your team. Without the media, you do not see or listen to the advertising that companies pay your team to show. Without the team's name in the media, the companies may stop paying for advertising because it's not worthwhile. If the companies stop advertising, they will stop paying and thus income to the team falls.

## Influence on the ownership of sports clubs

Many sports clubs are now owned by individuals. Football is the best example, with the majority of Premier League clubs owned by wealthy businesspeople. These people are wealthy because they are good at business. They are good at seeing opportunities to make a profit, so why are they buying Premier League clubs?

It probably isn't for profit as only half of the Premier League clubs are profit-making. Yet, English clubs are in high demand for foreign investors, with 13 of the 20 Premier League teams currently (2018) owned by overseas owners.

One explanation is that it has nothing to do with money. Several Premier League owners such as Mike Ashley at Newcastle and Roman Abramovich at Chelsea have put millions of pounds of their own money into the clubs. They appear to be using the clubs either as a hobby or a way of making themselves famous.

The Glazer family bought Manchester United in 2006. They saw the potential of using the brand name of the club to generate money. They borrowed the money to buy the club using the club itself as the guarantee for payments. The profits from selling the club's name and merchandise have been used to reduce the original loans and soon the Glazers will be in possession of a multi-billion-pound asset (Manchester United) with the loans paid off. This is simply good business.

## Sponsorship and advertising

**Sponsorship** is a relationship between a provider (of funds, goods or services) and an event, activity or person, which in return offers some rights and association that may be used for a commercial advantage. **Sponsorship is usually done as a form of advertising**.

**Classroom discussion**

How would football teams cope without the millions of pounds given to them by Sky Sports and BT Sport? What would sponsors do if the team they sponsor no longer appears on TV?

**Key term**

**Sponsorship** Where a company pays money to a team or individual in return for advertising their goods

The sport is sold to businesses as a means of advertising the business's product. The business sponsors the sport to obtain advertising space and publicise its product. The sport is shown via the media, which promotes the product, and the sports spectators see the advertising and buy the business's product.

### Links between media coverage and sponsorship

Broadcasting rights, sponsorship and ticket sales are all directly related to how interested people are in the sport. If there are millions of people watching, the price of the TV broadcast rights will be huge. This then directly affects sponsorship deals, as more exposure on TV means the sponsor will be required to pay more to be associated with the club or event. Similarly, if the event is popular, ticket prices can be increased to increase profit.

Businesses sponsor sport mainly as a means of advertising their product. If the sponsored sport is regularly in the media, then spectators will see the sponsor's name and this publicity may increase sales of the sponsor's products. Many businesses sponsor a sport in order to associate the name of the product with a successful or popular team or individual. The notion they are hoping to put into the spectator's head is that if this team is high quality, then the sponsor's product must be high quality.

The sponsor wants the spectator to buy its product. There are sponsors whose main aim is not so much to gain increased sales of its product, but rather to support the local community, and become well known in the local community. Local businesses will often support local sports teams simply with the intention of helping others. This is almost a form of charity.

### Different types of sponsorship and advertising in sport

Sponsorship appears to be a great benefit to sport. In fact, without sponsorship, sport as we know it would have to change, because of all the money involved. The sponsor is not always providing money; other forms of support such as company products are more usually provided. Sponsors may provide items such as equipment, clothing or footwear. Car manufacturers often sponsor teams by providing cars for the players. Similarly, the sponsorship is not always to a sport; there are **different types of sponsorship and advertising** seen in sport. Businesses can sponsor an individual player, a team, a competition, a stadium or a stand.

There are drawbacks to sponsoring a sport. The sponsor's name becomes linked to the activity, which is good provided that the activity is seen in a positive light by the spectators. But being linked to an activity, team or performer that is not performing well reflects badly on the sponsor. Similarly, any negative aspects to a sport, such as cheating, violence or bad results reflect, negatively on the sponsor's product.

**Group activity**

Make a list of different sponsors and the way they are involved in sponsorship (on shirts, providing kit, advertising around the grounds and so on).

## Adoption and rejection of sporting heroes by the media

The media promotes sport. Sports are played by individuals and therefore the media also promotes individuals. These individuals then become role models and sporting heroes for many.

The problem is that many sporting heroes are only heroes for as long as the media portrays them as heroes. The media is just as quick to **adopt a sporting hero as it is to reject one**.

For example, Sir Bradley Wiggins was a hero through his Olympic cycling and Tour de France successes, but when details of his use of (permitted) allergy medication were leaked by the media, he soon lost his hero status. Chris Froome has suffered the same fate – winning four Tour de France races and then being found to have high levels of an asthma drug in his body.

David Beckham went from hero to villain in one match after kicking an Argentinian player at the 1998 World Cup and receiving a red card. His return to hero status only occurred when he scored a last-minute goal against Greece in a 2001 World Cup qualifier.

## How scrutiny and criticism through the media have increased

It has been repeatedly said throughout this chapter that we are informed by the media. But with the development of social media, we also have the ability to give our own opinions rather than simply accept the opinions of others. What you post on Facebook, Twitter or Snapchat as your opinions are then made available to thousands of others.

Therefore, scrutiny and criticism through the media have increased. Sports performers, coaches, management and chairpeople are much more exposed to different forms of the media.

## The impact of pay-per-view

**The impact of pay-per-view** has not been as great as many people thought it would be. Although some boxing matches on pay-per-view have been seen by over 1 million subscribers, most matches have attracted smaller numbers than that.

The same sorts of figures are found for Ultimate Fighting Championship contests. These low viewing figures are probably why few other sports have entered into the pay-per-view market.

**Links to other units**

You can find further information on this topic in **Units R051, 53** and **55**.

## Know it!

1 Identify four sports that have more media coverage than most others.
2 Describe the relationship between sport, the media and business/companies/sponsorship.
3 Describe the impact of pay-per-view TV on sport.

## Assessment preparation

Think about the task/s that your teacher may set you to assess your knowledge of the relationship between sports and the media.

Make sure you:

- Know how the media uses sport to promote itself.
- Know how sport uses the media to promote itself.
- Know about sport as a commodity:
  ○ many sports are now much more dependent on media as a source of revenue
  ○ the influence on the ownership of sports clubs.
- Know about sponsorship and advertising:
  ○ links between the amount of media coverage and sponsorship that can be attracted
  ○ different types of sponsorship and advertising which are seen in sport.
- Know about adoption and rejection of sporting heroes by the media.
- Know how scrutiny or criticism through the media has increased.
- Know about the impact of pay-per-view.

### Mark scheme

| LO4 Understand the relationship between sport and the media | | |
|---|---|---|
| Mark band 1 | Mark band 2 | Mark band 3 |
| **Outlines some** aspects of the relationship between sport and the media. Provides **some basic** examples of their value to one another. Shows **little awareness** of the ways in which sport and the media influence each other or that this has changed over time. | **Describes a range** of aspects of the relationship between sport and the media, supported by **mostly relevant** examples of their value to one another. Attempts **some explanation** of the ways in which sport and the media influence each other, showing an understanding that this has changed over time. | **Describes a wide range** of aspects of the relationship between sport and the media, with **relevant** examples of their value to one another. **Explains** the ways in which sport and the media influence each other, showing a **thorough understanding** of **how** this has changed over time. |

# LO5 Be able to evaluate media coverage of sport

## Aspects which may influence coverage of a story or item

Several factors govern whether a story is 'worthy' of being covered by the media. **Aspects which may influence the coverage of a story** include the popularity of the sport, team or individual involved, the type of media that is presenting the story and the timing of the story.

### Type or 'brand' of media outlet

A **media outlet** is a publication or broadcast programme that provides news and feature stories to the public through various distribution channels. Media outlets include newspapers, magazines, radio, television, the internet and social media.

The **type of media outlet** involved can influence whether a story is reported. For example, broadsheet newspapers tend to emphasise themselves as an information service; they have less of the total paper devoted to sport, but a more varied coverage in terms of a wider range of sports. The broadsheets also tend to provide critical analysis of events and issues affecting sport.

The tabloid newspapers tend to sensationalise events and personalities. They tend to focus on a narrow range of popular sports, for example, football and horse racing, and have little coverage of minority sports. Most tabloids have a larger proportion of the total newspaper (up to a quarter) devoted to sport.

There is a considerable cost for television to be involved in reporting a story compared to social media. Television needs a reporter, a camera operator, a sound operator and possibly a director. It has now become common for social media to be the first to report a story and then for television to report it if the TV producer thinks it will make a 'good' story.

### Competition with other media outlets

There is **competition between media outlets** as they try to bring stories to the general public. In order to attract viewers or listeners, the different types of media try to find a different 'angle' for a report or story.

For example, television may show a story about a sport, and then radio may try to secure interviews with fans about how they feel about the story, while newspapers may print an 'exclusive' interview with one particular individual involved in the story.

**Key term**

**Media outlet** Publication or broadcast programme providing information through various distribution channels

## Target audience

A similar factor influencing coverage of a story is the **target audience**. If the majority of a media's readers or listeners are from one particular section of the population, then the media would do well to focus on an aspect of the story that appeals to that section of the population. For example, Snapchat is becoming the preferred media for younger people, while Facebook is becoming known for its use by older members of the population.

## Timing of the event, story or item

The **timing of the event, story or item** is important. When a story is published in the media, it will only last a certain amount of time before the public becomes disinterested and it is no longer newsworthy. If the sport, organisation or people involved are already in the news, it becomes important that the different media outlets make each new revelation about the story dissimilar to previous stories and possibly magnified to maintain interest.

## Popularity, notoriety or size of the individual, club or organisation being covered

Whether a story is newsworthy often depends on the **popularity, notoriety or size of the individual, club or organisation being covered**. In other words, who or what the story is about. For example, a story about a footballer who makes a bad pass is probably not worth publishing as it is too common, even though the sport is very popular. But a story about the same footballer being seen out late drinking, just before an important match, may be worth publishing.

Similarly, some sports or individuals may have a reputation that is worth talking about, so a story about a rugby player who gets sent off for the fourth or fifth consecutive match is probably worth a critical article.

Another aspect that influences whether a story is published is the status of the sport, organisation or individual. You would not expect a football TV channel such as LFCTV to show a programme criticising the Liverpool manager. In the same way, you would not expect Sky Sports to show a programme criticising its coverage of football.

This does not necessarily apply to social media, where criticism and opinions are much more likely to appear, as the content of what is posted is under fewer constraints.

## Features of the coverage which may vary from one media outlet to another

Different media outlets may have different ways of presenting news stories, so that **features of the coverage may vary from one media outlet to another**.

## Representation of the issue, organisation or individual involved

Different media outlets will **represent the issue, organisation or individual involved** in a story in different ways. It should be obvious that LFCTV and Chelsea TV would not report a match between Liverpool and Chelsea in exactly the same way.

Similarly, the Premiership rugby website will probably a have different focus when reporting on the performance of one of its referees compared to a fansite's comments on the referee from the same match.

## Method of reporting

The **method of reporting** in terms of the language used and the tone of the content will also vary between different media outlets. Comments posted on Facebook and WhatsApp will be different from those of the BBC's website.

## Format and presentation

The **format and presentation** in terms of the use of images, the balance between image and text, and the use of headlines and captions varies between different media outlets.

## Potential bias

As previously mentioned, some media outlets may have an agenda that makes them take a certain view on an issue. The reporting of a Liverpool v Chelsea football match by LFCTV has the potential for bias because the report is being produced for Liverpool fans.

## Extent of the coverage

The coverage given to a story by different media outlets will vary. The **extent of the coverage** can be measured by counting the number of lines or pages devoted to that story, or by calculating the column inches used.

**Group activity**

Identify a recent sports story and research two different ways that the story was reported in different media outlets. Suggest reasons for the differences between the two forms of reporting.

**Group activity**

Each person in the group researches a match report from the previous week. Measure the amount of coverage of the match by counting the number of lines of text (or words used).

**Stretch activity**

Using the same match report from the group activity, work out how many words of seven letters or more were in the report. This indicates the method of reporting being used.

## Duration of the coverage

Stories about sport only have a limited lifespan. The **duration of the coverage** varies, depending on the importance the media outlet gives to that story. Some stories go on for days, while others only exist for a few hours. It all depends on whether the media outlet feels that the story is still attracting viewers or listeners.

**Links to other units**

You can find further information on this topic in **Units R051** and **55**.

## Know it!

1 Describe the aspects of the media that may influence coverage of a story.
2 Describe how features of a story may vary from one media outlet to another.

## Read about it

Information on the different broadcasting contracts for different sports:
https://en.wikipedia.org/wiki/Sports_broadcasting_contracts_in_the_United_Kingdom

Read about sport on Amazon Prime:
https://www.radiotimes.com/news/2017-11-07/amazon-prime-video-live-sport

Which Premier League team is on TV the most?:
www.theweek.co.uk/premier-league/91634/premier-league-tv-rights-deal- sky-sports-bt-sport-2019-2022

Article about football on Amazon Prime: www.bbc.co.uk/sport/football/44396151

The best sports books:
https://www.telegraph.co.uk/sport/picturegalleries/12001859/The-50-best-sports-books-ever-written.html

List of available radio stations: https://media.info/radio/stations

One newspaper's sports blog: www.theguardian.com/sport/blog

Sports on TV: www.tvguide.co.uk/Sports

Premier League football website: www.premierleague.com

Rugby World Cup website: www.rugbyworldcup.com

Article about the success of British cycling:
www.theguardian.com/sport/2012/jul/14/british-cycling-world-beaters

Article about one footballer's behaviour problems: www.bbc.co.uk/sport/football/32436515

Article about off-field behaviour: www.bbc.co.uk/news/uk-england-gloucestershire-45201916

What is the most popular sport in England?: www.telegraph.co.uk/sport/2017/02/15/popular-sport-england

Background to lots of sports stars: www.sporting-heroes.net

Article on pay-per-view TV: https://en.wikipedia.org/wiki/Pay-per-view#United_Kingdom

## Assessment preparation

Think about the task/s that your teacher may set you to assess your ability to evaluate media coverage of sport.

Make sure you know:

- The type or brand of media outlet.
- How media outlets are in competition.
- The target audience.
- The timing of the event/story/item.
- The popularity/notoriety or size of the individual/club/organisation being covered.
- The representation of the issues/organisations/individuals involved.
- The method of reporting:
  - format/presentation
  - potential bias
  - extent of the coverage
  - duration of the coverage.

## Mark scheme

| LO5 Be able to evaluate media coverage of sport | | |
|---|---|---|
| **Mark band 1** | **Mark band 2** | **Mark band 3** |
| Evaluation of the coverage of a sports story/item by different media outlets is **basic**. | Evaluation of the coverage of a sports story/item by different media outlets is **detailed**. | Evaluation of the coverage of a sports story/item by different media outlets is **comprehensive**. |
| **Briefly** discusses a **limited range** of features of the coverage. | **Discusses a range** of features of the coverage. | **Fully discusses a wide range** of features of the coverage. |
| Consideration of aspects which may have influenced the coverage is **superficial**. | Aspects which may have influenced the coverage are **considered**. | Aspects which may have influenced the coverage are **considered in detail**. |
| **Few relevant** comparisons of the coverage between the different media outlets are made. | **Relevant** comparisons of the coverage between the different media outlets are made. | **Clear and relevant** comparisons of the coverage between the different media outlets are made. |
| There is **little attempt** to make an overall judgement about whether the way in which the media outlets have covered the item/story is appropriate. | An overall **judgement is made** about whether the way in which the media outlets have covered the item/story is appropriate. | An overall **judgement is made and justified** about whether the way in which the media outlets have covered the item/story is appropriate. |

# R055 Working in the sports industry

## About this unit

Within this unit, learners will start to develop an appreciation of some of the career paths linked to the sports industry. Although not all careers have a direct link to specific sports, many careers hold some correlation to aspects of the sports industry. This can include careers which encourage participation, progression or sports development. This unit will allow learners the chance to appreciate the breadth of sports-related opportunities that relate to administration, security, grounds-keeping, coaching, management, sports development and leisure management. Learners will begin to see the role that these jobs play and how development pathways within a career can progress. The unit also allows learners to explore how the sports industry affects society in Britain by looking at areas such as the economy, health and fitness, heritage, tourism and national identity.

## Learning outcomes

**LO1** Know the areas of employment within the sports industry

**LO2** Know the skills and knowledge required to work within the sports industry

**LO3** Be able to apply for jobs within the sports industry

**LO4** Understand the impacts which the sports industry has in the UK

## How will I be assessed?

This is assessed over 30 Guided Learning Hours. Approximately 10 hours of internal assessment will be worth 60 marks (60 UMS). This is centre-assessed and OCR moderated.

### For LO1

Learners need to have knowledge and understanding of:

- different areas of employment within the sports industry.

### For LO2

Learners need to have knowledge and understanding of:

- skills which can be applied to different roles within the sports industry
- knowledge which can be applied to different roles within the sports industry.

### For LO3

Learners need to have knowledge and understanding of:

- sources of information regarding job vacancies in the sports industry
- key aspects to consider in researching a specific job role within the sports industry
- how to create a curriculum vitae
- how to prepare for an interview
- key considerations when producing a personal career plan.

### For LO4

Learners need to have knowledge and understanding of the:

- economic impacts of the sports industry
- social impacts of the sports industry
- health impacts of the sports industry.

## LO1 Know the areas of employment within the sports industry

The sports industry generates billions of pounds every year across the world. It is a global phenomenon and, as a result, there is a wealth of different job roles which hold some link to the sports industry.

### Different areas of employment within the sports industry

This section will outline many of the different areas of employment that exist within the sports industry.

#### Administration/organisation

An **administrator** may be a secretary or someone who provides support to professionals in terms of communication, paperwork, and co-ordination and implementation of procedures. In relation to the sports industry, examples of administrative work include the following:

- An **HR manager** at a sports club who deals with the people who work there, e.g. contracts, pay, bank details, terms of work and so on.

> **Getting started**
>
> In pairs, list as many jobs as you can that have some form of link to the world of sport.

> **Key term**
>
> **Administration** The work of a secretary or someone who provides support to professionals in terms of communication, paperwork, and co-ordination and implementation of procedures

- A **receptionist** at a gym who administers membership details and meets and greets those attending.
- A **health and safety officer** at a leisure centre who administers all procedural details in relation to the health and safety of that leisure centre.

**Figure 5.1** Working as a leisure centre receptionist.

## Advertising and marketing

Advertising involves letting people know about something through sources of media or campaigns. Advertising is a part of **marketing**, which involves attracting, keeping and satisfying customers through marketing activity. Marketing activity can involve advertising to give the price of what is being marketed, information about the product being marketed, the place where it is available and the promotion or offer being marketed. Therefore, advertising or marketing jobs in the sports industry could include the following:

- **PR/marketing** for a sports club. PR stands for public relations. Therefore, the club marketer will look to attract, keep and satisfy customers of that club, for example, gain new fans for a rugby club.
- **Sports advertising**: working to advertise products and their qualities to the public, e.g. campaigns for Nike, Adidas, Puma and so on.
- **Graphic designers** design the graphics of logos and brands which are often used in marketing activity. For example, if a new pair of trainers is launched, the sports company will use graphic designers to design billboards, magazine adverts and store window displays.

## Coaching, leading, instructing

One common area of employment in the sports industry is working as a coach, leader or instructor. Earning different rates of pay

### Key terms

**Marketing** The process of attracting, keeping and satisfying customers through marketing activity

**PR** Public relations

### Group activity

Search online for some adverts for trainers from any of the global brands, e.g. Nike, Adidas, Puma, Under Armour, Asics, New Balance and so on. How do graphic designers try to make products look good in the adverts?

depending on the activity and level being instructed, coaches or leaders take charge of individuals or groups to ensure they progress and are safe in their activity. Specific examples include the following:

- **Local/regional/NGB coach**: A local, regional or national governing body (NGB) coach will work with groups of individuals to develop, progress and improve performance levels in certain activities. For example, a regional rugby development officer will provide opportunities for people to take part in rugby and deliver coaching sessions to help them improve.

- **Qualified fitness instructors** may work in private or public leisure centres, fitness clubs or local facilities and will provide fitness classes and/or advice to the public. This might be via advice to those using a gym or as an expert in specific fitness classes, e.g. Zumba, spinning or aerobics.

- **Outdoor activities leaders** provide supervision and teaching of outdoor and adventure activities. They must be qualified and possess specific knowledge about how to lead, develop and ensure the safety of a group of people, e.g. when rock climbing, canoeing, bouldering or hill walking and navigating.

**Figure 5.2** An aerobics instructor taking a session with a class.

## Facilities

There are many jobs within the sports industry that involve specific roles at specific sports facilities. For example:

- A **steward** at a sports venue works to direct the public to their seats in a stadium, ensuring health and safety procedures are maintained and followed by all in attendance.

- **Bar staff** at a sports club, e.g. golf club, who work behind the bar, serving food and drinks to the public.
- **Groundskeepers** look after the grounds and playing surfaces on which sports are played. For example, a groundskeeper at a cricket club will maintain the wicket and outfield. A groundskeeper at a football club will maintain the pitch. Groundskeepers (or 'greens keepers') on a golf course will maintain the upkeep and maintenance of the golf course, e.g. cutting grass, removing weeds and applying chemicals to the greens.

## Finance

Sport is a multi-million dollar business and, as a result, many jobs focus on the financial aspects involved. Examples include the following:

- treasurer for a local sports club
- sports auditing for a national governing body
- finance officer for a sports club/organisation
- accountant for a major sports club, e.g. Premiership football club.

## Government

The government has a major role to play in the organisation of sport within the UK. This includes the provision of facilities for the public and spending taxation to encourage public health and fitness. Examples of government work within the sports industry include:

- working for the **Department for Digital, Culture, Media and Sport**, which is responsible for sports participation and elite sports performance
- working for the **local council/local authority sport organisation**, which could include working on local sports development and opportunities to take part in sporting activities.

## Media

As sport is very popular, it attracts a lot of media coverage. Media is generally deemed to be television, newspapers, magazines, radio, online sources and social media. The BBC is a public-funded organisation with a 'flagship' website providing coverage of sport 24/7.

Media jobs within the sports industry include the following:

- **Local newspaper reporter**, covering news, stories and features about local sport, e.g. local football, rugby and cricket teams.
- **National newspaper reporter**, covering news, stories and features about sporting performance on a national basis, e.g. athletics results, tennis scores, cycling results.

**Key term**

**Groundskeepers** People who look after the grounds and surfaces on which sport is played

**Classroom discussion**

Discuss what local facilities require grounds maintenance. How well are these facilities kept? Do the groundskeepers do a good job to maintain a suitable playing surface?

- **Radio presenter**, providing radio-based coverage, news and features about sport either on a local or national stage. National radio stations such as Radio 5 Live Sport provide coverage of featured sports, including live commentary of chosen sports events.
- A **commentator/pundit** provides expert coverage, views and opinions about chosen sporting events. Commentators or pundits often provide analysis, explanation of tactics and strategies and viewpoints about how well or otherwise people have performed.
- **Sports photographers** are often close to the action, e.g. pitch-side or court-side, and receive special access to take photographs of sports performers to be used in various forms of the media.

> **Key term**
>
> **Commentator/pundit**
> Provides expert coverage, views and opinions about chosen sports

## National governing body

You may remember from Unit R051 that national governing bodies (NGBs) are privately run organisations that oversee the administration, management and organisation of a sport in a particular country. As a result, there are many jobs that exist within NGBs:

- **Fund raising**: working on campaigns to raise money and awareness within that sport. This may involve lobbying the government for further funding.
- **Regulatory work**: working to administer and act on regulations. This could include administering bans or fines for poor discipline or working on rule changes.
- **Monitoring work**: working with designated mentors and the athletes whom they mentor.

## Retail

As sports clothing is extremely popular for those taking part in sport, there is a huge marketplace for major sporting retailers to sell their sports clothes, equipment and footwear. Equally, as sports fans follow their sporting heroes, they often want to buy the merchandise, kit or colours of their favourite sports stars. The retail sector for sports-related merchandise is a huge business. Examples of specific jobs within the retail sector include the following:

- Working in a **high street sports shop**, selling sports-branded merchandise to the public. This can involve managerial work within the shop, being a specialist, e.g. footwear specialist, or a shop assistant providing the goods the customer wants.
- Working for an **internet sports retailer**, fulfilling any orders made online to ensure that customers receive the correct goods punctually, via the post.

**Figure 5.3** One job role within the sports industry is to work for a major sports retailer.

> ### 💬 Classroom discussion
>
> Which websites do class members buy sporting goods from? Are some websites better than others when purchasing sports goods? Think about:
> - the choice available
> - how easy or otherwise it is to navigate the site
> - how quickly goods arrive
> - how easy or otherwise the online retailer makes it to return unwanted goods.

## Professional sport

If talented enough, some people can make a career out of professional sport. Examples of this include the following:

- **Professional performer/athlete**. The professional performer dedicates their time to training and competing, although most professional performers have media and sponsorship duties to fulfil as well.

- **Professional coach/manager**. Those who manage or coach professional sports teams or individuals can make a lucrative career from this. Football managers at the highest level get paid a good salary, but do need to have achieved specific qualifications. However, their job security is also extremely fragile in such a results-based business.

- **Professional referee/official**. Professional referees are now used in many sports, with many of these officials doing this as their main job. Officials need to gain experience, achieve specific qualifications, and continually prove themselves to be reliable, fair and consistent.

- **Licensed agent**. A licensed sports agent acts on behalf of a performer or group of performers to arrange contracts, sponsorship and endorsements. Licensed agents take a percentage of the money that is acquired through their work. Highly paid sports performers usually have an agent who acts on their behalf.

## Sport development

Many job roles exist in sports development, working for either a governing body, local authority or as part of a specific campaign. Examples include:

- **Sports development officer for a council**: in charge of generating opportunities for people to take part in sports in the local area. Sports development officers often work with governing bodies and providers of facilities to promote the provision of clubs, sports camps and development opportunities for those who are able to play to a representative standard.
- **Sport development officer for a university**: carries out a similar role to a sports development officer for a local council, with the exception that they work solely on campus to generate sporting opportunities within the university.

## Sports events

Sports events can be one-off or regular and require a significant amount of organisation. Examples of roles in sports events include the following:

- **Event-organising committee member**: whereby the person sits on a committee, providing advice and guidance to ensure an event is a success.
- **An events promoter**: works to promote an event to the public through marketing activity, media and public relations work.
- **Specialist sports travel and events companies**: provide a bespoke experience for those looking to travel to or attend a sporting event.

## Sports-related gambling

**Gambling** is the act of betting money on the outcome or prospective features of a sporting event. Sports-related gambling is heavily regulated but is also seen as a growing market in the UK. Companies such as SportPesa have increased the number of jobs available in the UK. Jobs in sports-related gambling include:

- **Bookmaker**. A bookmaker owns or manages the company that provides betting services. There are high street bookmakers and

**Key terms**

**Licensed agent** Acts on behalf of a performer or group of performers to arrange contracts, sponsorship and endorsements of sporting events

**Gambling** The act of betting money on the outcome or prospective features of a sporting event

**Bookmaker** Owns or manages the company that provides betting services

online bookmakers. They take the bets and pay out winnings, as appropriate. Bookmakers can often be seen at race courses taking bets on horse races.

## Sport science

**Sport science** involves using the principles of science such as biology, chemistry, physics, biomechanics and kinesiology to explain, predict, analyse and evaluate sporting performance. Examples of jobs which exist within the field of sports science include the following:

- **Sport medicine**: involves the diagnosis of problems or symptoms in order to prescribe suitable legal medication to improve health, well-being and possibly performance. This could include helping performers to recover from injury or deal with symptoms such as asthma. Although many drugs are prohibited, some athletes can obtain a therapeutic use exemption (TUE) on medical grounds and are allowed to take the (normally) prohibited substance.

**Key terms**

**Sport science** Using the principles of science to explain, predict, analyse and evaluate sporting performance

**Sport medicine** The diagnosis of problems or symptoms in order to prescribe suitable legal medication to improve health, well-being and possibly performance

Figure 5.4 Physiotherapist using manual techniques to improve a patient's mobility.

- **Physiotherapists** work with sports performers to provide manual manipulation and techniques to improve range of movement, mobility or strength or simply to recover faster from an injury.

- **Sport psychologists** work with performers to help them with the mental aspects that can affect their performance. Some examples are given in Figure 5.5.

- **Personal trainers** work on a one-to-one basis (personally) with someone in need of advice about how to train or improve performance. Personal trainers often devise bespoke training programmes, specifically suited to the needs of the person receiving their advice. Personal trainers often work in gyms or occasionally on a freelance basis visiting people's houses.

**Key term**

**Personal trainers** Work on a one-to-one basis (personally) with someone in need of advice about how to train or improve performance

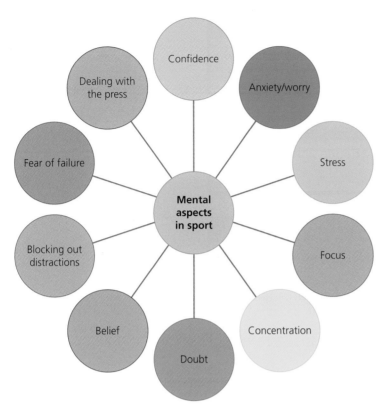

**Figure 5.5** Mental aspects in sports.

- **Nutritionists** provide dietary advice to performers about what to eat and drink to achieve the highest level of performance. As performance demands energy, which essentially comes from food sources, performers can be advised to eat suitably to meet their energy demands. Similarly, performers must stay hydrated to prevent an increase in reaction time and interrupted decision making.

**Figure 5.6** Personal trainer providing fitness advice to a client.

 **Key term**

**Nutritionists** Provide dietary advice to performers about what to eat and drink to achieve the highest level of performance

 **Classroom discussion**

Do you feel you eat the diet of an athlete? What dietary advice could you do with?

 **Group activity**

Research online to learn the average salaries of people in the jobs listed above. Share your findings amongst your group.

## Stretch activity

Try to visit someone who does any of the job roles described above. Carry out an informal interview with them, asking about their role.

## Links to other units

You can find further information on the synoptic links to this unit in **Units R051, 52, 53, 54** and **56**.

## Know it!

1 Name four areas in which you could work within the sports industry.
2 State two examples of specific jobs within each area (given in Question 1).
3 What is a physiotherapist?
4 State the different types of media.
5 Name two types of bookmaker.

## Assessment preparation

Think about the task that your teacher will set you in order to assess your knowledge and understanding of *different areas of employment within the sports industry*.

Make sure you are clear about:

● The areas of employment within the sports industry.
● A wide range of examples.

How will you demonstrate that you know these areas well and can support your work with a wide range of examples?

### Mark scheme

| LO1 Know the areas of employment within the sports industry | | |
|---|---|---|
| Mark band 1 | Mark band 2 | Mark band 3 |
| Identifies **some** of the areas of employment within the sports industry, supported by a **limited range** of examples. | Identifies **many** of the areas of employment within the sports industry, supported by a **range** of examples. | Identifies **most** of the areas of employment within the sports industry, supported by a **wide range** of examples. |

# LO2 Know the skills and knowledge required to work within the sports industry

## Skills that can be applied to different roles within the sports industry

There are many generic skills that can be beneficial in more than one role within the sports industry. Some examples are provided below.

### Sport-specific skills

**Sport-specific skills** refer to the specific skills, techniques and movements required when performing in a particular sport. These skills are obviously needed by the performer, but their coach may also need to be able to demonstrate these skills and, at the very least, is required to know how such skills should be performed.

### Literacy and numeracy skills

**Literacy** is the ability to read and write coherently, whereas **numeracy** is the ability to apply and use numbers. Both skills are required in some sports-related job roles; for example:

- **Financial or human resources roles**: where there is some financial management involved. This can be the management of a club's finances as a whole or of employees' wages within the business. This could also involve the transactional side of buying and selling items, such as players, resources or equipment. Reports may need to be written on employees, and sales and marketing reports will combine literacy and numeracy skills.
- **Administration**: many administrative roles involve literacy and numeracy skills. A leisure centre manager will have to write reports and plan financially, whereas a fitness instructor needs to write a training programme they have devised in a way that can be understood on paper.

### Information technology (IT) skills

There are very few job roles that do not make use of some IT skills. Computers are used for a wide array of purposes in most job roles, so a basic (or higher) level of IT literacy is important. Examples in the sports industry include the following:

- **Sports journalists** will tend to write their articles on a computer to be published by their local or national paper.
- **Graphic designers** will use specific software programs on their computer to design appropriate visual images.
- **Marketing or advertising executives** will write marketing plans on their computers and plan and publish reports and statistics via specially developed software packages.

**Getting started**

In pairs, choose a sports-related job outlined in section one (LO1 Know the areas of employment within the sports industry) and list the characteristics and qualities that you feel someone will need to be able to carry out such a role.

**Figure 5.7** Both coaches and performers need to know the correct technical model to perform suitable skills in that sport.

**Key terms**

**Sport-specific skills** The skills, techniques and movements required when performing in that sport

**Literacy** The ability to read and write coherently

**Numeracy** The ability to use and understand the use of numbers

- **Leisure centre receptionists** will administer bookings and attendance via an online system which would necessitate a basic understanding of IT skills.
- **Online shopping retailers** will process orders via their computer-based system.
- Gambling records are kept on computer-based systems which allow a simple barcode scan to find each bet that has been placed and calculate winnings. **Online gambling providers** will need a high level of IT skills to design gambling programs and manage the accounts of thousands of customers.

**Figure 5.8** Leisure centre receptionists require basic IT skills to administer bookings at the centre.

## People skills

**People skills** can be defined as the generic qualities and skills required to be able to communicate clearly and effectively with other people. It can therefore be argued that anyone who works with other people requires people skills. In the sports industry, examples of roles that particularly require good people skills include the following:

- **High street retailers** need to deal effectively with the public to welcome them, help them with enquiries and enable the customer to buy the goods they want.
- **Coaches and managers** need particularly good people skills to get the best out of the people they are coaching or managing. The relationship between a coach and their performer is key to ensuring that the performer listens and remains motivated.
- **PE teachers** plan, deliver and assess lessons on a daily basis. For those being taught, the success of a lesson is largely down to the people skills that the PE teacher has. They have to communicate effectively with their students to enable all students to progress in their learning.

## Communication skills

Communication skills are linked closely to people skills, although communication can be written, verbal or non-verbal. Several job roles require effective communication:

- A **manager** must be able to communicate his or her tactics and instructions to the team. These instructions must be clear, concise and easy to follow.
- **Instructors** are doing just that – instructing! Therefore, they must communicate their instructions clearly and without ambiguity. A fitness instructor must communicate effectively to those being instructed.
- **TV/radio presenters** are judged on their ability to communicate. They sometimes have to be flexible and innovative and respond to unexpected situations. Commentators aim to communicate a visual image of a sport through the spoken word.

 **Key term**

**People skills** The generic qualities and skills required to be able to communicate clearly and effectively with other people

## Organisational skills

It can be argued that all job roles require a degree of organisation. However, some roles have specific demands on a person's ability to organise; for example:

- An **events co-ordinator** must be incredibly organised to deal with the demands of an event. They may well have to organise a venue, health and safety, the order of events, sound, lighting, security and so on.
- **HR** consultants deal with human resources – i.e. people. Therefore, they must ensure that there is an organised process of review, that contractual obligations are adhered to and that employees receive their wages.

> **🔑 Key term**
>
> **HR** Human resources

## Team-working skills

Any job which involves working with other people can be said to need team-working skills. These can be very similar to both communication and organisational skills. However, some roles require team-working skills more than others; for example:

- Working within a **fund-raising team** requires a good team spirit to work together to raise the funds required.
- A **marketing team** is often in existence at large sports clubs, with people in the team working together to form different functions, e.g. PR, communications, agency work, advertising, internal communications and so on.
- Professional sports people who play in teams require certain abilities to work with others and show cohesion towards a team goal.

## Knowledge which can be applied to different roles within the sports industry

There are also many aspects of knowledge which can be beneficial in more than one sports-related job role. Some examples are provided below.

### Rules and regulations

Knowing the rules and regulations can be very important for those involved in sport. It is rather obvious to say that professional performers need to know the rules, but the following job roles also necessitate an in-depth knowledge:

- **Coaches** must know the rules and regulations so they can coach within the rules and maximise strategies to win or compete in the correct manner.
- **Officials** possibly more than anyone else need to know the rules and regulations as their role is to apply these rules and officiate within the laws of the sport.

## Consumer market

Knowledge of the **consumer market** basically means knowing who is likely to be interested in and willing to pay to be part of that market, i.e. who the fans are, who likes certain sports and so on.

- Knowing your market is a big part of **marketing**, with marketers aiming to target specific people, e.g. targeted e-shots (email). However, the law has recently changed and marketing teams can now only contact those people who 'opt in' to receive the information.

- Those working in **sponsorship** aim for their product or company to be of interest to those watching the sport. For example, Barclays was the main sponsor of the English Football Premier League for many years in the belief that a large number of those watching will see and be interested in their brand.

- Those working within the **gambling** field need to know who their market is and what they want. People are paid to design bet options that aim to entice those within the consumer market. For example, some companies sponsor half time at events and offer specific betting deals based on what they believe may or may not happen in the second half.

## Education/training

Most jobs require some form of formal training and/or qualification/s to enable the person to get the job in the first place. These qualifications may include the following:

- **GCSEs**: many jobs require a certain number of GCSEs. Jobs with literacy and numeracy requirements tend to stipulate that candidates need to have passed GCSE English and Maths.

- **A Levels**: university entrance tends to need A Levels or equivalent qualifications.

- **University degree**: e.g. journalists and marketing executives tend to have university degrees.

- **Vocational/industry standard qualifications**: e.g. Level 2 City & Guilds certificate in green-keeping for golf.

- **Coaching award**: most sports require coaches to work through different levels of coaching awards. A professional football manager must have their Pro-Licence Award. The LTA Level 1: Development Coach Award is a specific coaching award required to coach tennis.

- **College certificate**: for example, the college-based Introduction to Sport Level 1 certificate is designed for those who want to develop their readiness for work in a sports-related field. It is designed to improve your knowledge and understanding of sport, as well as your personal and social confidence.

**Key term**

**Consumer market** Those who are likely to be interested in and willing to pay to be part of a specific market

As you can see in the job advert below, the post demands that applicants must have an NGB Level 2 or Level 3 PE/Coaching Award in order to apply.

## PART-TIME SPORTS COACH

We are looking to recruit a part-time Sports Coach for 16 hours a week to work in our local primary schools.

The Sports Coach will be expected to:

- deliver fun, engaging physical activities at lunchtime
- structured sports clubs after school
- run physical activity breakfast clubs
- support the KSSP team to deliver additional primary festivals
- be able to motivate and engage primary age pupils
- be able to effectively communicate with children and adults
- hold an NGB level 2 coaching qualification or a Level 3 PE / Coaching Apprenticeship
- have their own transport (ideally)

Coaches will be employed for 16 hours a week on a term-time only contract (including holiday & sick pay and some car mileage). To view more information about the job please click on the job description and job specification links.

**Figure 5.9** Sample job advert for a sports coach.

### Legislation

It is important in any job role that you understand the relevant **legislation** that relates to that role. Legislation is deemed to be the laws that have been passed, affecting how that role is carried out. Examples include:

- **Child protection laws**: affecting all job roles in which there is some form of interaction with children. In all four home nations, there is a responsibility to identify children who are at risk of harm. This includes taking action to protect those children and prevent further abuse from occurring.

- **Licensing in outdoor and adventurous activities**: for example, the Adventure Activities Licensing Authority (AALA) came into existence in April 1996. It ensures that outdoor activity providers follow suitable safety management practices. In effect this ensures that young children are not exposed to situations where death or disabling injury is possible.

- **Governing the minimum standard of facilities**: e.g. the Disability Discrimination Act 1995 (DDA) lays out the measures that must be taken in the design of stadia to make reasonable adjustments to physical barriers and services for disabled spectators.

**Key term**

**Legislation** Laws that have been passed that affect how a role is carried out

## Role-related experience

**Role-related experience** refers to having previous experience within the same or similar role being applied for. Examples include:

- sales experience when applying for a job as a retail sales assistant
- managerial experience when applying for a job as a team manager or manager of a leisure centre.

## Health and safety

Health and safety are an important part of any job. The health and safety expectations within any job will be stipulated in the job description. Examples include:

- basic first aid requirements to be a PE teacher
- ability to write and carry out risk assessments when working in a sports centre
- ability to follow safety protocols when working as a steward in a stadium.

### Key term

**Role-related experience**
Having previous experience within the same or similar role being applied for

### Classroom discussion

Does anyone hope to gain a job in a sports-related field? If so, what skills and knowledge do you feel you need to develop further? Do you know how you could develop such skills?

### Group activity

Think about the skills and knowledge you have developed on this course. Try to link these to any of the job roles within this unit. Share your findings in small groups.

### Stretch activity

For each of the four careers listed below, research online to find out how and where you could gain the knowledge and skills required to become qualified in each role:

- Physiotherapist
- Sports journalist
- Fitness instructor
- Leisure centre manager.

## Links to other units

You can find further information on the synoptic links to this unit in **Units R052**, **53**, **54** and **56**.

## Know it!

1 Why do performers and coaches need to know sports-specific skills?
2 Give examples of the types of knowledge required to be a physiotherapist.
3 Give an example of a coaching qualification that can be gained.
4 Give an example of a job that requires 'people skills'.

## Assessment preparation

Think about the task that your teacher will set you in order to assess your knowledge and understanding of the skills and knowledge required to work in the sports industry.

Make sure you are clear about:

● Specific skills that can be beneficial when aiming to work in the sports industry.
● Specific knowledge that can be beneficial when aiming to work in the sports industry.

How will you demonstrate that you know these areas well and can support your work with a wide range of examples, related to specific, relevant job roles?

### Mark scheme

| LO2 Know the skills and knowledge required to work within the sports industry | | |
| --- | --- | --- |
| Mark band 1 | Mark band 2 | Mark band 3 |
| **Outlines** the skill and knowledge requirements for a **limited range** of careers and professions within the sports industry and **broadly** matches the requirements with **some** job roles. | **Describes** the skill and knowledge requirements for a **range** of careers and professions within the sports industry and matches the requirements with **mostly relevant** job roles. | **Describes in detail** the skill and knowledge requirements for a **wide range** of careers and professions within the sports industry and **clearly** matches the requirements with **specific, relevant** job roles. |

## LO3 Be able to apply for jobs within the sports industry

### Sources of information regarding job vacancies in the sports industry

Information about jobs within the sports industry can be gained from a variety of sources. These include:

- **Careers advisers**: provide advice about careers and how to get a job. There are often careers advisers in schools, universities and sometimes through local government.

- The **Connexions service** was a government-funded organisation that provided information to young people about careers. However, it has largely been disbanded due to government cuts, though some local authorities still provide a Connexions service. One main aim of the service is to help young people who have left school already but are not yet in education, training or a career.

- Libraries are great sources of information and often have online facilities and newspapers which contain job adverts.

- The internet is a source of many job sites advertising roles and vacancies.

- The Job Centre is a specialised place the public can attend to gain careers advice and to register their interest in types of employment.

- Local newspapers generally have a section within them detailing all available jobs in that area.

- Noticeboards at sports centres may contain information about jobs within the leisure centre or partnership.

- People employed in the workplace can inform others about available jobs through word of mouth.

- Specialist agencies exist to help those looking to work within the sports industry, e.g. Careers in Sport offers a specialist website for those interested in working within the sports industry.

- 'Prospects' offers a specialist website that aims to help students make the right choice in their chosen career. They aim to match skills and personalities to suitable jobs.

- National governing body (NGB) websites include information about careers and job vacancies. They advertise roles working at the NGB itself but also opportunities to work in the sport that they focus on.

- Many sports organisations provide information about job vacancies in the sports industry. These include:
  - UK sport: **www.uksport.gov.uk/**
  - Youth Sport Trust: **www.youthsporttrust.org/**

### Getting started

Write down a list of people that you think you could talk to, in order to gain advice about jobs in sport.

**Figure 5.10** Careers adviser providing advice about jobs and careers.

### 🔑 Key terms

**Careers adviser** A person who provides advice about careers and how to get a job

**Connexions service** Was a government-funded organisation that provided information to young people about careers

**Figure 5.11** Job Centres are a good place to go to see what job vacancies exist.

## Key aspects to consider in researching a specific job role within the sports industry

There are key aspects to be aware of when looking for a job in the sports industry. These aspects should be considered carefully and planned for so that you give yourself the best possible chance of being successful. These aspects include the following:

- The job description/specification, which outlines what the job entails.
- The company or organisation that the job role is with. For example, does the company have a good reputation of looking after its employees? Is the company financially sound and unlikely to go out of business? Does the company offer a particular pension scheme or any benefits for employees, e.g. private healthcare?
- Skills and knowledge required. It is common for job descriptions to have a separate section which outlines the skills and knowledge required. For example, they may stipulate a certain level of education or coaching award.
- What progression may be available in terms of a development route? In other words, if you were successful in your application, would there be any potential for promotion and new opportunities within the company, e.g. progressing from being a gym supervisor to gym manager?
- Considering your own suitability for the role. This could involve identifying your own strengths and weaknesses. Do you and your experience and qualifications match the expectations of the job role?

## How to create a curriculum vitae

A **curriculum vitae (CV)** is a written overview of a person's details, education, experience and qualifications. This is usually typed and printed out in a neat and organised manner. Particular features of an appropriate CV include:

- No spelling, grammar or punctuation mistakes: i.e. proof-read it before you send it out!
- An appropriate length. A CV is usually no more than three pages long. It has to be clear and concise, i.e. to the point.
- Details of all appropriate qualifications, awards and experience.
- Relevant information and experience that is tailored to the job role.

 **Key term**

**Curriculum vitae (CV)**
Written overview of a person's details, education, experience and qualifications

# CURRICULUM VITAE

**PERSONAL DETAILS**

**SUMMARY OF THE PERSON**

**EDUCATION AND QUALIFICATIONS**

**RELEVANT EXPERIENCE**

**RELEVANT TRAINING ATTENDED**

**INTERESTS**

**DETAILS OF REFEREES**

**Figure 5.12** Example layout of a CV.

Generally speaking a CV is accompanied by a **covering letter**. This is a letter sent with, and explaining the contents of, your application.

An example covering letter is shown below:

> 10 Downing Place
>
> London XB1 CR2
>
> **Position applied for: Part-time leisure centre assistant**
>
> Dear Sir/Madam
>
> I wish to apply for the advertised position of part-time leisure centre assistant at New Kenton Leisure Centre. I have been studying sport studies at school, completing the OCR Cambridge National in Sport. As part of this course I have gained an understanding of the skills that I feel will help me in this role, including leadership and sports organisation.
>
> As a coach at my local badminton club, I have gained an appreciation of the importance of facilities being organised and equipment being readily available.
>
> As captain of two different sports teams, I possess leadership skills and would be happy to make use of these as a leisure centre assistant.
>
> I enclose a copy of my CV for your perusal.
>
> Yours faithfully
>
> Frank Sauzee

## How to prepare for an interview

Preparation is key prior to an interview so that you can think through what you may be asked or required to do. Further details to consider include the following:

- Prepare answers for common questions, e.g. Why do you want to work here? What strengths and weaknesses do you have? Why should we employ you ahead of the other candidates?
- Consider research undertaken about the job role, e.g. what you have discovered about the role and the organisation. Do you need to remember anything, e.g. protocols that staff follow, or do you need to take particular evidence with you, e.g. certificates or awards?
- Prepare for assessment tasks that you know you will be asked to carry out, e.g. presentations to be given, role-play activities or team tasks.
- Prepare some questions as you will certainly be asked if you have any questions. It is always good to have one or two to take with you, e.g. Are there clear career progression routes within the company? Do you provide training for your staff?

## Key considerations when producing a personal career plan

Many people write or at least consider the details behind a **personal career plan**, in other words, what pathway or route they hope their career may follow. In doing so, it is advisable to consider:

- **SMART** targets. SMART stands for specific, measurable, attainable, realistic and timely.
  - ○ **Specific** means that the goal should be specific to the person and their aspirations.
  - ○ **Measureable** means that you should be able to measure if the goal was met.
  - ○ **Attainable** means that it is attainable within the ability level of the person.
  - ○ **Realistic** means that it is realistic to achieve within the realms and demands of the person's life.
  - ○ **Timely** means that it should be set over a designated period of time so that the person knows how long it should take to achieve.

Example of a SMART target:

> 'I aim to become a leisure centre manager by the age of 25.'
>
> - Specific to the person
> - Measurable in that they either become this or don't
> - Attainable as long as they have the ability
> - Realistic that they can complete the study required and bridge the skill gaps
> - Timely in that the target is set by age 25

- Achievements should be considered when producing a personal career plan. In other words, what has been achieved so far and what could be achieved to gain the qualifications for the next level in their career path.
- **Skills gaps** should be acknowledged and then addressed. Skills gaps are areas in which the person is lacking in order to progress through their career path. For example, the person may need specific qualifications or need to gain experience in certain aspects of their role.
- In order to address skills gaps, the person must work out their training needs, e.g. courses to attend, qualifications to attain, experience to gain, etc.

### Key terms

**Personal career plan** What pathway or route a person hopes their career may follow

**Skills gaps** Areas in which a person is lacking in order to progress through their career path

**Figure 5.13** Goals set within a personal career plan should be SMART.

### Classroom discussion

What skills gaps do you feel you have? Are there any obvious areas that you need to develop to fulfil your personal career path?

### Stretch activity

Start to write your CV on a computer and aim to lay out all the information in a clear, concise and organised fashion.

### Group activity

Search online for providers of training in aspects that you may need to develop, e.g. look on a national governing body's website to see if they have any courses that relate to that sport.

## Know it!

1 State two ways that you can gain advice on careers.
2 State three ways that you can find out what jobs are available.
3 State three things that a CV must include.
4 What is meant by the term 'covering letter'?
5 What is meant by a 'personal career plan'?

## Links to other units

You can find further information on the synoptic links to this unit in **Units R052, 53, 54** and **56**.

## Assessment preparation

Think about the task that your teacher will set you in order to assess your ability to apply for jobs within the sports industry.

Make sure you are clear about:

- How you can find out about job roles available.
- How to lay out a CV.
- How you will research into a specific job role within the sports industry considering **all** of the key aspects.

How will you compile and present a personal career plan, making appropriate use of SMART targets and relevant references to achievement, skills gaps and training requirements?

| LO3 Be able to apply for jobs within the sports industry | | |
|---|---|---|
| Mark band 1 | Mark band 2 | Mark band 3 |
| Identifies a **limited range** of sources of information regarding job vacancies with **some relevance** to the sports industry. | Identifies a **range** of sources of information regarding job vacancies, **many of which are relevant** to the sports industry. | Identifies a **wide range** of sources of information regarding job vacancies that are **specific** to the sports industry. |
| Research into a specific job role within the sports industry is **basic** and considers **few** of the key aspects. | Research into a specific job role within the sports industry is **detailed** and considers **most** of the key aspects. | Research into a specific job role within the sports industry is **extensive** and considers **all** of the key aspects. |
| Mark band 1 | Mark band 2 | Mark band 3 |
| Creates a **simple** CV that contains **some appropriate** personal information and has **limited relevance** to the job role being applied for. | Creates a **detailed** CV that contains **appropriate** personal information and is **mostly relevant** to the job role being applied for. | Creates a **thorough** and **concise** CV that contains **considered** personal information and is **completely relevant** to the job role being applied for. |
| Preparation for an interview is **brief**, with **limited** consideration of research undertaken and potential questions and tasks. | Preparation for an interview is **thorough**, with **appropriate** consideration of research undertaken and potential questions and tasks. **Some** questions to ask at the interview are identified. | Preparation for an interview is **extensive**, with **detailed** consideration of research undertaken and potential questions and tasks. **Appropriate** questions to ask at the interview are planned. |
| Mark band 1 | Mark band 2 | Mark band 3 |
| Personal career plan is **superficial**, with **limited** use of SMART targets and **few** references to achievement, skills gaps and training requirements. | Personal career plan is **detailed**, with **appropriate** use of SMART targets and references to achievement, skills gaps and training requirements. | Personal career plan is **comprehensive**, with **appropriate** use of SMART targets and **frequent** and **relevant** references to achievement, skills gaps and training requirements. |

# L04 Understand the impacts which the sports industry has in the UK

## Economic impacts of the sports industry

**Economic impact** refers to the additional expenditure, within a defined area, which has happened due to a specific event. For example, how much more have people received or had to spend due to a sports event? The economic impact can be as a result of many different factors, such as those listed below.

### Tourism

Increased tourism (the number of visitors who live in other areas/countries) results in an increase of income as tourists spend money in hotels, shops and restaurants. This includes things such as:

- package holidays to major sporting events, e.g. to the Olympic Games
- cities with 'world famous' football teams which attract tourists, e.g. tourists vising Barcelona to watch FC Barcelona.

**Figure 5.14** Any sports event can impact on tourism, particularly when the competitors are from different countries, e.g. Grand Prix Formula 1 racing, Wimbledon tennis, international athletics meets and European football competitions at grounds such as Anfield in Liverpool.

### Employment

Sporting events can make an impact on employment figures within a specific area.

- Growing areas increase employment. The advent of the sports village at Manchester City has increased the employment rate within the area. Tottenham Hotspur's new stadium (due to be finished in 2019) will provide new and exciting facilities not just for the club but also for the local residents. Employment opportunities will increase through jobs such as stewards, bar staff, staff for external events and staff to work in the Extreme Sports Hub, the Tottenham Experience, the Sky Walk and the enhanced plaza. Tottenham Hotspur advocates that 'local residents will find a multitude of new activities to be enjoyed on their doorstep 365 days a year'.

**Getting started**

Start a simple list of positives and negatives for a British city bidding to host a major sporting event.

**Key term**

**Economic impact** The additional expenditure within a defined area that has happened due to a specific event

**Classroom discussion**

What sports and what teams within the UK do you feel attract the most tourists and why?

- There is an increase in internet shopping, causing high street retailers to go out of business. However, employment opportunities exist in larger numbers as part of the internet shopping business to take orders and process deliveries from large warehouses.

## Consumer expenditure

**Consumer expenditure** refers to the goods or services that the public buy. The sports industry involves selling a lot of products and merchandise to the public.

- Sports clothing is extremely popular and specialist shops exist to provide sports clothing to the public. Many members of the public follow specific sports or teams and regularly buy branded merchandise from their favourite club.
- **Satellite channel subscription** is the term used to describe the payment made to companies who provide sports channels at a cost. **Terrestrial TV** (free to watch) does not have the rights to show all sport on TV, so many members of the public choose to pay a subscription to watch certain sports or events, e.g. on Sky TV.
- Money is made through attendance at live events, with members of the public paying to watch the event in person. The attendees often pay for transport or parking, their entrance ticket, food and drink and possibly even a programme at the event.

> ### 🔑 Key terms
>
> **Consumer expenditure** Goods or services that the public buy
>
> **Satellite channel subscription** Term used to describe the payment made to companies who provide sports channels at a cost
>
> **Terrestrial TV** Free to watch TV

**Figure 5.16** Fans who attend events pay money for the entrance tickets.

## Foreign investment

Many sports bring in foreign investment into the UK economy as a result of foreign ownership. In September 2018, only seven of the twenty Premier League football clubs had some ownership based within the UK. Even the second tier (the Championship) is predominantly overseas owned. High profile billionaires like Roman Abramovich, who bought Chelsea in 2003, have put millions of pounds into UK clubs. There is also huge investment from overseas-based TV channels to access the rights to sport within the UK.

**Figure 5.17** Roman Abramovich, who bought Chelsea FC in 2003.

## Productivity

**Productivity** refers to how productive a person is, i.e. how well they carry out everyday tasks. Sports success, either as a participant or spectator, can increase productivity in the workplace, as the employee feels fitter and happier.

Employees occasionally may need to take time off sick due to sports-related injuries, having suffered an injury whilst playing.

Sport can also teach employees about the value of working as a team, having witnessed good or bad teamwork on the sports field.

## Social impacts of the sports industry

There are many social impacts of the sports industry, affecting how people interact and live together. Such social impacts include some of the following issues.

### Crime/anti-social behaviour

The sports industry can have an impact on the level of crime and **anti-social behaviour** recorded in the UK. Anti-social behaviour refers to behaviour that is not deemed as desirable by society.

- Participation in sport helps decrease anti-social behaviour in youths as they are being productive and using their time usefully. It can also foster a sense of community, which may make anti-social behaviour less likely.
- Gambling on sport can be addictive and can lead people into debt. It is then possible that the person will commit crime in order to pay off their debt.
- Investment in security by sports clubs can lead to a reduction in violence and hooliganism as potential hooligans will know they will be seen and potentially caught.

### Public services

One social impact of the sports industry can be the effect on public services. The police and ambulance services can be stretched on match days. This is particularly the case when local derbies are played and when violence may be expected or inevitable. The Metropolitan Police in London spend approximately £7 million per year policing football matches.

### Education

The sports industry can have a positive or negative effect on the level of education a person receives. Many professional sports clubs provide a high level of education for those involved at the club, providing access to teaching staff and qualifications. Research carried out in the USA showed that learners involved in sport perform better in the classroom, with exercise boosting their cognitive skills, attitudes and academic behaviour. It can, however, be argued that those involved in sport or aspiring to become professional athletes may neglect their studies.

> ### Key terms
>
> **Productivity** How productive a person is, i.e. how well they carry out everyday tasks
>
> **Anti-social behaviour** Behaviour that is not deemed as desirable by society

**Figure 5.18** Gambling in sport can become addictive and lead people into debt.

**Figure 5.19** Policing at sports events can come at a huge cost to society.

## Culture

The culture and environment that a person is exposed to affects and influences their desire or ability to take part in sporting activity. Sports provision is more readily available in cities and towns rather than rural areas, with larger facilities such as indoor snow-zones, climbing centres and athletics tracks more likely to be available.

Different sports events or clubs target their advertising to different demographic groups, which can encourage social division.

## Identity

The identity of a group or occupants of an area or city can be affected by the sporting attachment that they have. For example, a town with a mountain biking centre may be 'attached by association' to being known as 'the place where you go mountain biking'. Equally, the host city or venue for a major sporting event may be reflected on badly if the event is poorly managed or organised. The converse to this can also apply, i.e. people of a city are reflected well due to a well run event. This is perhaps what happened to London as a result of a successful 2012 Olympic Games. A well run and well equipped leisure centre or sporting venue can promote an area for visitors.

**Figure 5.20** The London area of Wembley is strongly attached in identity to the stadium.

## Environment

The environment is a major concern to all areas of the planet. Therefore, the increased popularity and promotion of sport may encourage local councils to maintain green space for sports facilities. It is arguable that it is more environmentally friendly to maintain grass sports facilities than to invest in a building that consumes energy. However, as the number and size of sports buildings increases, their energy consumption and carbon footprint also increase, thus harming the environment. Popular sports attract large audiences and match days can cause traffic congestion and pollution.

## Health impacts of the sports industry

There are many health benefits and impacts that occur as a direct result of the sports industry.

**Classroom discussion**

As a group, who do you feel that local clubs or facilities target with their advertising?

**Figure 5.21** Green spaces can be protected for sports use.

### Increased awareness

Millions watch sport and the health benefits of exercising can be advertised in tandem with the coverage. Campaigns by sports clubs or retailers can highlight the benefits of sport on health and fitness in order to sell their products. For example, sportswear companies may promote products through their benefits, e.g. the use of trainers to get you fit and healthy.

Some athletes are used in **endorsements**, whereby their name is attached to products to promote them. Although these change all the time, in 2018 examples included Jessica Ennis for Santander Bank, Roger Federer for Gillette and Mo Farah for Quorn.

The NHS uses sports events to raise awareness about healthcare. An example of this is NHS walking clubs.

### Research

It is common for sports science to be the first to discover or influence a technique or scientific discovery that is then adopted within the health service (NHS). For example, the world of sports science has led the way in research on obesity. Also, advances in prosthetic limbs in sport are now adapted within aspects of NHS care. Some physical rehabilitation techniques now available on the NHS were first discovered by sports scientists looking to aid athletes' recovery. One example is **hyperbaric oxygen therapy** (HBOT) chambers that were used by divers before being available for certain conditions via the NHS. These chambers supply the body with 100 per cent oxygen and are believed to speed recovery.

### Increased participation

The availability of sporting facilities can obviously impact on the participation rate within society. The availability of gyms, sports clubs and youth centres can enhance participation rates as people have more opportunity to participate. Many facilities are free and readily available, e.g. in local parks. Leisure centre activities are often subsidised and very affordable. It can also be relatively good value to purchase sports clothing or specialist clothing and equipment. As purchases are easy to make in store or online, participation in sport can be positively influenced.

**Group activity**

Find out how your local doctors' surgery, walk-in centre or hospital tries to promote the value of exercise.

**Key terms**

**Endorsements** Where a celebrity and their name is attached to products to promote them

**Hyperbaric oxygen therapy** Treatment in a chamber, where the body receives 100 per cent oxygen to speed recovery

**Figure 5.22** The more sports facilities available, the more potential there is for participation.

**Classroom discussion**

Do you feel that sport holds more positive values for society than negatives?

**Group activity**

Look on TV for adverts that make use of sporting celebrities to endorse their products.

**Stretch activity**

Research online to discover if crime rates rise or fall during major sporting events.

## Know it!

1 State three economic impacts of the sports industry.
2 Describe how sport can have a positive social impact.
3 Give an example of how the sports industry can be used to promote positive health impacts.
4 Give one example of how a group of people can hold an identity that is inspired from a sporting context.

## Links to other units

You can find further information on the synoptic links to this unit in **Units R052, 53, 54** and **56**.

## Read about it

Have a look at www.bbc.co.uk/sport to see the degree of sports coverage available.

Job search sites: www.indeed.co.uk; www.jobisjob.co.uk; www.topendsports.com/resources/jobs-in-sport.htm

Visit the Careers in Sport website: https://careers-in-sport.co.uk

Visit Prospects: https://www.prospects.ac.uk

Read about hyperbaric oxygen therapy chambers: www.medicalnewstoday.com/articles/313155.php

## Assessment preparation

Think about the task that your teacher will set you in order to assess your ability to show you understand the impacts which the sports industry has in the UK.

Make sure you are clear about:

- Economic impacts of the sports industry.
- Social impacts of the sports industry.
- Health impacts of the sports industry.

How will you show a wide range of examples from the specification, drawing upon knowledge from other units?

### Mark scheme

| LO4 Understand the impacts which the sports industry has on the UK | | |
|---|---|---|
| Mark band 1 | Mark band 2 | Mark band 3 |
| **Outlines** a **limited range** of economic, social and health impacts the sports industry has on the UK supported by **basic** examples. | **Describes** a **range** of economic, social and health impacts the sports industry has on the UK supported by **relevant** examples. | **Explains in detail** a **wide range** of economic, social and health impacts the sports industry has on the UK supported by **clear** and **insightful** examples. |
| Draws upon **limited** skills/knowledge/understanding from other units in the specification. | Draws upon **some relevant** skills/knowledge/understanding from other units in the specification. | **Clearly** draws upon **relevant** skills/knowledge/understanding from other units in the specification. |

# R056 Developing knowledge and skills in outdoor activities

## About this unit

Outdoor activities are group or individual activities that take place in a natural, outdoor environment, giving people the opportunity to participate in and test themselves against the natural environment. They include a vast range of activities, from rock climbing to mountain biking, windsurfing to skiing. These activities usually involve meticulous planning and preparation and enable participants to develop skills that are useful and transferable in everyday life. For this reason, many organisations use outdoor and adventurous activities as the basis for team away-days and team-building exercises, requiring individuals to work collaboratively and develop their problem-solving and communication skills as a group.

By completing this unit, learners will know about the range of outdoor activities that are available in the UK and be able to identify organisations that provide access to these activities. They will also be able to appreciate the reasons why people become involved in these activities and the risks they face when participating. Learners will consider how to plan an outdoor activity and be able to participate in one. They will gain an understanding of health and safety and risk assessments in outdoor scenarios, of detailed planning for a group activity with multiple variables, and they will develop their communication, decision-making and leadership skills in challenging scenarios and environments.

## Learning outcomes

**LO1** Know about different types of outdoor activities and their provision

**LO2** Understand the value of participating in outdoor activities

**LO3** Be able to plan an outdoor activity

**LO4** Be able to demonstrate knowledge and skills during outdoor activities

## How will I be assessed?

This optional unit is internally assessed through a written assignment set and marked by your centre. It is worth 50 per cent of the overall mark for the OCR Level 1/2 Cambridge National Award in Sport Studies or 25 per cent of the overall mark for the OCR Level 1/2 Cambridge National Certificate in Sport Studies. It is estimated that the assignment will take about 10 hours to complete and is worth 60 marks.

OCR provides a model assignment for this unit: http://ocr.org.uk/qualifications/cambridge-nationals/cambridge-nationals-sport-studies-level-1-2-j803-j813/assessment/

### For LO1

Learners need to know:

● the definition of an outdoor activity

● examples of outdoor activities

● provision of outdoor activities in the UK.

### For LO2

Learners need to understand:

● the general benefits of participating in outdoor activities

● how participating in outdoor activities can help skills development.

### For LO3

Learners need to understand:

● the key considerations to make when planning an outdoor activity

● hazards to be aware of when planning outdoor activities.

### For LO4

Learners need to understand:

● care and use of equipment

● safe practice

● communication skills

● decision-making skills

● team-working skills

● problem-solving skills.

## LO1 Know about different types of outdoor activities and their provision

### Definition of an outdoor activity

The idea of outdoor activities is limited to those activities that are reliant on a natural resource such as a lake or a mountain. An **outdoor activity is defined** as a leisure, recreation or sport activity undertaken in a natural, rural space that can be done as an individual or part of a group. There are many activities that take place outdoors, such as football and cricket, that are not classed as

### Getting started

The introduction to this unit listed four outdoor activities: rock climbing, mountain biking, windsurfing and skiing. Make a list of ten other activities that take place in the outdoor natural environment.

outdoor activities because you can play these games on any suitable surface anywhere, even in cities.

## Examples of outdoor activities

There are numerous **examples of outdoor activities**. Some take place on water – they are water-based. Others are land-based, and some are even air-based.

### Water sports

There are many **water sports** that are outdoor activities, ranging from those involving a single person such as scuba diving and windsurfing to those involving teams, such as sailing.

Most present-day **canoeing** is done as a sport or recreational activity and involves paddling a canoe with a single-bladed paddle.

**Kayaking** is different in that the kayaker sits in a kayak, while a canoeist kneels. Also, a kayaker uses a double-bladed paddle while a canoeist's paddle has a single blade.

Canoeing and kayaking are popular activities and are available to a wide range of people as individuals or in pairs. The activity may be done in the sea, on rivers and canals, and on lakes. Different styles of kayaks and canoes are made to suit different situations.

**Sailing** uses the wind acting on sails to move a boat on the surface of the water over a chosen course. You can also sail on ice in an iceboat, or on land in a land yacht. The craft can vary in size, from dinghies for individual sailors to yachts over 20 metres in length carrying several crew. Sailing usually takes place on lakes, coastal waters and in the oceans.

**Figure 6.1** Canoeing.

**Figure 6.2** Kayaking.

**Figure 6.3** A sailing dinghy.

**Figure 6.4** A yacht.

**Windsurfing** is a water-based activity that uses a board with a sail attached and, similarly to sailing, relies on the wind for propulsion. Windsurfing is usually learned on flat lakes but can be done at sea in waves. Variations on windsurfing include kitesurfing, wakeboarding and kiteboarding.

### Trekking

**Trekking** is a long journey undertaken on foot in areas where there are usually no other forms of transport. It is walking, sometimes for a number of days, on paths that are sometimes uncharted, in challenging environments that are often hilly or mountainous.

## Key terms

**Canoeing** Paddling a water craft with a single paddle

**Kayaking** Paddling a water craft with a double paddle

**Sailing** Floating water craft propelled by wind

**Windsurfing** Floating flat board propelled by wind

**Trekking** Walking in the natural environment

Walking is one of the most popular outdoor activities in the UK. The word 'hiking' is sometimes used, but it essentially means the same thing. Walking as an outdoor activity takes place in the natural environment on paths and trails.

Walks or hikes undertaken in upland country, moorland and mountains, especially where it includes climbing to the top of a hill, are called **hill walking**.

**Figure 6.5** Windsurfing.

**Figure 6.6** Hill walking is a popular outdoor activity in the UK.

**Orienteering** is an activity that requires the skills of using a map and compass to navigate from point to point in unfamiliar terrain, whilst moving at speed. Participants are given a specially prepared orienteering map, which they use to find control points as quickly as possible. This involves deciding the best route between control points and the best pace to use on different terrain.

Orienteering can be done in forests, on sand dunes, or on open land. Often hill walking requires some elements of orienteering to get to the desired locations.

**Figure 6.7** Orienteering involves using a map and a compass to navigate from point to point.

> ### Key terms
>
> **Hill walking** Walking in a hilly natural environment
>
> **Orienteering** Using a map and compass to follow a route

> ### Classroom discussion
>
> Which outdoor activities have members of the teaching group been involved with? What was good/bad about that activity?

**Mountaineering** is climbing and trekking in the mountains. Hiking in the mountains can also be a simple form of mountaineering if it includes some scrambling over rocks or some simple rock climbing.

## Camping

**Camping** is an outdoor activity involving overnight stays away from home in a shelter, such as a tent. Usually, those involved leave developed areas to spend time outdoors in more natural areas in pursuit of enjoyment.

**Figure 6.9** Camping site.

**Wild camping** is the idea of camping without the provision of facilities such as running water, toilets and shower blocks. Wild camping means that, as well as your tent and sleeping bag, you'll be carrying all your food, fuel, water and other supplies with you.

## Climbing

**Climbing** is the ascent of a steep incline using the hands, feet, or any other part of the body. It is usually done with the aid of specialist equipment such as ropes and harnesses to protect the climber from falling. Climbing often includes the use of specialist climbing shoes that have a smooth, sticky rubber sole to obtain the grip needed.

**Figure 6.11** Rock climbing.

**Figure 6.8** Mountaineering involves climbing or trekking in the mountains.

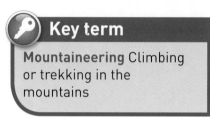

**Key term**

**Mountaineering** Climbing or trekking in the mountains

**Figure 6.10** Wild camping.

**Figure 6.12** Belaying for a climbing partner.

Climbing normally involves two people working together to support one another. The pair use a variety of techniques to exert tension on a climbing rope, a process called belaying, so that a falling climber does not fall very far. A **belay** is the term used to describe the position where the support climber is located. A **pitch** in rock climbing is a section of a route that is climbed between two belay points, using a rope for protection from falling. The number and difficulty of the pitches on a climbing route indicate the climb's difficulty rating.

Climbing activities include:

- Bouldering, which is climbing over boulders or small outcrops of rock. Rather than ropes for safety, a crash mat is used to prevent injury.
- Free climbing is a form of rock climbing where the climber uses equipment such as ropes and other climbing equipment, but only to prevent injury should they fall.
- Ice climbing involves ascending ice formations using specialised equipment such as ice axes and crampons.
- Indoor climbing uses artificial walls with holds bolted into the surface.
- Rock climbing is ascending rock formations using equipment such as bolts and pitons to safeguard against falls, but also as artificial aids.
- Traditional climbing does not use fixed anchors and bolts; rather the climber places such protection in position as they climb.
- Solo climbing or soloing is where the climber climbs alone, without the protection of a rope.

**Abseiling** is the name given to a controlled descent off a vertical drop, such as a rock face, using a rope. The technique is used by climbers to descend when it is too dangerous to do otherwise. It involves using a variety of techniques to increase the friction on the rope, so the speed of descent can be easily controlled.

## Caving

**Caving**, often called **potholing**, is the exploration of caving systems. Caves come in different shapes and sizes, but they all lack light, so caving relies on torches and lamps. Caving may involve pitches in much the same way as climbing but may also involve crawling and squeezing through narrow gaps. Some caves are dry, but many are flooded and these may involve another activity called cave diving.

> ### Key terms
>
> **Belay** To secure a climbing rope
>
> **Pitch** Section of a climbing route
>
> **Abseiling** Using a climbing rope to descend
>
> **Caving** Exploration of caving systems, also called **potholing**

**Figure 6.13** Abseiling is the controlled descent off a vertical drop using a rope.

**Figure 6.14** Caving, also known as potholing.

**Mine exploration** is an outdoor activity where people visit abandoned mines and quarries. It usually involves more walking and less crawling than caving.

## Cycling

**Cycling** involves the use of bicycles for recreation. Cycling in towns or to and from school does not really fit into the category of an outdoor activity because it is not usually sufficiently in the natural environment. The two main outdoor activities involving bicycles are mountain biking and trail biking.

**Mountain biking** is the outdoor activity of riding bicycles off-road, often over rough terrain using specially designed mountain bikes. The bikes are reinforced to cope with the continuous punishment on the rough terrain. They have thicker tyres than road bikes for extra grip and use suspension to soften impacts. They also have many gears to allow for both uphill and downhill tracks. The activity requires endurance and balance, together with good bike-handling skills. Mountain bikers usually ride on country roads, bridleways and dedicated cycle ways.

 **Key terms**

**Mine exploration** Walking through mines and quarries

**Mountain biking** Off-road cycling on specialised bikes

**Figure 6.15** Mountain biking in the Swiss Alps.

**Trail biking** is using a mountain bike on short, steep, highly technical and specially constructed trails. Trail bike routes are generally designated as such and waymarked. They may form single routes or be part of a complex known as route centres. Trail biking is often a long-duration activity but there are relatively few trails in the UK.

**Key term**

Trail biking Mountain biking on specialised trails

## Snow sports

A snow sport is an outdoor activity which takes place on snow or ice. Most **snow sports** are variations of skiing, ice skating and sledging. Traditionally, these activities could only be undertaken in cold areas of the UK during winter, but the development of artificial ice and snow allows more flexibility.

Snowboarding is an outdoor activity that involves descending on a snow-covered slope while standing on a snowboard that is attached to the rider's feet. Snowboarding is a fairly recent innovation – the first board being built in the 1960s.

**Figure 6.16** Snowboarding.

Since its inception as an outdoor activity, snowboarding has developed various styles, each with its own specialised equipment and technique. The most common styles in use are:

- freeride – a style of snowboarding performed on natural terrain
- freestyle – involves the use of tricks
- freecarve – snowboard racing.

**Skiing** is a recreational outdoor activity in which the participant uses skis to glide about on snow. The two main types of skiing are Alpine skiing and Nordic skiing.

Alpine skiing is also called **downhill skiing**. Alpine skiing often takes place on a marked ski run or piste at a ski resort. In the UK there are many snow-covered indoor ski facilities. In Alpine skiing, both the heels and toes of the skier are fixed to the skis.

**Figure 6.17** Downhill skiing.

Nordic or **cross-country skiers** rely on themselves to get across the snow, rather than ski lifts and slopes. Cross-country skis use bindings at the toes but not the heels. It may be practised on designated trails on undeveloped back country areas.

**Snowshoeing** is a form of hiking (see page 177) on snow where the participant wears specialised snowshoes. These distribute the person's weight over a large area, so they do not sink into the snow too deeply. Walking in snow without snowshoes is very tiring as your feet sink down, often up to your knees. Snowshoeing is claimed to be the fastest growing winter sport in the world.

**Figure 6.18** Nordic or cross-country skiing.

## Gliding

**Gliding** is an air-based activity where pilots fly unpowered aircraft using natural currents of rising air to remain airborne. The gliders are launched by powered aircraft or winches from airfields.

**Hang gliding** is an outdoor activity in which a pilot flies a lighter-than-air craft called a hang glider. The pilot is attached to the lightweight airframe by a harness. The airframe contains a synthetic sailcloth. The pilot controls the aircraft by shifting their body weight in the harness. The hang glider is usually launched by running into an updraft on a hill. Powered harnesses are now available. The idea is to stay airborne for as long as possible, which can involve long journeys over many miles.

**Figure 6.19** Snowshoeing.

**Figure 6.20** Hang gliding.

**Figure 6.21** Paragliding.

**Paragliding** involves flying under a canopy adapted from a parachute. The lightweight canopy is highly efficient at catching and holding air currents, which help it maintain lift. Most paragliders use hills and mountains as launch sites in a similar way to hang gliders, although it is possible to tow-launch from a winch or a boat.

## Other land-based activities

**Canyoning** is the idea of travelling through canyons or gorges using a variety of other outdoor activities such as walking, scrambling, abseiling and swimming. Canyoning is usually done in remote areas and frequently needs map-reading and other outdoor activity skills.

Canyoning is often done where water goes through narrow gorges with numerous drops and waterfalls. Canyoning requires extensive equipment, including climbing gear, ropes, helmets, wetsuits, specially designed shoes and rucksacks.

**Gorge walking** is similar to canyoning, involving scrambling up or down a river or stream. It is the type of river that makes the difference between an easy stroll and an arduous adventure. Rivers with steep gorges produce various natural challenges, from abseiling down or climbing up waterfalls, jumping into plunge pools and many other activities.

**Sea-level traversing** is similar to gorge walking but involves climbing and scrambling along coastal rocks above the sea. Ropes are often used to make steep sections safe or are used as a method of crossing between gaps across the sea. **Coasteering** involves much the same idea, involving movement along the seashore of a rocky coastline on foot or by swimming, without the aid of boats, surf boards or other craft. Coasteering may include swimming, climbing, scrambling, jumping and diving.

**Figure 6.22** Gorge walking involves scrambling up or down a river or stream.

**Figure 6.23** Sea-level traversing.

A **high ropes course** is a challenging outdoor activity which usually consists of a professionally installed course, built of poles, cables and bolts from which various types of rope are suspended.

A high ropes course can also be hand-built in a wooded area, where ropes and wires are attached to different trees. Participants are attached to an upper wire or belay cable, with ropes for safety. The idea of the courses is to provide an adventure involving climbing, abseiling and high rope walking. Some high ropes courses are designed to explore group interaction, problem solving, leadership and teamwork.

**Figure 6.24** A high ropes course.

## Provision of outdoor activities in the UK

**Provision of outdoor activities in the UK** refers to how easy it is for people to participate and where each activity takes place. Provision is affected by several factors, including:

- Media – the amount of positive coverage affects provision.
- Location – outdoor activities are dependent on the environment. No water available means no water-based activities available. No mountains nearby means no mountainous activities available.
- Finance – many outdoor activities require expensive equipment, which may limit provision.

Local provision is concerned with centres and clubs providing opportunities for participation. This may need providers to work with local councils and schools to promote and provide opportunities for the activity.

National provision is usually through the national governing body for the activity, which has various roles and responsibilities. They employ staff to organise activities that are designed to increase current and future participation. The national governing body's responsibilities include:

- promotion of the activity
- organising events and competitions

- safety regulations
- developing training schemes
- providing grassroots opportunities.

## Outdoor activity providers

There are many organisations that provide opportunities for people to become involved in outdoor activities. These can be organised as intensive residential courses or shorter courses run in outdoor activity centres.

Typical **outdoor activity providers** offer several activity centres around the country that are available to schools, groups and families, offering qualified instructors, a range of facilities and accommodation for residential stays. Activity centres usually provide a range of outdoor activities, so visitors can sample several different activities during their visit.

Most national governing bodies' websites offer guidance on how to get involved in an activity.

## National Sports Centres

There are three **National Sports Centres** as part of Sport England's policy to create elite world-class sporting talent. One of these, Plas y Brenin in North Wales, is the National Mountain Centre for the UK.

Plas y Brenin provides instruction in all aspects of mountaineering, mountain biking and paddling, as well as in rescue. It also supports a range of organisations to develop new coaching and leadership awards and works with a large range of groups to get more people involved in outdoor activity as part of its national centre role.

A range of courses are offered at Plas y Brenin, from those active in university clubs to those working professionally in the outdoors. Courses are run all year round, not only in North Wales but in the north west of Scotland and in the Alps.

As well as the natural environment of Snowdonia that surrounds the centre, on-site facilities include:

- 13-metre climbing wall and a training wall
- indoor canoe training pool
- fitness room.

There are conference facilities and residential accommodation. Equipment is available to hire.

Holme Pierrepont in Nottinghamshire used to be a National Sports Centre, but it now exists as the National Water Sports Centre, located within Holme Pierrepont Country Park.

The centre has three distinct pieces of water:

- a regatta lake featuring a six-lane rowing course
- a purpose-built white-water canoe slalom course
- a water ski lagoon with ski jump and a ski cableway.

The River Trent is also nearby. The facilities provide a full range of award courses in:

- sailing
- canoeing
- kayaking
- powerboat handling
- raft guide training.

Holme Pierrepont Country Park also has an outdoor adventure park, which includes a high ropes course and other adventure activities, and two gyms. The park also offers team-building activities. The site has residential facilities, as well as conference and meeting facilities.

## Voluntary organisations

There are many **voluntary organisations** in the United Kingdom that have been established to provide services to people under the age of 18.

The Scouts is a voluntary organisation that encourages young to people enjoy fun and adventure while developing skills such as teamwork, leadership and resilience.

Different age group programmes exist within the Scouting movement:

| Section | Ages | Activities | 2017 Membership |
|---|---|---|---|
| Beaver Scouts | 5¾–8 | Emphasis on having fun | 128,224 |
| Cub Scouts | 8–10½ | Introduction to Scoutcraft and activities | 157,994 |
| Scouts | 10½–14 | Further development of Scouting skills | 127,176 |
| Explorer Scouts | 14–18 | Emphasis on personal challenge and adventure | 43,749 |
| Scout Network | 18–25 | More flexible with greater personal choice | 7,544 |

Scouts may take part in a vast range of outdoor activities, from abseiling to kayaking to zip wires.

The Guides, now officially known as Girlguiding, is the largest girl-only youth association in the UK.

Girlguiding activities include canoeing on rivers, leading their own camps, or simply having fun and trying new things with girls of the same age. Girlguiding operates different age group programmes:

| Section | Ages | Activities |
|---|---|---|
| Rainbows | 5–7 | A fun and exciting programme, all about learning by doing |
| Brownies | 7–10 | Go on camps, holidays, day trips and sleepovers. Meet friends regularly and learn new hobbies, get creative, explore other cultures and have outdoor adventures |
| Guides | 10–14 | What you do in Guides is up to you, from taking part in lots of exciting activities at regular meetings to special events and trips away |
| Senior section | 14–25 | Travel to countries or take on a leadership role within the organisation – the opportunities are endless |

The Duke of Edinburgh's Award (DofE) is a youth awards programme that takes between one and four years to complete and must be finished by the participant's twenty-fifth birthday.

The programmes are at three progressive levels which lead to a Bronze, Silver or Gold Duke of Edinburgh's Award. Participants select and set objectives in each of the following areas:

- Volunteering: undertaking service to individuals or the community.
- Physical: improving in an area of sport, dance or fitness activities.
- Skills: developing practical and social skills and personal interests.
- Expedition: planning, training for, and completion of an adventurous journey in the UK or abroad.
- At Gold level, participants must do an additional fifth residential section, which involves staying and working away from home for five days, doing a shared activity.

To achieve an award, the participant must work on each section for a minimum period of time. Each progressive level demands more time and commitment from the participant. Participants are required to show regular involvement in the activities and commitment to the award for the duration of their DofE programme, which is usually at least one hour per week.

## Examples of local and national providers of the different outdoor activities identified

There are dozens of different types of outdoor activities. Each of these activities are available through different outdoor activity providers. National providers were described on page 184. Local providers are just that, local; they will be close to where you live, and you need to find out about who they are, where they are and what they offer.

### Stretch activity

Choose one water-based, one land-based and one air-based outdoor activity. For each activity you choose, write a description of what that outdoor activity is and research how that activity is provided at a national and local level.

### Links to other units

You can find further information on this topic in **Units R051** and **R055**.

## Know it!

1 Define, using four examples, the term outdoor activity.
2 Identify four outdoor activity providers in the UK.

## Stretch activity

Make a list of six different outdoor activities. Research and identify a local and national provider for each activity.

## Assessment preparation

Think about the task/s that your teacher may set you to assess your knowledge of the different types of outdoor activities and their provision.

Make sure you know:

- The definition of an outdoor activity.
- Examples of outdoor activities:
  - water sports
  - trekking
  - camping
  - climbing
  - caving
  - cycling
  - snow sports
  - gliding
  - other land-based activities.
- Provision of outdoor activities in the UK:
  - outdoor activity providers
  - national sports centres
  - voluntary organisations
  - examples of local and national providers of the different outdoor activities identified.

### Mark scheme

| LO1 Know about different types of outdoor activities and their provision | | |
|---|---|---|
| **Mark band 1** | **Mark band 2** | **Mark band 3** |
| Definition of outdoor activities is **limited**. | Definition of outdoor activities is **accurate** with **some detail**. | Definition of outdoor activities is **accurate** and **detailed**. |
| **Some** different outdoor activities are **briefly** described with a few examples given. | A **range** of outdoor activities are described in **detail** with **mostly relevant** examples given for each. | A **wide range** of outdoor activities are described in **detail** with **clear** and **relevant** examples given for each. |
| **Outlines** the provision of outdoor activities in the UK using **few** examples. | **Describes** the provision of outdoor activities in the UK using a **range** of examples. | **Comprehensively** describes the provision of outdoor activities in the UK using a wide **range** of examples. |

## LO2 Understand the value of participating in outdoor activities

### General benefits of participating in outdoor activities

The **general benefits of participating in outdoor activities** may be summarised under four headings: physical; social; emotional; and intellectual.

The physical benefits include those associated with participation in general, such as an increase in general fitness and corresponding improvements in health.

Outdoor activities are invariably done in the company of others, so there are social benefits to be gained through opportunities to work and co-operate with others and become involved in teamwork. This togetherness will also involve becoming aware of the safety issues associated with a particular outdoor activity.

Outdoor activities involve emotional benefits with the person choosing what to become involved with, and they include making use of 'free time' to possibly escape from stress by reducing anxiety and having the opportunity to relax.

There is also the intellectual benefit of being in a different environment, which means that people have to learn to cope with a challenge and become more self-reliant, and even overcoming fear. Participants can also learn new skills while involved in outdoor activities.

### Increased confidence

By participating in outdoor activities, the individual will **increase in confidence** and gain a sense of fulfilment by completing a task that they have possibly never attempted or even thought of attempting before.

The sense of achievement developed from successfully completing a task in an outdoor activity will also increase the individual's self-esteem.

### Enjoyment and challenge

Taking part in outdoor activities provides both **enjoyment and challenge**. Whether a person takes part in outdoor activities or not is usually a decision made by that person. Most people choose to do something because they expect to enjoy doing it.

The challenge in outdoor activities is that the activity is different and the participant expects there to be a certain amount of danger involved with it. Taking part in the activity means that the person

**Getting started**

Make a list of the potential benefits of taking part in outdoor activities.

**Figure 6.25** Children on a rope course.

concerned must show some level of bravery and possibly overcome an inbuilt fear of participating in that activity.

The participant in outdoor activities will find out about their own personal limits and appreciate that there is an element of risk involved. The challenge to the individual is to realise the risk, and successfully cope with that risk in completing the task. This will depend on their capacity to rely on their own skills and abilities. For this reason, outdoor activities improve self-reliance.

**Figure 6.26** Hiking is an accessible form of outdoor fitness.

## Improved health and fitness

Involvement in outdoor activities results in **improved health and fitness**. Any form of physical activity is known to reduce minor and harmful illnesses. Outdoor activities, in particular, help to burn off more calories and tone the whole body because of aspects such as wind resistance, and uneven ground or slopes. A full day's canoeing, snowboarding or orienteering will develop various components of fitness such as stamina, strength and agility.

Improvements in general fitness through outdoor activities will have a benefit to an individual's overall health. Increased fitness will reduce the risks of health problems such as heart attacks, obesity, diabetes and cancer.

## Greater environmental awareness

Outdoor activities, by definition, take place outdoors. Many people who live in cities may be unaware of the problems of our rural surroundings and, by taking part in outdoor activities, more people will develop a **greater environmental awareness**.

Participation in activities such as hill walking, orienteering and sailing will make people more aware of environmental issues such as pollution, deforestation, industrialisation and conservation through an increased appreciation of the natural environment.

## Increased motivation

Outdoor activities are great for keeping a healthy mind. The activities are generally fun and that **increases motivation**. It has already been said that people benefit mentally through improved confidence and self-esteem, and socially through making friends. They become happier people. This benefits children in particular, at school and at home. Fresh air and exercise will increase their oxygen intake, which releases chemicals in the brain that make children feel good, and the change in scenery stops them from getting bored. Many outdoor activities are long-duration and relatively strenuous. Motivation may be needed to complete the activity.

## Opportunity to socialise

Participation in outdoor activities provides **opportunities to socialise**. For example, activities such as rock climbing, potholing and paragliding all require others to be involved to make sure the activity is safely completed. In reality, most outdoor activities are designed to be undertaken with other people present. Working with others and being part of a team are important aspects of most outdoor activities.

**Figure 6.27** A walk in the park can be sociable as well as healthy.

## How participating in outdoor activities can help skills development

**Taking part in outdoor activities helps skills develop**. Some activities such as kayaking, windsurfing and rock climbing require specific skills to be learned in order to do the activity. Other activities help participants to learn more general skills such as survival skills, map-reading skills, and camping skills. The skills developed through outdoor activities, such as people skills, social skills and communication skills, are called soft skills.

### Social skills

Many outdoor activities require participants to work with others and so develop **social skills**, such as being part of a team, trusting others and being dependent on others. For example, when wild camping, everybody has to become involved in things such as setting up camp, cooking and cleaning up. In order to do this successfully, you must communicate and work together with the rest of the party.

### Team-building skills

In some outdoor activities, the participants develop **team-building skills** such as teamwork, leadership and response to leadership. For example, the sailing team needs to co-operate to get the best out of the yacht; the gorge-walking or snowshoeing group needs to work well as a group and go at the pace of the slowest. In order to do these things, somebody needs to take control of the situation and act as a leader, and the others must be willing to follow the leader.

### Decision-making skills

While involved in outdoor activities, participants will develop their **decision-making skills**. Whether it's deciding whether to go left or right while canoeing in a river, or whether to continue along a certain footpath while orienteering, or moving your hand up to a particular hold while rock climbing, outdoor activities require almost constant decision making, and decision-making skills improve in terms of speed and clarity the more you become involved in the activity.

## Planning and organisation skills

Taking part in outdoor activities develops **planning and organisational skills**. Participants cannot just go out and do outdoor activities – it takes careful preparation and research before the activity can be undertaken.

Even with a relatively simple outdoor activity such as mountain biking, the logistics of getting to the activity site, getting the bikes ready, checking which route to follow, making sure that all safety matters have been attended to, what to do about food and drink, and what to do if something untoward happens all require careful planning.

## Problem-solving skills

**Problem-solving skills** are common in outdoor activities, because there is a high level of unpredictability in these activities. You never know what might happen next and the ability to find appropriate solutions to problems is important. For example, what do you do when canoeing if the boat gets damaged and you are still a long way from home? Do you carry on and hope the damage is not too severe? Do you stop and attempt emergency repairs? Do you abandon the canoe and telephone for a lift home? Problems such as these need solving.

**Figure 6.28** Climbers assess a cliff face.

## Communication skills

The **communication skills** that are involved in outdoor activities are not just about speaking to other people. In activities such as rock climbing, there are strict guidelines as to the words and phrases that need to be used to clarify what is happening between the climber and the belayer. This is because you do not want any confusion over who is doing what in a situation where there may be little visual contact.

 **Classroom discussion**

Which three outdoor activities could be made available for your group? Every suggestion must be backed up with reasons why you recommend that particular activity.

## Know it!

1 State four general benefits of participating in outdoor activities.
2 Suggest how participating in outdoor activities can help skill development.

## Links to other units

You can find further information on this topic in **Units R051, R052, R053** and **R055**.

## Assessment preparation

Think about the task/s that your teacher may set you to assess your understanding of the value of participating in outdoor activities.

Make sure you know:

- The general benefits of participating in outdoor activities:
  - increased confidence
  - enjoyment and challenge
  - improved health and fitness
  - greater environmental awareness
  - increased motivation
  - opportunity to socialise.
- How participating in outdoor activities can help skills development:
  - social skills
  - team-building skills
  - decision-making skills
  - planning and organisational skills
  - problem-solving skills
  - communication skills.

### Mark scheme

| LO2 Understand the value of participating in outdoor activities | | |
|---|---|---|
| Mark band 1 | Mark band 2 | Mark band 3 |
| **Outlines a few** of the general benefits of participating in outdoor activities. | **Describes some** of the general benefits of participating in outdoor activities in **some detail**. | **Describes most** of the general benefits of participating in outdoor activities **in detail**. |
| **Identifies some** of the skills which can be developed by participating in outdoor activities. | **Describes most** of the skills which can be developed by participating in outdoor activities and how they are developed, providing a **range** of reasons as to why they are of value to the individual. | **Explains most** of the skills which can be developed by participating in outdoor activities and how they are developed, providing a **wide range** of reasons as to why they are of value to the individual. |
| **Outlines** how a **few** of these skills are developed, providing **limited** reasons as to why they are of value to the individual. | | |

## LO3 Be able to plan an outdoor activity

### Key considerations to make when planning an outdoor activity

The **key consideration to make when planning an outdoor activity** is to focus on the precise activity you wish to do. A table such as the one below might help.

| Target client | Activity idea | Aims and objectives | Location | Numbers |
|---|---|---|---|---|
| Who is this activity for? | What do you want to do? | Why do you want to do it? | Where do you want to do it? | Overall size of activity? |

In the early planning stage, you may have a number of ideas. That's fine, just make sure that all the ideas are listed in the table. The table is going to change as you and other people who become involved think about some other ideas or get rid of others as being too difficult to organise. As you refine these ideas, you will realise that there are many things to consider when planning an outdoor activity.

### Health and safety

It is important that **health and safety** are considered when planning an outdoor activity. This should include thoughts such as whether the activity is suitable for the group concerned, and whether all potential risks have been identified.

It is important to get the right balance between protecting the group from risk and allowing them to learn from the activity. For example, there are risks involved in hill walking such as changes in the weather and stumbling and falling over rocks. But being over-protective by postponing the trip if there is a chance of rain, or making sure everybody is roped together, even when walking across a flat field, is taking safety too far.

Most national governing bodies publish guidelines on safety and good practice.

### Personnel

The numbers, experience and qualifications of the **personnel** who are leading the trip need to be considered. Aspects of the planned trip such as the ratio of leaders to participants, and the level of qualification and experience of the members of the leadership team, provide guidance as to the suitability of the activity.

For example, most outdoor activity providers offer a student to instructor ratio of 1:8 to 1:12, depending on the provider and the activity.

### Getting started

Make a list of three outdoor activities that you would like to take part in. For each activity, write down what you would like to achieve if you took part in each activity, where you could take part in each activity and when you could take part in each activity.

### Adventure Activities Licensing Authority

The **Adventure Activities Licensing Authority** (AALA) was founded in 1996. The idea behind adventure activities licensing is to provide assurances to the public about the safety of those activity providers who have been granted a licence.

A licence indicates that the activity provider has been inspected by the Adventure Activities Licensing Authority, with particular attention paid to their safety management systems, and the Authority has found that the provider follows the nationally accepted standards of good practice for the delivery of adventure activities to young people, with due regard to the benefits and risks of the activity.

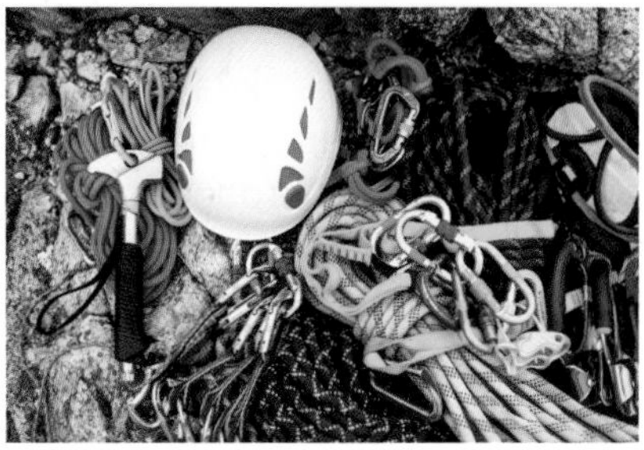

**Figure 6.29** Rock climbing equipment.

### Clothing and equipment

Specialised outdoor activities require specialist outdoor **clothing and equipment**. For example, a wide range of equipment is used during rock climbing, including ropes, helmets, harnesses, carabiners and belay devices that are commonly used to protect a climber against the consequences of a fall. Such equipment must not be damaged and should be checked prior to and after use.

Rock climbing can be done wearing almost anything, but some clothing is better suited to climbing rocks than others. It is important to wear clothes that are loose, comfortable, and protective. Different clothes may be needed for winter and summer, but whatever the season, the clothes shouldn't be torn or have loose bits that could catch on a rocky outcrop. Nor should the clothes be so tight that they restrict movement. Rocks can be climbed in trainers, but if you get seriously involved in the activity, you may wish to buy specialist rock-climbing shoes.

### Location

Outdoor activities need to be conducted at a suitable **location**. There is a big difference between kayaking on a canal, on a lake or on the sea. Beginners will find it much easier to kayak on the flat calm of a canal, rather than in the white water of a river or the waves and swell of the sea. On land, the terrain is also important. There is a big difference between trekking across fields, through forests and up steep hills. The location needs to be suitable not only for the activity, but also the experience and ability of the participants.

### Supplies

It is important that there are sufficient **supplies** available for any outdoor activity. 'Supplies' means food and water. Things to consider about supplies include who provides the food and drinks, and will the participants carry their own, or will the provisions be left at a suitable location?

The duration of the activity may dictate the need for food in terms of meals, but it is always a good idea to have access to an energy bar or something similar to top up energy levels during strenuous activity. Water is probably more important than food as everybody has a need for water intake at regular intervals.

## Emergency procedures

Circumstances can change at any time and during any outdoor activity. The people involved in the activity must be prepared and ready to implement **emergency procedures**.

There must be an alternative escape route in place for activities where part of the activity is following a specific route. For example, when hill walking, rock climbing or mountaineering, an escape route would be used following a fall, illness or a sudden change in the weather.

There must be a first aider available and there must be a suitable first aid kit containing basic items such as plasters, blister dressings, small wound dressings, bandages and painkillers.

Mobile phones are useful for summoning help, but coverage must be checked beforehand, as hilly and mountainous areas often have limited coverage, and hills can block signals. Mobile phones must be charged before setting out.

If there is no mobile signal, the usual practice is for the group to remain with the casualty, while two people set off for help to the nearest habitation or road to call for help.

## Contingency plans

There must be a **contingency plan** in place to deal with any eventualities that may occur. An alternative route should be available in case there is an unexpected obstruction, such as a tree falling over a path or stream when orienteering or canoeing.

Spare equipment should be carried, such as spare ropes and harnesses if abseiling, in case any break.

## Shelter

If weather conditions have the potential to change, or if the activity requires an overnight stay, then **shelter** needs to be available. This is usually in the form of a tent, and so camping out may become part of the activity. This would be appropriate and expected in fairly strenuous hill walking and mountaineering activities.

## Weather forecast

The organisers of any outdoor activity need to have knowledge of the **weather forecast** to make sure that the weather conditions remain suitable for the activity. A change in weather conditions may

**Figure 6.30** Emergency supplies.

necessitate a change of plan as regards continuing the activity, as some weather conditions may cause a potential risk during the activity. For example, the forecast of rain may mean that a rock-climbing activity may need to be cut short as climbing on wet rock can be dangerous.

## Timing

It is important that the organisers of the activity have due regard of **timing**. They need to make sure that the length of time allocated to the activity is suitable. For example, an afternoon's kayaking is quite restricted if the actual kayaking requires a two-hour drive to reach the activity site. There will also be a two-hour drive back. Similarly, activities will have to be shorter in the winter because the earlier onset of darkness will mean that activities may need to finish sooner than in the summer.

## Hazards to be aware of when planning outdoor activities

It is important that the organisers are **aware of any hazards when planning outdoor activities**. These hazards may be general, such as changes to the weather, or specific to the activity, such as hitting an obstruction and damaging the craft while sailing.

### Inappropriate supervision/tuition

There must be sufficient staff to supervise the activity. Many national governing bodies issue guidelines as to the appropriate ratio of instructors to participants. There may be legal consequences if there is **inappropriate supervision/tuition** of an activity.

The qualifications of the instructors must also be appropriate and up to date. The instructors should also have knowledge of the local terrains, tides and weather so that they are not taken unaware by any sudden changes in conditions.

### Poor or incorrect equipment

The organisers need to make sure that the correct equipment is available for those taking part in the activity. The use of **poor or incorrect equipment** is hazardous. The equipment should be thoroughly cleaned and seen to be in good working order before setting out on an activity. For example, buoyancy aids must be checked before going sailing.

The clothing worn by the participants must also be appropriate for the activity. This is possibly most important in terms of footwear, and the provision of fully waterproof outer clothing in activities such as hill walking. Similarly, when walking, the rucksack being used must not be too heavy or the wrong size for the person carrying it.

## Unforeseen weather conditions

Most outdoor activities take place in an open, rural environment, where changes to the weather have an impact. The organisers must be prepared for **unforeseen weather conditions**. For example, if the activity involves hill walking in winter, then the possibility of snow blizzards is increased and should be anticipated.

Changes to the weather can lead to people not enjoying the activity because, for example, they get wet in unexpected rain. It can also lead to more serious consequences such as hypothermia when the temperature suddenly drops and people who are already wet also suffer from extreme cold.

Hot weather also impacts upon participants in outdoor activities. This involves not only the potential problem of overheating, but also the possibility of dehydration, and the likelihood of sunburn.

Water-based activities need careful planning to take into account sudden changes in weather. Rivers can sometimes be subject to flash floods, the tides can change when in the sea and, if linked to the wind, can cause swell to increase, which can be dangerous for canoeists and sailors. Changes in wind direction can also affect conditions on lakes.

## Illness or injury

The potential for **illness or injury** needs to be considered when planning an outdoor activity. This becomes even more important if the activity is taking place in a more remote area.

Illnesses could include a reaction to an insect bite or nettle stings. As already mentioned, participants could suffer from heat exhaustion, dehydration or hypothermia. Under extreme conditions, people could suffer frostbite.

Injuries may occur from stumbling or falling on rough ground, which could lead to anything from cuts and bruises to sprains and fractures.

These illnesses and injuries will all be unplanned, but if anticipated, should not present serious problems. As previously mentioned, all groups involved in outdoor activities should have a simple first aid kit, someone qualified to use the first aid kit, and a plan of action for what to do in an emergency.

## Poor organisation

**Poor organisation** can lead to those involved in an outdoor activity not enjoying the activity. In extreme cases, poor organisation can lead to the activity becoming dangerous or even life-threatening.

For example, a group may set off for a hill-walking activity. Through poor organisation, there is a lack of clearly defined roles. Nobody has checked the weather forecast and so rain is not anticipated. Not only that, but through a lack of organisation, nobody has checked that the clothing and footwear of the group are suitable for any changes in weather. When the rain comes, several members of the group get very wet. The walk continues, but again through poor organisation, nobody has realised that the stops for changing into waterproof clothing have slowed the group down, and that walking in rain is slower than walking in the dry, so the group is delayed and their timings to reach the end of the walk are inaccurate. They are now walking in the rain and it's getting dark. Nobody had anticipated this and they have not brought flashlights or torches. The potential for injury and illness has increased considerably.

Good organisation is essential when planning an outdoor activity. It is often said that planning for the next activity should begin as soon as you return from the current activity.

### Getting lost

**Getting lost** shouldn't really happen if the activity has been carefully planned. Organisers should make sure that there are sufficient people in each group who are competent map readers and can use a compass. Do not rely on mobile phone maps; they do not show as much detail as ordnance survey maps, and a mobile signal is often weak in rural areas. Planning should incorporate what to do if a group becomes lost – for example, when hill walking, the idea might be to simply walk down the slope and off the hill.

### Unstable terrain

Changes in circumstances may mean that outdoor activities may take place on **unstable terrain**, where mud slides, rock falls or avalanches may occur. Planning should take into account such possibilities with a simple to follow 'What to do if ...' plan.

### Animals and insects

The presence of **animals and insects** during an outdoor activity should be expected rather than be a surprise. Planning should include the expectation of insect bites through the provision of suitable first aid equipment. The possibility of animals being encountered and even scavenging food should not be the cause of alarm.

> **Links to other units**
>
> You can find further information on this topic in **Units R051**, **R052**, **R053** and **R055**.

> **Know it!**
>
> 1  Identify five key considerations to make when planning an outdoor activity.
> 2  Identify five hazards to be aware of when planning outdoor activities.

## Classroom discussion

Each member of the group suggests a potential outdoor activity that the group could participate in. In turn, each member of the group attempts to justify why that activity is potentially suitable for the group, while the rest of the group suggest reasons why that activity is unsuitable.

## Assessment preparation

Think about the task/s that your teacher may set you to assess your ability to plan an outdoor activity.

Make sure you know:

- Key considerations to make when planning an outdoor activity:
  - health and safety
  - personnel
  - Adventure Activities Licensing Authority
  - clothing and equipment
  - location
  - supplies
  - emergency procedures
  - contingency plans
  - shelter
  - weather forecast
  - timing.
- Hazards to be aware of when planning outdoor activities:
  - inappropriate supervision/tuition
  - poor/incorrect equipment
  - unforeseen weather conditions
  - illness/injury
  - poor organisation
  - getting lost
  - unstable terrain
  - animals and insects.

### Mark scheme

| LO3 Be able to plan an outdoor activity | | |
|---|---|---|
| **Mark band 1** | **Mark band 2** | **Mark band 3** |
| Produces a **basic** plan which considers **limited** requirements for an effective and safe outdoor activity session with **some** prompting from the teacher. | Produces an **appropriate** and **detailed** plan which considers **many** of the requirements for an effective and safe outdoor activity session with **little** prompting from the teacher. | Produces an **appropriate** and **comprehensive** plan which covers **most** of the requirements for an effective and safe outdoor activity session independently. |
| Draws upon **limited** skills/knowledge/understanding from other units in the specification. | Draws upon **some relevant** skills/knowledge/understanding from other units in the specification. | **Clearly** draws upon **relevant** skills/knowledge/understanding from other units in the specification. |
| **Mark band 1** | **Mark band 2** | **Mark band 3** |
| Shows a **limited** awareness of safety considerations and emergency procedures related to the activity and equipment to be used. | Shows **some understanding** of safety considerations and emergency procedures related to the activity and equipment to be used. | Shows a **well-developed understanding** of safety considerations and emergency procedures related to the activity and equipment to be used. |
| Gives little consideration to the environment the activity will take place in and the personnel used. | Gives **some** consideration to the environment the activity will take place in and the personnel used. | Gives **thorough** consideration to the environment the activity will take place in and the personnel used. |

# LO4 Be able to demonstrate knowledge and skills during outdoor activities

## Care and use of equipment

The **care and use of equipment** used in outdoor activities is very important; it could prevent you from getting wet, cold, ill or injured.

Different outdoor activities require different types of equipment. Some of it is designed to make it easier to do the activity; some of it is designed to protect you from the weather; some of it is designed to make sure you do not get injured. Whatever equipment you use, you must make sure that it is working properly and fit for the purpose it was designed for. This check must be done before starting the activity.

### Understanding of correct purpose and use of activity-specific equipment

You need to make sure that you **understand the correct purpose and use of activity-specific equipment** and use it appropriately during your chosen outdoor activity.

Much of the equipment you may be using is specifically for a certain type of activity. For example, a twin-bladed paddle is essential for kayaking, but of little use, in fact is quite a hindrance, when rock climbing!

Some of the equipment used in certain activities may not be obvious in what it is supposed to do until it is needed. For example, a rock-climbing harness just appears to be a mass of webbing until you actually go rock climbing, put it on and realise how valuable it is when climbing.

### Ability to use activity-specific equipment

You will be assessed on your **ability to use activity-specific equipment**. This obviously varies from activity to activity, but it is important that you get used to using all potential equipment.

For example, there are many different shaped pitons that can be used when rock climbing and you may only use a certain one very occasionally, but you must be able to use it.

### Appropriate storage to avoid damage

One of the commonest ways to damage equipment is by not putting it away properly. After an exhausting day involved in an outdoor activity, it is all too easy just to throw equipment into a storage area. It is really important to use **appropriate storage to avoid damage** to equipment.

For example, when involved in water-based activities, buoyancy aids must be stored only after they have been washed and thoroughly dried, otherwise they are liable to rot. Make sure you clean any equipment you have been using and put it away properly.

## Safe practice

It is essential that you are seen to be following **safe practice** when involved in your chosen outdoor activity.

### Follow instructions closely

One very important aspect of safe practice is being able to **follow instructions closely**. During your outdoor activity, make sure you listen carefully to any instructions given, by paying attention to the person delivering the instructions and not appearing uninterested. Having followed the instructions, make sure you understand what has been said. Always ask if not sure.

### Ensure you have the prescribed clothing/equipment

You must **ensure that you have the prescribed clothing/equipment** for the activity being undertaken. This could involve you getting the clothing together yourself if, for example, you are going hill walking or canoeing. For some activities, such as caving, the clothing, possibly a wet suit, may be provided. If it's provided, you must try it on and make sure it fits and works before you take part in the activity.

### Make sure you are aware of emergency procedures

You must **make sure that you are aware of the emergency procedures** that accompany the activity. You must know what to do if anything goes wrong, such as a change in the weather, or somebody becoming ill or getting injured. Be aware of any escape route; know who the qualified first aider is and where the first aid kit is; who has a mobile phone and who to ring if need be; what to do if there is no mobile signal.

## Communication skills

It is important that you demonstrate the use of good **communication skills** during the activity.

### Verbal

**Verbal** communication skills are those involving the voice. They are normally spoken, but can be shouted, and can involve screaming. You must demonstrate your ability to use verbal communication during your activity. This will mean talking (and listening) to others.

Make sure you use appropriate language for that activity. For example, it's a canoe, not a boat; it's a belay, not a rest point; it's near the bow, not near the front. In rock climbing, for example, there are clear verbal signals that are used between the climber and the belayer that provide all the information each of them needs because quite often they may not be able to see each other.

## Non-verbal

In some outdoor activities the use of **non-verbal** communication is more appropriate and must be demonstrated. For example, in scuba-diving, there are standardised non-verbal (hand) signals that every diver must know.

## Activity-specific language/terminology

Many **activities have specific language/terminology** that must be understood and, if necessary, used by you. Some of these terms have different meanings in different activities. For example, a 'shaft' in caving is a vertical passage, whereas in fishing the 'shaft' is part of the fishing rod. In canoeing a 'back stroke' is a paddling technique, but in swimming it is a type of arm action.

# Decision-making skills

Most outdoor activities involve many **decision-making skills**. You must demonstrate your ability to make decisions during your activity.

## Defining and clarifying an issue

There will be situations that occur when you are taking part in outdoor activities where you have to make decisions and take greater responsibility for your own learning by **defining and clarifying an issue**.

For example, when canoeing in a river, you may see that there are trees over-hanging the river and that the river gets shallow near the bank. You will have to decide which course to take so that you avoid the shallow water and the trees. You will also have to decide which strokes to use to stay in the middle of the river and avoid the issues.

## Gathering facts about issues and understanding their causes

During your activity you will be assessed on your ability to **gather facts about issues and understand their causes**.

For example, when mountaineering in a group, one of the issues is safety. Because of that issue, you need to proceed at the pace of the slowest and not let the group split up.

## Generating/brainstorming possible solutions

You need to **generate/brainstorm possible solutions** to issues. For example, in rock climbing, when working with a group, you will need to listen to others in the group before deciding what is going to be the best route up a pitch.

## Comparing the pros and cons of the options

Invariably when a decision needs to be made, you will have to **compare the pros and cons of the options**. Should we do this or should we do that? You will be assessed on your ability to weigh up the options. For example, when hill walking there may be several ways to get to the top of the hill. Do you go straight up the steepest part of the hill to get to the top in the shortest time, or do you take a longer route that will take more time, but is not as strenuous?

## Selecting the best option

Having compared the available options, it will eventually become time to **select the best option**. The final decision may be yours or it may be collaborative. You may have the agreement of everybody or there may be a few dissenting voices. You are going to be assessed on your ability to select the best option.

# Team-working skills

The ability to work well within a group is a **team-working skill**. You will be assessed on how well you work within a group; for example, working with the rest of your hill-walking group on a long descent off the hill.

## Reliability

A key team-working skill is **reliability**. Being reliable means that you can be depended on for your qualities such as honesty, achievement and accuracy. For example, can you be relied on to go to the front of an orienteering group and set a pace that the rest of the group can also maintain? This forms part of your assessment.

## Active listening

**Active listening** is a communication technique that requires the listener to understand, interpret and evaluate what they hear. Another way of thinking about this is to call it attentive listening. You need to be seen not only to listen to what's being said, but to take on board what is being said.

## Active participation

**Active participation** is the idea that everybody is involved in the activity. Active participation improves motivation. You do not want to be seen as the straggler at the back who is just following along.

## Collaborative working

**Collaborative working** is working with others. You need to be seen as part of the group, involved in helping others. It would be good if, at the end of the activity, other people were able to describe you as 'helpful', 'reliable' or 'supportive'.

## Demonstrating commitment

It is important that during the activity you **demonstrate commitment** to the activity. This may be seen when you are keen to do something, motivated to do well, always at the front, not sulking at the back, encouraging, not complaining.

## Treating others with respect

During your activity you need to **treat others with respect**. This means listening to other people's ideas, not making all the decisions without asking others.

# Problem-solving skills

During the activity, you must show your **problem-solving skills**.

## Prioritise issues

When solving problems, it is important that you **prioritise issues**. During your activity there will be a variety of problems that may arise. Problems need to be prioritised. This means putting them in order of importance: 'We'll deal with this before we worry about this.'

## Set targets for resolution

Problem-solving may often involve **setting targets for resolution**. Resolution means solving a problem. For example, it is important to find a suitable overnight campsite before it gets dark. If hill walking in warm weather, it is important to return to base before the group runs out of water.

## Use experience to help resolve problems

This is common practice. People who have done things before can **use their experience to help resolve a problem**. For example, you might find that on a rock-climbing wall you encountered a similar problem with a hand-hold and can use this particular grip to resolve the problem on a different climb.

## Monitor performance in resolving a problem

Problem-solving doesn't always work. You need to **monitor your performance in resolving a problem**. Be secure enough in your own abilities to say that if this isn't working, I'll try something else.

## Evaluate performance in resolving a problem

Finally, you need to be seen to be able to evaluate your own performance in resolving a problem. You need to be able to think or talk about what you are going to do next time when faced with the same problem. Maybe next time it will be better if you do something else first.

### Know it!

1 Describe how to take care of equipment and follow safe practice.
2 Describe two ways of communicating.
3 What should you consider before making a decision when involved in outdoor activities?
4 Describe four features of team-working skills.
5 Describe the best ways of using problem-solving skills.

### Links to other units

You can find further information on this topic in **Units R051**, **R052**, **R053** and **R055**.

### Read about it

Mountain bike trails: https://en.wikipedia.org/wiki/List_of_mountain_bike_areas_and_trails_in_the_United_Kingdom

How to snowshoe: www.snowshoemag.com/first-timers

Website about range of outdoor activities: www.outdoorpursuits.co.uk

Mountain biking website: www.britishcycling.org.uk/getintomountainbiking

Canoeing website: www.britishcanoeing.org.uk

Climbing website: www.ukclimbing.com

Hang gliding website: www.bhpa.co.uk

Plas y Brenin: www.pyb.co.uk

Holme Pierrepont: www.nwscnotts.com

Youth organisations: https://en.wikipedia.org/wiki/Youth_organisations_in_the_United_Kingdom

Scouts website: https://members.scouts.org.uk/supportresources/search/?cat=26,407,351

Girl guiding: www.girlguiding.org.uk

Duke of Edinburgh's Award: www.dofe.org/

List of outdoor activities: www.activeoutdoors.info/outdoor-activities-list

Values and benefits of outdoor activities: www.englishoutdoorcouncil.org/Values_and_benefits.htm

Planning outdoor activities: http://www.outdoorrecreationni.com/wp-content/uploads/2012/04/Community-Toolkit-to-Success-Planning-Outdoor-Activities_ORNI-2012.pdf

Safety and good practice guide: https://www.britishcanoeing.org.uk/uploads/documents/Event-Safety-Guidance-5.pdf

Adventure Activity Licensing: www.hse.gov.uk/aala/index.htm

How to dress for rock climbing: www.wikihow.com/Dress-for-Rock-Climbing

## Assessment preparation

Think about the task/s that your teacher may set you to assess your ability to demonstrate your skills and knowledge during the outdoor activity session.

Make sure you know about:

- Care and use of equipment:
  - understanding of correct purpose and use of activity-specific equipment
  - ability to use activity-specific equipment
  - appropriate storage to avoid damage.
- Safe practice:
  - follow instruction closely
  - ensure you have the prescribed clothing/equipment
  - make sure you are aware of emergency procedures.
- Communication skills:
  - verbal
  - non-verbal
  - activity-specific language/terminology.
- Decision-making skills:
  - defining and clarifying an issue
  - gathering facts about issues and understanding their causes
  - generating/brainstorming possible solutions
  - comparing the pros and cons of the options
  - selecting the best option.
- Team-working skills:
  - reliability
  - collaborative working
  - active listening
  - demonstrating commitment
  - active participation
  - treating others with respect.
- Problem-solving skills:
  - prioritise issues
  - set targets for resolution
  - use experience to help resolve problems
  - monitor performance in resolving a problem
  - evaluate performance in resolving a problem.

### Mark scheme

| LO4 Be able to demonstrate knowledge and skills during outdoor activities | | |
| --- | --- | --- |
| Mark band 1 | Mark band 2 | Mark band 3 |
| Demonstrates a **limited** range of relevant skills and knowledge during outdoor activities. | Demonstrates a **wide** range of relevant skills and knowledge during outdoor activities. | **Confidently** demonstrates a **wide** range of relevant skills and knowledge during outdoor activities. |
| Mark band 1 | Mark band 2 | Mark band 3 |
| Cares for and uses equipment in a **limited** manner and needs **some prompting** from the activity leader to follow safe practice. | Cares for and uses equipment in a **competent** manner and needs **little prompting** from the activity leader to follow safe practice. | Cares for and uses equipment in an **effective** manner and follows safe practice **independently**. |

# Glossary

**Abseiling** Using a climbing rope to descend

**Access** Being able to get to or into a facility

**Adaptable** Being flexible with your plans and willing to make changes if necessary

**Administration** The work of a secretary or someone who provides support to professionals in terms of communication, paperwork, and co-ordination and implementation of procedures

**Ambitious** Hoping and expecting to achieve

**Annually** Every year

**Anti-doping** Preventing the use of prohibited performance-enhancing drugs

**Anti-social behaviour** Behaviour that is not deemed as desirable by society

**App** Application software designed to run on smartphones and other mobile devices

**Arousal** Physical and mental state of excitement

**Autocratic** Leadership style in which the leader does not value the opinion of others. They do not ask for opinions or welcome suggestions

**Awareness** How aware or knowledgeable a particular group is about something

**Barriers** Factors that may make participation particularly difficult

**Belay** To secure a climbing rope

**Biennially** Every second year

**Blog** Informal journal provided online

**Bookmaker** Owns or manages the company that provides betting services

**Broadsheet** More informative type of newspaper

**BT Sport** Group of sports channels provided by BT

**Cable** TV images sent through an underground fibre-optic cable

**Canoeing** Paddling a water craft with a single paddle

**Careers adviser** A person who provides advice about careers and how to get a job

**Caving** Exploration of caving systems, also called potholing

**Children** Human beings under the age of 18, unless the law in a country permits otherwise

**Citizenship** Acting in a way that citizens of a country should

**Closed skill** Skill made within an unchanging/ stable environment

**Commentator/pundit** Provides expert coverage, views and opinions about chosen sports

**Commodity** A product that can be sold

**Complex skill** Skill made with many decisions

**Composition** Art of creating and arranging

**Connexions service** Was a government-funded organisation that provided information to young people about careers

**Consumer expenditure** Goods or services that the public buy

**Consumer market** Those who are likely to be interested in and willing to pay to be part of a specific market

**Consumers** People who buy commodities

**Cool-down** Gradually reducing the pulse and breathing rate whilst stretching muscles to remove waste products

**Corrective actions** Actions to correct or reduce the chances of the risk from taking place

**Covering letter** A letter sent with, and explaining the contents of, an application

**Creativity** Solving a problem using different ideas

**Curriculum vitae (CV)** Written overview of a person's details, education, experience and qualifications

**DAB** Digital audio broadcasting – a type of digitised radio signal

**DCO** Doping control officer

**Delivery style** The style and manner in which you lead the session

**Democratic** Leadership style in which the leader consults the group when making decisions

**Demonstrations** A visual way to show the group how to do something

**Digital terrestrial television** Digital form of TV signal for terrestrial channels

**Direct tourism** Visitors visit the host city as a result of attending a major sporting event

**Disabled** People who have a physical or mental condition that affects their ability to carry out movement, use senses or undertake everyday activities

**Economic impact** The additional expenditure within a defined area that has happened due to a specific event

**Economically disadvantaged** Someone who does not have enough income to meet basic needs and qualifies for state-organised benefits

**Endorsements** Where a celebrity and their name is attached to products to promote them

**Engaging** How well the session will hold the participants' attention

**Equipment** Fixed equipment or portable equipment that can be moved

**Ethics** The moral principles that govern a person's behaviour

**Ethnic minorities** A group within a community that is of a different culture, religion or nationality from the main group in that area

**Etiquette** The unwritten rules concerning player behaviour

**Evaluation** To judge something's worth, appropriateness and level of success

**Excellence** Striving to be the best that you can

**Extrinsic motivators** Something is offered to create motivation from an external source. This can be tangible or intangible

**Fair play** Appropriate, polite behaviour, which involves respecting fellow competitors and adhering to the rules and does not involve illega doping

**Fanzines** Non-official publications produced by sports fans

**Fixed practice** Repetitive practice, best for closed skills

**Gambling** The act of betting money on the outcome or prospective features of a sporting event

**Gamesmanship** Bending the rules, making use of dubious methods that are not strictly outside of the rules to gain an advantage

**Grassroots level** For ordinary people, rather than those who are specialists

**Groundskeepers** People who look after the grounds and surfaces on which sport is played

**Hill walking** Walking in a hilly natural environment

**HR** Human resources

**Hype** Extravagant or intensive publicity or promotion

**Hyperbaric oxygen therapy** Treatment in a chamber, where the body receives 100 per cent oxygen to speed recovery

**Inclusion** Being included in a team, competition or structure

**Indirect tourism** Visitors visit the host city after the event, as they have been made aware of the city when following the event via the media

**Individual sport** Involves a single performer competing against one or more other performers

**Intangible** Rewards that cannot be touched, e.g. praise from a coach

**Internet** Global system of interconnected computer networks

**Kayaking** Paddling a water craft with a double paddle

**Laissez-faire** Leadership style in which the leader does not intervene and allows an activity to follow its own natural course

**Leader** Person who holds responsibility and respect and has followers they can influence

**Leadership** The action of leading a group of people

**Legacy** The long-term effects and positive impact of having hosted a major sporting event for the country, its people and its provision of sporting activities

**Legislation** Laws that have been passed that affect how a role is carried out

**Licensed agent** Acts on behalf of a performer or group of performers to arrange contracts, sponsorship and endorsements of sporting events

**Literacy** The ability to read and write coherently

**Lobbying** Presenting an argument that seeks to influence another's decision

**Marketing** The process of attracting, keeping and satisfying customers through marketing activity

**Match analysis** Use of motion recording to analyse tactics and team performances

**Media** Forms of mass communication such as television, newspapers, magazines, radio, and internet

**Media outlet** Publication or broadcast programme providing information through various distribution channels

**Mental rehearsal** Picturing perfect performance to control arousal

**Mine exploration** Walking through mines and quarries

**Mobility exercises** Moving a limb through its full range of movement

**Motivation** The desire or drive to accomplish something

**Mountain biking** Off-road cycling on specialised bikes

**Mountaineering** Climbing or trekking in the mountains

**National pride** A sense of pride in the name, culture and practices of a country

**Numeracy** The ability to use and understand the use of numbers

**Nutritionists** Provide dietary advice to performers about what to eat and drink to achieve the highest level of performance

**Objectives** What you hope to achieve

**Olympic and Paralympic values** Friendship, respect and excellence – along with the four Paralympic values – determination, inspiration, courage and equality

**Olympic creed** The Olympic message

**Olympic symbol** Five interlocking rings to represent the union of the five continents of the world that take part

**Open skill** Skill made within a changing environment

**Optimal level of arousal** When performance is at its highest level

**Orienteering** Using a map and compass to follow a route

**P2P** Peer-to-peer file sharing

**Part practice** Skill broken down and only part of it practised

**Participation** Taking part

**Pathways** Structured routes for performers to progress through

**Pay-per-view** Service provided by a broadcaster where the subscriber pays to watch an event

**PEDs** Performance-enhancing drugs

**People skills** The generic qualities and skills required to be able to communicate clearly and effectively with other people

**Personal career plan** What pathway or route a person hopes their career may follow

**Personal trainers** Work on a one-to-one basis (personally) with someone in need of advice about how to train or improve performance

**Pitch** Section of a climbing route

**Podcasts** Digital audio recording available to download

**Potholing** Exploration of caving systems, also called caving

**PR** Public relations

**Proactive** Making decisions to eliminate any problems before they happen

**Productivity** How productive a person is, i.e. how well they carry out everyday tasks

**Promotion** Promotion involves any type of marketing used to persuade a targeted audience

**Provision** What is provided or available

**Ratio** The number of leaders required for the number of students

**Reaction time** Time taken to decide what to do

**Reactive** Reacting to problems by changing what you are doing

**Recurring** Periodically repeated in the same place

**Regular** Happens often at set intervals

**Regulations** Define the playing area

**Ring-fenced** Sports events that the government prevents TV companies from charging to watch so that everyone can watch for free

**Risk assessment** Used to identify and eliminate risks where possible, protecting participants from harm

**Role models** Well known people who others aspire to be like

**Role-related experience** Having previous experience within the same or similar role being applied for

**Rules** Define how to win fairly

**Safeguarding** The action taken to protect the welfare of children and protect them from harm

**Sailing** Floating water craft propelled by wind

**Satellite** TV images sent from a geo-stationary satellite

**Satellite channel subscription** Term used to describe the payment made to companies who provide sports channels at a cost

**Shop window effect** The city and country are advertised to the world

**Simple skill** Skill made with few decisions

**Single parents** Any adult who is bringing up a child or children on their own

**Skill** Learned combination of movements

**Skills gaps** Areas in which a person is lacking in order to progress through their career path

**Sky Sports** Main subscription-based sports channel provider in UK

**Social development** Improving the well-being and interaction of those in society so they can feel safe and secure, reach their potential and communicate effectively with others

**Spectatorship** Attending an event as against watching on media

**Sponsors** The act of supporting an event, activity, person or organisation through the provision of finance, products or merchandise

**Sponsorship** Where a company pays money to a team or individual in return for advertising their goods

**Sport medicine** The diagnosis of problems or symptoms in order to prescribe suitable legal medication to improve health, well-being and possibly performance

**Sport science** Using the principles of science to explain, predict, analyse and evaluate sporting performance

**Sporting behaviour** Behaving in a way that shows sportsmanship – involves appropriate, polite and fair behaviour while participating in a sporting event

**Sports Council** There are five: Sport England, Sport Scotland, Sport Wales, Sport Northern Ireland and UK Sport

**Sportsmanship** Fair and generous behaviour or treatment of others in a sporting contest

**Sports marketing** Promotion of sport and associated products

**Sport-specific skills** The skills, techniques and movements required when performing in that sport

**State-sponsored doping** Wide-scale doping programme organised and supported by government agencies

**Stereotyping** A widely held but simple and sometimes unjust viewpoint of or idea about a particular type of person

**Strategies** Overall plan of how best to perform

**Tabloid** More sensationalist type of newspaper

**Tactics** Plans used against opponents' weaknesses and for own strengths

**Tangible** Rewards that can be touched, e.g. a certificate

**Team spirit** The feeling of pride and loyalty that exists among the members of a team that makes them want their team to do well or to be the best

**Technical advice** Advice on equipment, venues and surfaces

**Technique** Method used to perform a skill

**Teenagers** Human beings aged from 13 to 19 years

**Terrestrial** Signals sent from a transmitter to an aerial or receiver

**Terrestrial TV** Free to watch TV

**Tolerance and respect** Willingness to accept others' differences

**Trail biking** Mountain biking on specialised trails

**Trekking** Walking in the natural environment

**TUE** Therapeutic use exemption (for a drug) – the process by which an athlete can obtain approval to use a prescribed prohibited substance or method for the treatment of a legitimate medical condition

**UKCC** United Kingdom Coaching Certificate

**User groups** The different groups of people who face barriers to participation

**Variable practice** Changing the practice – best for open skills

**Video analysis** Use of motion recording to analyse individual techniques

**Virgin Media** Main cable TV operator

**Vision** What an NGB feels they are focused on achieving

**WADA** World Anti-Doping Agency

**Warm-up** To include a pulse-raising activity, stretches and familiarisation or skill-based activities

**Webcasting** Radio broadcast on the internet

**Webzines** Online versions of fanzines

**Whole practice** Skill performed in its entirety

**Windsurfing** Floating flat board propelled by wind

**World wide web** Part of the internet used for interlinked information

# Index

The Publishers would like to thank the following for permission to reproduce copyright material.

# Photo credits

**p.1** © ChiccoDodiFC/stock.adobe.com; **p.3** © Photographee.eu/stock.adobe.com; **p.5** © Salajean/123RF; **p.6** *t* © David Burrows/Shutterstock.com, *b* © Halfpoint/stock.adobe.com; **p.8** *t* © Antonioguillem/stock.adobe.com, *b* © RioPatuca Images/stock.adobe.com; **p.9** t © BasPhoto/Shutterstock.com, b © Bnenin/stock.adobe.com; **p.12** © LIGHTFIELD STUDIOS/stock.adobe.com; **p.13** © Chris Gill/Alamy Stock Photo; **p.14** *t* © Mitch Gunn/Shutterstock.com, *b* © Gary Mitchell, GMP Media/Alamy Stock Photo; **p.17** *t* © Michael Preston/Alamy Stock Photo, *c* © John Locher/AP/REX/Shutterstock, *b* © International Olympic Committee; **p.18** *t* Sport Relief is an initiative of Comic Relief registered charity 326568 (England/Wales); SC039730 (Scotland), b © Davidf/E+/Getty Images; **p.23** © Alexander Zemlianichenko/AP/REX/Shutterstock; **p.24** © 279photo/stock.adobe.com; **p.25** © Jimmie48 Photography/Shutterstock.com; **p.26** © Jason Coles/123RF; **p.27** © A.RICARDO/Shutterstock.com; **p.28** © Chris Harvey/Shutterstock.com; **p.31** © International Olympic Committee; **p.34** © Matthew Peters/Manchester United/Getty Images; **p.37** © Stadium Bank/Alamy Stock Photo; **p.38** © Shutterstock/Monkey Business Images; **p.40** © Shariff Che'Lah/stock.adobe.com; **p.45** © Halfdark/Getty Images; **p.47** *l* Carine06, https://www.flickr.com/photos/43555660@N00/7107958053/https://creativecommons.oor/licenses/by-sa/2.0/, *r* © PCN Black/PCN Photography/Alamy Stock Photo; **p.48** *t* © BVDC/stock.adobe.com, *b* © Andriy Bezuglov/stock.adobe.com; **p.50** © Kzenon/stock.adobe.com; **p.51** © Mark Kolbe/Getty Images; **p.52** © Biker3/stock.adobe.com; **p.54** © Pixland/Thinkstock/Getty Images; **p.56** © Michael Dodge/Getty Images; **p.57** © Johnny Lye/stock.adobe.com; **p.58** © .shock/stock.adobe.com; **p.60** © Action Plus Sports Images/Alamy Stock Photo; **p.62** © Juergen Hasenkopf/Alamy Stock Photo; **p.63** © Leremy/stock.adobe.com; **p.65** © Photographer S.I./stock.adobe.com; **p.69** © Brian McEntire/iStock/Thinkstock; **p.70** © WavebreakmediaMicro/stock.adobe.com; **p.71** © REX/Shutterstock; **p.78** © JackF/stock.adobe.com; **p.81** *t* © Rawpixel.com/stock.adobe.com, *c* © Seventyfour/stock.adobe.com, *b* © Cathy Yeulet – 123RF.com; **p.82** © Dziurek/stock.adobe.com; **p.85** © WavebreakMediaMicro/stock.adobe.com; **p.87** © alexandre zveiger – Fotolia; **p.89** © crdjan – Fotolia; **p.90** *t* © Sergey Ryzhov/stock.adobe.com, *b* © WavebreakMediaMicro/stock.adobe.com; **p.92** © Pressmaster/stock.adobe.com; **p.95** © Maskot/Getty Images; **p.96** © Monkey Business/stock.adobe.com; **p.97** © Creative Crop/Digital Vision/Getty Images; **p.106** © Baytunc/E+/Getty Images; **p.109** Courtesy of BBC Sport; **p.110** © Sky Sports; **p.112** © PA Photos/TopFoto; **p.115** © Alexander Zemlianichenko/AP/REX/Shutterstock; **p.116** © Sebastian Crocker/stock.adobe.com; **p.118** © ThomasDeco/Shutterstock.com; **p.130** © Simonkr/E+/Getty Images; **p.144** © DragonImages/stock.adobe.com; **p.146** © Andresr/E+/Getty Images; **p.147** © Syda Productions/stock.adobe.com; **p.150** © Michaeljung/stock.adobe.com; **p.152** © New Africa/stock.adobe.com; **p.153** © Dusanpetkovic1/stock.adobe.com; **p.155** © Highwaystarz/stock.adobe.com; **p.156** © Mladen/stock.adobe.com; **p.162** *t* © Monkey Business/stock.adobe.com; *b* Jobcentre Plus logo by permission of Department for Work and Pensions (UK); **p.166** © Art3d/123RF; **p.168** © PhotoLondonUK/Shutterstock.com; **p.169** *l* © Matushchak Anton/Shutterstock.com, *r* © Magicinfoto/Shutterstock.com; **p.170** *t* © Monika Wisniewska/stock.adobe.com, *b* © Clive Chilvers/Shutterstock.com; **p.171** *t* © Tanasut Chindasuthi/Shutterstock.com, *b* © Nebojsa/stock.adobe.com; **p.172** © Prostock-studio/stock.adobe.com; **p.174** © Jakub Cejpek – Fotolia.com; **p.176** *tr* © Yongkiet/stock.adobe.com, *cr* © Ammit/stock.adobe.com, *bl* © smuki/stock.adobe.com, *bc* © De Visu/stock.adobe.com; **p.177** *tr* © Paweł Mruk – Fotolia, *c* © RadeLukovic/123RF.com, *b* © WavebreakMediaMicro/stock.adobe.com; **p.178** *tr* © Ribtoks/123RF.com, *tl* © Federicofoto – Fotolia.com, *cr* © Duncanandison/stock.adobe.com, *bl* © Simon Dannhauer/stock.adobe.com, *br* © Juananbarros/stock.adobe.com; **p.179** © Pedrosala/stock.adobe.com; **p.180** *t* © Pedrosala/stock.adobe.com, *b* © Eyetronic/stock.adobe.com; **p.181** © Dennisvdwater/stock.adobe.com; **p.182** *tl* © ARochau/stock.adobe.com, *tr* © ARochau/stock.adobe.com, *cr* © Vetal1983/stock.adobe.com, *bl* © Alexandra Lande/stock.adobe.com, *bc* © Jenny Thompson/stock.adobe.com; **p.183** *t* © Dorset Media Service/Alamy Stock Photo, *b* © Alex Ekins Adventure Photography/Alamy Stock Photo; **p.184** © Sylv1rob1/stock.adobe.com; **p.189** © Kzenon/stock.adobe.com; **p.190** © Jeannot Weber/stock.adobe.com; **p.191** © Photoinsel/stock.adobe.com; **p.192** © Hero Images Inc./Alamy Stock Photo; **p.195** © yanik88/stock.adobe.com; **p.196** © Maksym Kaharlyk/Shutterstock.com.